AN INTRODUCTION TO CHILDHOOD AND YOUTH STUDIES AND PSYCHOLOGY

This exciting new book provides a novel interdisciplinary introduction to Childhood and Youth Studies and Psychology. Its accessible approach illuminates holistic understandings of children and young people's lives by drawing from multiple disciplines and theoretical frameworks and wide-ranging research examples, including case studies from around the world, featuring children and young people's perspectives throughout.

Weaving insights from education and cultural studies, social anthropology, and sociology with social, cultural, and developmental psychology, it covers children and young people's experiences and development from infancy to young adulthood (0–23 years) and their rights. Chapters explore key contemporary topics such as the following:

- Digital childhood and youth
- Children's embodied experiences
- The social and cultural origins of selves
- Diverse families
- Race and ethnicity
- Global childhoods
- Models for understanding health and disability
- Children's rights and agency
- Gender in childhood and youth

An essential reading for students on childhood and youth, psychology, and education courses, *An Introduction to Childhood and Youth Studies and Psychology* is also a valuable introductory resource for practitioners working with children and young people and for parents and policy makers with an interest in how we understand children and young people's lives today.

Victoria Cooper is Senior Lecturer at The Open University who specialises in research focused on marginalised children and young people's experiences. She is co-author of *Parenting the First Twelve Years: What the Evidence Tells Us* (2018) and co-editor of *Exploring Childhood and Youth* (2021).

Mimi Tatlow-Golden is Senior Lecturer of Developmental Psychology and Childhood at The Open University. She co-directs the Centre for Children and Young People's Wellbeing and the RUMPUS Group researching fun. Her transdisciplinary research argues for dialogue between Childhood and Youth Studies and Psychology and showcases its benefits.

This Reader forms part of the module 'An introduction to childhood studies and child psychology' (E104), an interdisciplinary module, which develops theoretical knowledge about children and young people across the world. This is a key module in the Open University BA (Hons) in Childhood and Youth Studies qualification, a leading interdisciplinary programme, which offers a range of critical perspectives on children's and young people's lives in the 21st century. It is designed for anyone working with children and young people or with a general interest in the field. Details of this and other Open University modules can be obtained from Student Recruitment, The Open University, PO Box 197, Milton Keynes MK7 6BJ, United Kingdom (tel. +44(0)3003035303; email general-enquiries@open.ac.uk). www.open.ac.uk.

AN INTRODUCTION TO CHILDHOOD AND YOUTH STUDIES AND PSYCHOLOGY

Edited by
Victoria Cooper and
Mimi Tatlow-Golden

Routledge
Taylor & Francis Group

LONDON AND NEW YORK

The Open
University

Designed cover image: © Getty Images

First edition published 2023
by Routledge
4 Park Square, Milton Park, Abingdon, Oxon, OX14 4RN

in association with
The Open University, Walton Hall, Milton Keynes MK7 6AA, United Kingdom,
www.open.ac.uk

and by Routledge
605 Third Avenue, New York, NY 10158

Routledge is an imprint of the Taylor & Francis Group, an informa business

© 2023 The Open University

British Library Cataloguing-in-Publication Data
A catalogue record for this book is available from the British Library

Library of Congress Cataloging-in-Publication Data
Names: Cooper, Victoria, 1967– editor. | Tatlow-Golden, Mimi, 1963– editor.
Title: An introduction to childhood and youth studies and psychology / Victoria
  Cooper & Mimi Tatlow-Golden.
Description: New York : Routledge, 2023. | Includes bibliographical
  references and index. | Identifiers: LCCN 2023007151 (print) |
  LCCN 2023007152 (ebook) | ISBN 9781032415956 (hbk) |
  ISBN 9781032415932 (pbk) |ISBN 9781003358855 (ebk)
Subjects: LCSH: Child psychology. | Youth—Psychology.
Classification: LCC BF721 .I558 2023 (print) | LCC BF721 (ebook) |
  DDC 155.4—dc23/eng/20230501
LC record available at https://lccn.loc.gov/2023007151
LC ebook record available at https://lccn.loc.gov/2023007152

ISBN: 978-1-032-41595-6 (hbk)
ISBN: 978-1-032-41593-2 (pbk)
ISBN: 978-1-003-35885-5 (ebk)

DOI: 10.4324/9781003358855

Typeset in News Gothic
by Apex CoVantage, LLC

Printed and bound in Great Britain by Bell and Bain Ltd, Glasgow

CONTENTS

List of contributors   vii

Introduction: Understanding children and young people's lives   1
Mimi Tatlow-Golden and Victoria Cooper

1   **What is Childhood and Youth Studies?**   10
Heather Montgomery

2   **The psychology of childhood and youth**   24
Mimi Tatlow-Golden

3   **Children's bodies**   43
Victoria Cooper and Vicky Preece

4   **Making sense of the self**   58
Mimi Tatlow-Golden

5   **Diverse families**   75
Michael Boampong

6   **Young people's mental health**   90
Victoria Cooper

7   **Education, schools, and learning**   107
Amber Fensham-Smith

8   **Models of disability and their effects on children's lives**   123
Kieron Sheehy, Budiyanto, Sri Widayati, and Khofidotur Rofiah

9   **Race(ism) and ethnicity**   139
Anthony Gunter

10   **Global childhoods**   154
Afua Twum-Danso Imoh and Heather Montgomery

11   Gender in childhood and youth   **170**
Naomi Holford

12   Digital childhood and youth: Life with screens   **186**
Lucy Caton and Mel Green

13   Adolescents, teenagers, and youth: A time of change   **200**
Victoria Cooper, Mimi Tatlow-Golden, and Heather Montgomery

14   Transitions to adulthood   **218**
Anthony Gunter and Naomi Holford

Glossary terms   *233*
Index   *236*

CONTRIBUTORS

Michael Boampong
The Open University
Milton Keynes, England
&
ChildFund International
Virginia, USA

Budiyanto
Universitas Negeri Surabaya
Surabaya, Indonesia

Lucy Caton
Bolton University
Bolton, England

Victoria Cooper
The Open University
Milton Keynes, England

Amber Fensham-Smith
The Open University
Milton Keynes, England

Mel Green
The Open University
Milton Keynes, England

Anthony Gunter
The Open University
Milton Keynes, England

Naomi Holford
The Open University
Milton Keynes, England

Heather Montgomery
The Open University
Milton Keynes, England

Vicky Preece
The Open University
Milton Keynes, England

Khofidotur Rofiah
Universitas Negeri Surabaya
Surabaya, Indonesia

Kieron Sheehy
The Open University
Milton Keynes, England

Mimi Tatlow-Golden
The Open University
Milton Keynes, England

Afua Twum-Danso Imoh
University of Bristol
Bristol, England

Sri Widayati
Universitas Negeri Surabaya
Surabaya, Indonesia

Introduction

Understanding children and young people's lives

Mimi Tatlow-Golden and Victoria Cooper

Introduction

How can we understand children and young people? How do we gain insight into their lives and experiences? Why is childhood and youth experienced differently within countries and around the world? How can we best support children to develop, grow, and be well? Can we learn from them? What do they have to teach *us*? What *is* childhood?

These are questions that motivate people who want to learn about childhood and youth, including psychology – and they have motivated the authors of this Open University Reader. To guide you through the main topics, and the under-lying ideas that we explore throughout, we introduce them to you here.

The very notions of what 'childhood' and 'youth' *are* may seem utterly obvious – and yet as you will learn, they are really not that obvious at all. Childhoods and youth vary substantially from place to place and over time. They arise from social and cultural ideas about what is valued, what is deemed best for children, and how children develop and learn. These ideas affect how children are understood and treated, how they experience the world, and how they navigate the many transitions of their lives – whether into or out of schools, into or out of new or familiar activities, communities, friendships, relationships, into adolescence and adulthood, and out of dependence. Many social, biological, psychological, historical, and cultural factors shape these ideas about children and childhoods, and indeed, politics, policy, and economics do too.

Studying childhood and youth

Childhood and Youth Studies with Psychology

This Reader is novel in applying an interdisciplinary approach that first intro-duces you to Psychology and Childhood and Youth Studies separately and then combines insights from both in every subsequent chapter. Our goal is to acknow-ledge the rich perspectives on childhood and youth gained from combining theor-etical ideas and research findings across these disciplines and to offer broader and deeper understandings of children and young people's lives. Even though

DOI: 10.4324/9781003358855-1

historically, Psychology and Childhood and Youth Studies set themselves in contrast to one another and highlighted differences in their views and approaches,
a complementary overlap is often found, too, particularly in social and cultural
developmental psychology, and biological insights that can enhance the social
view. Interdisciplinary psychologist Mimi Tatlow-Golden and social anthropologist
Heather Montgomery (2020) argued for dialogue across difference, and in this
Reader, we place the disciplines in conversation with one another, describing and
integrating many different approaches to research that illuminate childhoods and
youth, with an emphasis on hearing from children and young people themselves.

When studying childhood and youth, it would be overwhelming to try and account for
everything, everywhere, all at once, and so researchers separate various elements out
from one another to be able to describe them more clearly. This Reader does so, too,
teaching topics one by one: bodies, the self, families, mental health, education, disability, race, gender, global childhoods, hybrid 'digital' childhoods, adolescence, and
transitions to adulthood. Yet it is essential to remember that all of these are interlinked.
For example, every child has a body, a self, and mental health. Most also have families
and receive an education. These factors, along with their experiences of race, ethnicity,
and gender, all connect and influence one another whether all at once or at particular
times, and together, they shape children and young people's lived experiences.

In teaching these topics, the Reader takes you through four groups of chapters. To
get you started with *Understanding children and young people's lives*, we first introduce
you to Childhood and Youth Studies and Psychology, the two main academic
perspectives that we combine in every subsequent chapter. We explain how their
different, sometimes contrasting but often complementary, ways of thinking about
childhood and youth provide rich insights and a more holistic view of children and
young people's lives than either perspective can offer alone. We then introduce
embodied childhoods: how children's bodies, characteristically thought of as biological, are also social. We show how children and young people's views of their bodies
and those of others reveal social power relations that define, celebrate, categorise, and
control bodies according to their age, size, place, race/ethnicity, and gender.

How do children and young people become themselves? How are they shaped by
their family experiences? How can we best understand and support their emotional wellbeing and their ability to learn? These are some of the questions answered by the
second group of chapters, *Social, emotional, and cognitive development*. We explore self-
concept and self-esteem, how they are formed in early childhood (and differently across
cultures), and how children and young people value aspects of their selves that adult
psychological researchers overlook. Drawing upon children and young people's points
of view as well as psychological evidence, we examine diverse family experiences across
the world and consider many different kinds of adult supports that are linked to children and young people's wellbeing. The chapter on mental health shares young people's accounts of experiences of mental ill-health in their own words and outlines how
researchers have created biological, psychological, and social models to understand
and support them and the differences in these models' goals and limitations. This

Figure 0.1 Children and young people's lived experiences and development vary depending on many factors beyond their individual differences, including their culture, its social constructions of childhood and youth, and the opportunities they encounter.

Source: FatCamera; andresr; monkeybusinessimages; pixelfusion3d; AzmanL; gorodenkoff; FG Trade; LeoPatrizi via Getty Images

second group closes with a chapter on children's education and schooling and invites readers to consider what a 'good' education means before exploring different understandings of how children learn and why inequalities persist within systems of formal schooling.

The third group of chapters, *Diverse childhoods and youth*, shows how children's lives and everyday experiences are shaped by their bodies, psychologies, and geographies, and by social and cultural ways of thinking about them. You will learn about disability and ways of understanding it and creating worlds in which children are not disabled by society. Addressing race and ethnicity, you will learn how young children respond to race and about racism experienced by children and young people – and how race is not biologically founded but rather socially created, with interpretations that vary across place and time. You will also learn about gender and how children and young people experience and enact gender identities and about childhoods and psychologies in the global South. The final group of chapters considers *Changing childhoods and youth*. Here you will learn how childhood and youth have, for many children around the world, now become 'hybrid', a fluid mix of off- and online lives that combine to create their daily lived experience, and you will consider potential implications for their wellbeing, positive as well as negative. The chapter on the teenage years examines a time of transformation, vulnerability, and opportunity by exploring young people's development from social, psychological, neuropsychological, and political perspectives. Finally, you will examine the processes involved in becoming an adult and the changes, challenges, and prospects that many young people encounter.

Within these individual topics are themes that echo through each of the chapters. The very first theme many people (including children) think about in relation to childhood is *development*. Throughout the Reader, we explore how children and young people *change over time* as they grow and learn. You will see how development involves not just growth but rather a flux of *gains* and also, surprisingly, *losses*. As you will see, the key point to bear in mind is that development brings new capacities – but challenges too.

With a widespread societal and psychological focus on development, we can see that childhood is often talked about as an entirely 'natural' phenomenon, a sort of automatic process in which children grow and change. Yet in fact children are both biological and social: all their development is co-created by both biological and sociocultural influences and the interplay between these. Indeed, the very concepts of 'childhood' and 'youth' are not natural categories but rather they are created by society and culture. By this, we mean that different societies and their cultures (in different regions and countries, different classes and nations, and at different times) all have different ideas about what childhood is, about what is right for a child, what children and young people should do, how children should behave, and what childhood should look and feel like. For example, your grandfather might have (had) different views on what's right for children from the views you have now, and a parent in a rural village in China today might have quite different views from a parent living in London or in Johannesburg. These *social constructions* (or deep-seated, influential socio-cultural ideas) about childhood and youth affect how children are treated, how they are gendered and racialised, and even what kind of a self they develop.

The context for both development and society – *culture* – can be hard to 'see'. Our culture is the immediate and wider world we live in – and cultures vary by country or region but also by communities whether urban or rural, wealthy or experiencing poverty, as you can see in Figure 0.1. In addition to food and care, children require relationships, society, and culture for healthy growth, as humans are social beings who need meaning in life and children can't thrive without others to co-create meaning with them. Culture and its meanings are taken for granted, so much so that people may think of them as 'normal' – though it's important to note that we will be making the case that there is actually no such thing as 'normal', as ideas of 'normal' vary from one place and time to another. People who have migrated to another region, or country, often find culture easier to 'see', as they notice how people's assumptions, activities, and behaviours differ from what they experienced elsewhere. How do you think social constructions of child- hood and youth are expressed differently in the images in Figure 0.1?

How even biology can be socially constructed: The example of race

The idea that childhood, which seems so 'natural', is socially constructed (created by ideas in society and culture) may seem puzzling at first. To start you thinking about this, here, we look at how even *biology* can be socially con- structed, taking the example of race. We highlight two aspects of 'race' that show how human ideas, language, and actions materially affect people's experi- ences and can even shape bodies and health.

First, society *uses biological language* about race to suggest that visible vari- ations in skin, hair, and facial appearance indicate fundamental underlying phys- ical differences between groups of people. Yet in fact, as you will learn in Chapter 9, there are almost no genetic differences between socially defined 'races' and indeed there is more genetic variation *within* them. Race is a socially created idea that was, and often still is, used to 'sort' people, based on the idea that some human groups are inherently more valued than others. Visible superfi- cial physical variations do not map consistently on to other genetic differences, such as blood type, lactose intolerance, malaria resistance, bone density, coeliac disease, or sickle cell disease (Cerdeña *et al.*, 2020; Fausto-Sterling, 2008; Morning, 2014) which exist in quite different patterns. This socially constructed nature of 'race' is further shown in shifting ideas about who belongs in which 'race'. For example, in the US, the idea of who is White has changed 'dramatic- ally over time – to include or exclude Jews, Irish people, Laplanders, Hispanics, South Asians, Middle Easterners, and Ethiopians' (Morning, 2014, p. 191). It, therefore, makes no sense to see 'race' as *based on* biology. How we imagine 'race' is created by people – it is socially constructed.

Ironically, however, even though 'race' doesn't have a biological basis, the very social construction of race can *create biological effects* in those who are racialised as belonging to a less valued group. Children of minoritised communities that experience disadvantage and/or prejudice often grow up with chronic stress, for example, that leads to inflammatory responses, creating greater susceptibility to certain illnesses. Racially minoritised communities often experience poverty, with fewer resources and services that itself create biological effects, seen in group differences in health outcomes. And, furthermore, where health care professionals hold inaccurate ideas about biological differences, or hold prejudiced racial beliefs about certain groups, this has been found to result in poorer health care, with effects on their health and wellbeing. In these ways, the social construction of bodies has identifiable effects on people's lives.

Similarly, socially held beliefs about childhood affect people's attitudes and actions towards children. As you will learn in this Reader, these have substantive outcomes on children and young people's bodies, selves, health, and experiences.

The authors in this Reader emphasise the importance of understanding childhood and youth, including development, as a social or cultural construction. They stress the need to look at how cultures, societies, and communities think about children's lives: how they 'construct', by thinking about and then seeking to enact, what constitutes a 'good' childhood. As you read, you will not only come to appreciate that children and young people's lives are *diverse* but also that *inequalities* shape everyday experiences because some children are treated better than others. These inequities can be understood as *intersectional*. By this we mean that different aspects of children and young people's lives connect – and intersect – in multiple ways that shape their experiences. So rather than focusing solely on individual topics such as gender, social class, or ethnicity, for example, an intersectional view invites closer scrutiny of how these aspects of childhood come together and collide, and as they multiply, they can create significant and enduring inequalities (Crenshaw, 1989). As you read about any topic in this Reader, and as you reflect on diverse experiences of childhood and youth such as those shown in Figure 0.1, we encourage you to bear this in mind.

Learning about childhood can be sensitive for most people

We have all been children and young people, and despite this – and also, crucially *because* of it – understanding childhood and youth is not always easy. You, and everyone else who reads this Reader, may find yourself challenged at times by research findings and accounts of children and young people's experiences that can feel unsettling and challenging if they resonate personally with you. We have certainly had that experience ourselves. Indeed, the topics that challenge can surprise us, as many of us are not always aware of what feels sensitive until experiencing a response. From our own experience of learning about, and teaching, the topics featured in this Reader – whether self-esteem, attachment, bodies, family stories, mental health, race, gender, and more – we recommend bearing the following in mind. First, you are not alone in having (often powerful) responses to learning about childhoods; it's an entirely typical reaction. Second, it's critical to remember that research findings reporting childhood and youth outcomes are giving the *group averages for overall outcomes* and this *cannot* predict individual trajectories. Finally, if you do feel uncomfortable when reading particular topics, step away from your reading and take a break. You may wish to connect to educational, personal, or professional sources of support available to you.

Fundamental to all the authors is the recognition that all children and young people have *rights*. This principle underpins our stance on childhoods and youth at The Open University, and as you will learn in Chapter 1 and hear more about throughout the Reader, it is based on the United Nations Convention on the Rights of the Child (UNCRC, 1989). The UNCRC articulates children's rights to life and also to health, development, play, education, freedom from exploitation, and crucially, to be consulted in matters concerning them. Discussions about rights build upon the understanding that children and young people have *agency* which describes their autonomy and power (if given the opportunity by the adult world) to make choices, decisions, and participate fully in their lives.

Central to this Reader and closely linked to the concept of rights is the principle that to understand childhood and youth, we must explore *children and young people's perspectives*. The idea of listening to children and young people, and providing opportunities for them to share their experiences and have a *voice*, challenges approaches to consultation and research where their views and experiences have been somewhat absent (Cooper, 2023). The UNCRC's repositioning of the status of those aged under 18 years mandated policy makers to engage with children and young people through enhanced engagement, including more effective listening and consultation processes (Cooper and Kellett, 2017). Yet a significant number of children and young people throughout the world still report experiences of not being listened to, and frustration when their views are heard but not acted upon (see Cooper, 2022).

Talking and listening are not only everyday activities but are also used formally by policy makers and researchers interested in the lives and experiences of children and young people. In this Reader, you will be introduced to academic authors spanning disciplines including psychology, childhood studies, sociology, and social anthropology, who draw from different approaches – and different research methods – to examine and understand the lives of children and young people. To ask questions about childhoods and youth, and to observe or study behaviours and experiences, involves selecting particular methods. Throughout this Reader, we introduce experiments, surveys and questionnaires, interviews, observations, and other methods. When looking at how particular methods provide different lenses for exploring and understanding childhood and youth, we also consider their strengths and weaknesses.

Researchers themselves debate these, but our view is that different methods permit researchers to illuminate childhood and youth in different ways.

A word about words: Language and terminology in this Reader

Words matter a great deal. As a child, you may have heard, or chanted yourself, 'Sticks and stones can break my bones, but words can never harm me!' This common incantation is really an act of bravado: it could not be further from the truth, as almost every child knows, because words can be used to insult and demean very effectively. The 21st century is a time of more rapid change than ever, arising from asking hard questions about prejudice and challenging how society constructs 'difference' – which varies from one society and culture to another. Frequent areas for prejudice include gender, race, disability, and mental health. Social shifts since the 20th century in some cultures seeking to recognise human equality, rights, and respect – including for children – are reflected in rapid, regular shifts in language, as people seek to leave behind words designed to insult, or words used as insults. The aim is to use words that are considered respectful, inclusive, and not demeaning.

Beyond terms to refer to certain groups of people, there are contested terms referring to groups of countries. Formerly widely used terms such as 'Third World' or 'developing' country imply a hierarchy in which some are 'first' and others behind. The idea that countries are ranked hierarchically is a racist, colonialist construct, and we, therefore, generally use the terms global South and North in this Reader.

The global South is also referred to as the Majority World, as most of the world's population lives here. It refers to countries in Asia, Africa, or South America. Many have a history of being colonised and marginalised for their beliefs, customs, and religions and many experience poverty. The term global North (or Minority World) refers to North America, Europe, and parts of Australasia. These countries used to be referred to as 'the West' (and the term Western is still regularly used). The global North overall is much more wealthy than the global South, although there are pockets of considerable deprivation and poverty within global North countries. Politically, many countries of the global North are much more powerful than those in the global South, and this leads to unequal relationships between them with uneven distribution of, and access to, resources.

It is important to remember that preferences for the terms used to refer to people or to groups of countries, vary culturally, historically, and also from person to person. In this Reader, you will learn about topics that are often considered sensitive and where language and terminology vary. We use currently preferred terms with the aim of respecting diversity while acknowledging that usage changes over time and that some terms are open to interpretation. Terms will continue to evolve, and some may have changed by the time you read this Reader.

Finally, we note that looking closely at childhood and youth reminds us that development is a lifelong process, as studying childhood and youth offers adults many opportunities to gain greater insight and understanding. Critical reflection thus lies at the heart of this Reader, as a process through which diverse academic authors, different global practices, and the perspectives of adults as well as those of children and young people are brought together. We have asked the authors, and now invite you as a reader, to reflect on what it means to be a child and a young person and how insights into diverse perspectives on childhood and youth can enhance our understanding.

References

Cerdeña, J. P. *et al.* (2020) 'From race-based to race-conscious medicine: how anti-racist uprisings call us to act', *Lancet*, 396, pp. 1125–1128.

Cooper, V. (2023) 'Child focused research: Disconnected and disembodied voices', *Childhood*, 30(1), pp. 71–85. https://doi.org/10.1177/09075682221132084.

Cooper, V., and Kellett, M. (2017) 'Listening to children', in J. Moyles, J. Georgeson, and J. Payler (eds.) *Beginning Teaching, Beginning Learning in Early Years and Primary Education*. Milton Keynes: McGraw Hill Education/Open University Press, pp. 229–240.

Crenshaw, K. (1989) 'Demarginalizing the intersection of race and sex: A Black feminist critique of antidiscrimination doctrine, feminist theory and antiracist politics', *University of Chicago Legal Forum*, 1989(1), article 8 (online: Accessed 26th November 2022).

Fausto-Sterling, A. (2008) 'The bare bones of race', *Social Studies of Science*, 38(5), pp. 657–694.

Morning, A. (2014) 'Does genomics challenge the social construction of race?', *Sociological Theory*, 32(3), pp. 189–207.

Tatlow-Golden, M., and Montgomery, H. (2020) 'Childhood studies and child psychology: disciplines in dialogue?', *Children & Society*, 35(1), pp. 3–17.

1 What is Childhood and Youth Studies?

Heather Montgomery

What is Childhood and Youth Studies, and how does it help us understand children's lives?

Childhood and Youth Studies (often abbreviated to CYS) is a vibrant and dynamic area of study which focuses on the role of children and young people in society and on their relationships and experiences. It analyses ideas about the nature of childhood, examining how adults, children, and young people think about, understand, and represent the experience of being young. It asks questions such as 'What is a child?', 'What do the terms *childhood* or *youth* mean?' and 'What constitutes a good childhood, and how can adults make this possible?' Perhaps most importantly of all, CYS recognises that the experts on childhood and youth are often children and young people themselves. By asking children and young people their views and foregrounding their experiences, CYS academics have been able to influence both policy and practice by ensuring that children and young people's voices are heard and taken into consideration in schools, at home, and across the many varied settings and institutions they connect with.

Childhood is a universal stage of the human life-cycle. Neither anthropologists and sociologists (those who study human cultures and societies in both the present and past) nor historians have ever found a society which did not differentiate between older and younger people or which did not assign special protections to its youngest members. Differences in how childhood is understood and how children are treated, however, are infinitely varied across both time and place, and it was not until relatively recently that academics began to focus on these differences and to look directly at children and young people's own experiences. They argued that in order to understand children's lives, you had to look at children themselves rather than at families, and at children's experiences of school rather than how they were taught. They also began to look at how young people themselves navigated their paths to adulthood and examined children and young persons' perspectives and the meanings they gave to their experiences. They also examined difference, analysing, for example, why girls' childhoods were different to boys' or why young people from diverse ethnic communities had different everyday experiences from others. At the heart of this was listening to children and young people themselves, finding out what changes they wanted and needed,

DOI: 10.4324/9781003358855-2

Figure 1.1 Finger flutings are the lines that human fingers leave when drawn over a soft surface. Palaeolithic people drew these on cave walls and ceilings. Recently, it was discovered that both adults and children made these flutings and that adults would hold up their children to draw – or maybe let them sit on their shoulders to do their art – suggesting rather touching similarities and continuities in parent-child relationships across millennia. The image above is of children's finger flutings in the French caverns of Rouffignac drawn approximately 13,000 years ago.

and working alongside them. This work was underpinned by conceptualisations of children's rights and explicitly driven by an agenda of improvement and social justice, using research to learn about children's lived experiences, to formulate changes in professional and practice settings, as well as in personal spaces, which might improve children's lives.

Expertise in Childhood and Youth Studies

CYS attracts many different people and is not the sole preserve of academic experts. Anyone reading this book will have experience of being a child and – on one level – will 'know' what being a child is all about and what it means. Some readers are attracted to the subject because they work with children and young people – as educators or community and youth workers or in various health and social care fields – and want to know more about how ideas of childhood and youth shape modern lives.

Others will be parents, sometimes of children with additional needs, who will already be highly accomplished and knowledgeable in understanding and advocating for their children. Others are interested in childhood in a more theoretical way. No one needs to have children, or work with them, to be interested in their lives or concerned about their welfare. Everyone reading this book, therefore, already has some expertise, experience, and understanding of children and young people's lives. The great paediatrician and children's advocate, Dr. Benjamin Spock, said this of childrearing, and it is equally pertinent to studying children and young people: 'Trust yourself. You know more than you think you do' (1946, p. 1).

The rest of this chapter (and the book) does not replace the knowledge you already have but will deepen, broaden, and contextualise it and – ideally – help you think about ways this knowledge might be put into your practice whether professionally or as a parent, family member, carer, or citizen.

Key points

- Childhood is a universal stage in the human life-cycle. All societies see older and younger people as different, although how childhood is understood and how children are treated are infinitely varied.
- CYS emphasises the importance of children's experiences and views and uses this to influence both policy and practice across many personal and professional settings.
- Understanding and having an interest in childhood is not confined to academics; parents and professionals also have particular expertise as, importantly, do children themselves.

Childhood is a social construction

A central strand of theory in CYS is that categories such as 'childhood' and 'youth' are *social constructions*. This means that children are thought about and understood very differently in different places and at different times, so that, for example, 100 years ago in the UK, children were most usually seen as less important and even inferior to adults. There was even a common saying that they should be 'seen and not heard'. Today, such an attitude towards children seems old-fashioned, unfair, and is rarely true in a society where relationships between adults and children are generally more mutually respectful. In this simple example, we see how children are thought about in general in society. How they are socially constructed informs not only adult attitudes but also the way they treat children and the way children might behave as a consequence.

It is sometimes hard to analyse our own beliefs and expectations of children. There is much we all take for granted or see as common sense, so to start to explore further what the social construction of childhood means, the boxes in the next section contain examples of how young children are regarded and behaved towards in two different societies. The first box concerns 3-year-old children in a Japanese nursery and the other one, 3-year-old children in an upper-middle-class community in Manhattan, New York.

Children in Japan – robots or social people?

Joy Hendry has spent many years as an anthropologist looking at how children are thought about in Japan and how they are raised. Japanese parents told her that they believed the early years of children's lives were particularly important because they thought that children's characters were fully formed by the age of three and that it was important to ensure children's happiness and family harmony in these years to protect them from longer-term problems. Despite this belief, however, children are not encouraged to express their individual desires and independence is not valued or encouraged. Children are socialised to be part of the collective. Hendry describes a Japanese kindergarten:

> Once children enter a kindergarten or a day nursery, they find themselves in a highly structured situation. Usually they are divided by age so that most of their contact with other children will be with peers, great emphasis being placed on the ideal that all the children should be friends (*tomodachi*) and get on well with one another. Best friends are not particularly encouraged, indeed there is not really a concept at this stage. . . . Conflict and competition is discouraged, and each child is expected to participate equally in the many and varied communal activities. Duties are allocated to each member of the class each day, but every child has a turn eventually to serve and to discipline the others.
>
> Much is made of the equality and sameness of the 'friends' surrounding one in an establishment such as this. Some have complete uniforms, little distinguishing one child from another, most have at least overalls and caps which are identical for boys and girls, except perhaps their caps are different colours to indicate the classroom to which they belong. They have identical sets of equipment kept in identical drawers and shelves.
>
> Thus the child who has been much fussed over, and attended to night and day, now finds itself among perhaps thirty-nine other children, each equally important in the eyes of the teacher, and each equally entitled to her attention.
>
> This is not aimed to turn the children into little robots or automatons, as some Western observers like to see it, but to impress upon the child that the world is full of people just like itself whose needs and desires are equally important. Their names are known – the register is read out every day when each child must answer clearly – and their quirks and character differences become common knowledge as the children move through the classes and often into the school together. Fun and enjoyment are perfectly possible in a kindergarten – indeed they are among the aspects most stressed by teachers and parents alike, but they require co-operation and consideration, and the other members of the peer group become forceful agents of socialisation into this stage of development.
>
> (Hendry, 1986/2017, pp. 165–166)

Children in the USA – cutthroat competitors or successful individuals?

Another anthropologist who is interested in how parents see their children and how they treat them is Adrie Kusserow, who researched an upper-middle-class community in a suburb of New York, which she calls Parkside. Here, parents express very different views of childhood, child-rearing, and what they expect from a nursery. She writes:

> It was quite evident that by age three Parkside children were already considered little competitors – small but complete 'little people' with their own tastes, desires, needs, and wants. All of the Parkside parents I interviewed had their children enrolled in private preschools. Among the Parkside parents, competition to get into private preschools was fierce. There was quite a complex and long application process, consisting of multiple interviews with the parents and the child, the parents alone, and finally the child alone. Intelligence tests and recommendations were also required. Many parents experienced a great deal of angst over whether their child would perform well during the interview process in the preschool they had chosen. The parents knew the child was amazing, but the challenge was to get him to show this to the interviewer.
>
> Interestingly enough, it was among the fathers of the Parkside parents that the language of individualism and competition was often linked. . . . [A] father, a lawyer named David whom I also interviewed in his office, said of his extremely bright and precocious child, Chaz, 'There's a great deal of metaphor possibility between the venture capital business and the upbringing of a child. . . . This has to do with what children are like. Entrepreneurs, successful entrepreneurs are absolutely driven and single minded and megalomaniacal and in many respects they are children'.
>
> Another father, Jordan, spoke proudly of the dogged, 'entrepreneurial' qualities of his daughter: 'She's a risk taker, self-determined. I think it's a personality trait that in the end will serve her well, somebody who's willing to try new things, to be successful . . . be smart, stick to it, be very aggressive and perseverant'.
>
> Of all the strands of individualism, appreciating and developing one's psychological uniqueness and individuality was perhaps most strongly emphasised and linked to success and happiness. One parent stated very simply, 'I think you have to be individually oriented to achieve'.
>
> Another mother said, 'I want my children to be the best that they can be. We are fairly competitive . . . I believe in individual excellence. I do not believe in the lowest common denominator. I think America is really clinging toward the most common denominator in all aspects of our society. I don't believe in that at all. I really fight it, and that's why I don't believe that if

everybody does what you do, that's a judge of what you do, ever. I do believe in the golden rule, but I think the only interesting thing in life is being different . . . better than everybody else'.

One mother, Celia, spoke candidly . . . 'I'm not interested in the normal, I'm interested in the best. I don't approach anything from the normal, so if there are certain things that will give them an advantage, whether or not they can use that or how they can use that is up to the individual. My daughter is extraordinary at chess and ice skating, for which I pay through the nose for her to be extraordinary at'.

(Kusserow, 2004, pp. 81–82)

What is social constructionism?

A theory highlighting the way that ideas, meanings, or categories are shaped by people who share assumptions about the world. Childhood means different things in different societies and cultures across the world and across different periods in history.

Each of these vignettes tells us what the adults in these two communities think about children and their ideas and expectations of childhood – in other words, *how childhood is socially constructed*. Each group of parents have very different ideas about what constitutes a good childhood and how best to achieve it. Hendry's account suggests that when Japanese children go to nursery, they are socialised to be cooperative and collaborative and to understand that their own individual desires and preferences are much less important than social cohesion and equality. They also learn that other children are 'forceful agents of socialisation' (i.e., that peer pressure and conformity are important parts of learning in the kindergarten). In contrast, the parents in New York view childhood as a time of learning the basics of how to grow up as an economically and socially successful individual who can compete, excel, and win against others.

These two short accounts provide a snapshot of specific communities at certain times, and while they show great differences between two notions of childhood, it is important not to generalise too broadly, or to stereotype, or to judge, different societies negatively because they are different to one's own. There are, of course, great differences within societies as much as between them. Not all parents in New York see their children in this way. Indeed, Adrie Kusserow also spent time in a much poorer, working-class community in a different borough, where children were thought about and talked about very differently. Here, life was more of a struggle. Children were 'toughened up' and taught to stand up for themselves not so they might compete and win against others or become miniature venture capitalists but so that they might survive in an unfriendly and sometimes hostile environment. Similarly in Japan, not all parents or all nurseries emphasise the importance of cooperation and conformity. Furthermore, Hendry's research was carried out in the 1980s, and as Japanese society has changed, so, too, have many ideas about childhood: nurseries in contemporary Japan may strive to instil different values in children.

Seeing childhood as a social construction allows us to acknowledge that childhoods are different, depending on where and when they happen, and that children and young people's lives are affected by the expectations adults place on them which reflect wider political, social, cultural, and economic factors. Understanding categories such as 'boys', 'girls', 'children', or 'youth' as social constructions allows us to recognise that ideas about children and young people differ between societies and change over both time and place. It is, therefore, important not to think that one's own culture, society, or community (wherever that might be) is the 'norm' or the 'best' one while others are different and possibly inferior. Instead, understanding *all* childhoods, including our own, as socially constructed allows us to recognise the varieties of childhood. If we can see that childhood is very different and children's lives are shaped by these different ideas of childhood *across* cultures, then it becomes easier to recognise and acknowledge a more diverse range of childhoods *within* cultures. In doing this, it is essential to start questioning our own 'common sense' or 'taken-for-granted' ideas of childhood. This will be explored in several chapters in this book, including Chapter 4 which explores how we make sense of self; Chapter 11 which examines the impact of gender on constructions of childhood; and Chapter 9 which looks at how the construction of 'youth' is often heavily racialised and how the expectations and stereotypes of certain groups of young people can have devastating impacts on their experiences.

Key points

- Understanding *childhood as a social construction* enables us to examine ideas about children and young people and to discover how they are thought about and treated. It allows us to examine the social meanings given to childhood across and within societies.
- Children in different countries and in different communities lead very different lives, and their parents have very different ideas about their nature, their needs, and what is best for them. This is what is meant by the phrase 'childhood is socially constructed'.

Different specialist areas within Childhood and Youth Studies

When you start studying Childhood and Youth Studies, you will come across a wide variety of terms and different specialist subject areas which focus specifically on the needs and capabilities of children and young people of different ages. You will sometimes come across categories such as early childhood (or early years), middle childhood, and youth. Indeed, Early Childhood or Youth Studies are sometimes considered disciplines in their own right but can also be usefully brought under the umbrella of CYS, each adding more pieces to the jigsaw puzzle to build up a holistic picture of children and young people's lives.

The term early childhood is generally used to cover the study of children in the first few years of their lives and focuses on their educational and developmental needs.

Middle childhood is often seen as starting around the age of 6 and ending approximately at 11 years. This is usually the age that many children across Europe and the United States start formal education, such as primary school (although children in the UK and Ireland start school earlier). They make their own friends and develop distinct preferences for friends of their own sex. It is the age when they start to build relationships away from the home and their families.

Terms for young people (those who are not still seen as children but are not yet adult) are also used differently, and the phrase young people usually refers to children over the age of 12 or 13. While childhood is defined as 0 to 18, youth is often seen as going past this, sometimes up to the age of 25 or even 30. There are also many names for this stage of life: 'teenage', for instance, is a word which came to prominence after World War II as an advertising term, referring to an emerging market of newly independent young people. It tapped into the growing distinctive youth culture of the post-war period (which you will explore in more detail in Chapter 13 on adolescence), and while the term 'teenage' is very common in everyday language, it is used more rarely in academic work. 'Adolescence' tends to be used by psychologists, health workers, and doctors and refers to the period after puberty (which can begin as early as 8 years in some contemporary societies) and before full adult growth is reached and is seen as a time of particular biological milestones or behaviours. In contrast, sociologists, anthropologists, and historians use the term 'youth' to suggest a flexible definition of young people which covers their lives from the early teenage years, around 12 or 13, and on into their middle 20s. The field of Youth Studies has a long and distinguished history as an interdisciplinary subject area which draws particularly on sociology, cultural studies, and education and has looked at youth subcultures, young people's political engagement, social rebellion, and at how young people are thought about and treated within society (see Chapter 14 on transitions). More recently, Youth Studies has turned its focus to youth activism and young people finding innovative ways and places outside school and home to enact social change.

An emerging but important subcategory of CYS is Disabled Children's Childhood Studies. This raises important questions about what society considers 'normal' or typical in childhood and allows for an examination of social attitudes towards disabled or neurodiverse children. While looking at many of the same ideas and asking the same questions as CYS, Disabled Children's Childhood Studies also focuses on those children who are 'different' or marginalised in some ways (this will be discussed further in Chapter 8 which addresses disabled children). It also questions some of the assumptions that scholars in CYS make when they study children, for example, that all children can be asked about their experiences and ideas and articulate their opinions and/or that stages of development are associated with specific ages, which may not be relevant to disabled children. Disabled Children's Childhood Studies calls upon academics in CYS to think about ways of fully integrating disabled children into research as well as into society and the best ways that research can help improve these children's lives and support them and their families (Curran and Runswick-Cole, 2013).

Figure 1.2 Learning to farm at a Thai school.

Key points

- Childhood and youth can be differentiated and studied according to particular ages and stages within development, including early childhood, middle childhood, and youth.
- There are different specialisms within CYS, such as or Early Childhood or Youth Studies, but they can all usefully be seen as part of a broader CYS and can work together to build up a holistic picture of children and young people's lives.
- Disabled Children's Childhood Studies is a new and vibrant part of CYS which looks at disabled children's experiences and roles in society and challenges ideas of what is 'normal' or typical.

Children's rights and why they are important

The idea that children have rights is a central component of Childhood and Youth Studies and one that shapes both the theories of the field as well as ways of researching children and young people's lives. The key point to remember when studying children's rights is that *children's rights are human rights*. Children have rights in international and national law because they are human beings, although it is recognised, in addition, that they may need special protections because of their social and physical vulnerability and because of their dependence on others. While the term most usually used is 'children's rights', it is perhaps more accurate to think of them as 'children and young people's human rights'.

Discussions of children's rights have been around for many decades. The first ever international legislation concerning children's welfare, the Geneva Declaration of the Rights of the Child, was adopted internationally in 1924. The most significant, however, is the United Nations Convention on the Rights of the Child (UNCRC) which was opened for signature in 1979. Since then, every country in the world has signed it (expressing their intent to comply with it) and every country except the USA has rati-fied it (meaning that governments have approved an international agreement internally and consent to be bound by it and pledge to change their own national and domestic laws to ensure they fulfil the UNCRC's provisions).

The UNCRC is made up of 54 articles covering, among other things, children's right to life, health care, education, nationality, and legal representation. The UNCRC is not simply a list of children's basic needs or an expression of what adults think is best for children. It emphasises their right to be taken seriously, listened to, con-sulted, and for their views to matter and be considered. It starts with a statement which affirms children's humanity and their requirement for special protections, as well as their need to be brought up in the 'spirit of peace, dignity, tolerance, freedom, equality and solidarity' (UNCRC, 1989). It defines a child as 'every human being below the age of 18 years' (Article 1) and takes as its fundamental principle: 'All actions concerning the child shall take full account of his or her best interests' (Article 3).

The rights set out in the UNCRC are often grouped into three categories known as the '3 Ps': children's right to *provision* (such as their rights to food, housing, or educa-

Figure 1.3 A mural about children's rights from Uganda.

tion), their right to *protection* (against exploitation and abuse), and (the most contro-versial) their right to *participation* (meaning that children have the right to express their views and that adults have an obligation to listen to them and to promote their parti-cipation in all matters affecting them). In the UK, the 1989 Children Act was the first piece of legislation brought in by the UK government in response to the UNCRC. The Act emphasised the importance of listening to children and, for the first time in the history of the British legal system, ruled that courts should regard the wishes and feel-ings of the children concerned, dependent on their age and understanding. Children were allowed, by the courts and within the welfare system, to voice opinions on matters such as where they would prefer to live after a parental divorce or whether they wished to remain at home or go into care when there were concerns about child protection. The Act, however, was not universally popular, and concerns were expressed over its potential to undermine parental responsibility and unsettle family relationships. Some commentators called it a 'Brat's Charter' and warned of children divorcing their parents if they did not have enough pocket money or demanding the right to do whatever they wanted (Lansdown, 1994).

Although this reaction looks slightly exaggerated in retrospect and no child ever tried to divorce their parents over pocket money (and indeed, there was no sugges-tion that they would ever be allowed to do so), it did highlight some of the difficulties of ensuring that children's participation rights worked in practice. Few would argue with the need for children to be fed or educated, but not everyone thinks that chil-dren's best interests are served by allowing them to make important decisions, or agrees about when they may have the capacity or full knowledge to do so, or indeed whether they should have to shoulder the responsibility of doing so. A 12-year-old child may have a preference about where she wants to live after a parental divorce, but asking her to make that decision and communicate it to a court may place a great burden on a child who does not wish to upset either parent. For others, the idea of children's autonomy and right to make decisions clashes with what they see as their responsibilities as parents. In 2006, Sue Axon sought a declaration from the courts that if any of her daughters, while under the age of 16, sought advice from a doctor about contraception, sexually transmitted infections, or abortion, she should be informed and the doctor was not obliged to keep this confidential. Mrs. Axon lost her case and the judge stated:

> The ratification by the United Kingdom of the United Nations Convention on the Rights of the Child in November 1989 was significant as showing a desire to give children greater rights . . . concerning their own future while reducing the super-visory rights of their parents. . . . [T]he right of young people to make decisions about their own lives by themselves at the expense of the views of their parents has now become an increasingly important and accepted feature of family life.
>
> (quoted in Cornock and Montgomery, 2014, p. 168)

It is still a balancing act, however, and there may be instances where regardless of young people's right to make a decision about their own lives, this right is superseded by what adults perceive are their best interests. Many of the most controversial cases have focused on medical decisions and children's competence and autonomy in being able to make decisions about their own bodies. In Norway, for instance, the Children's Ombudsman (the official in charge of the protection and promotion of the rights of children and young people) demanded a legal ban on cosmetic surgery for those under 18 – despite protests from girls of 16 who felt fully competent to make informed decisions about their bodies (Montgomery, 2003). Similarly, in England and Wales, the courts can and do intervene in cases where judges believe that the child's 'best interest' supersedes other rights so that, for example, a devout adolescent Jehovah's Witness cannot refuse a blood transfusion if it will save their lives.

More controversially, in 2020, the High Court in the UK ruled that the Gender Identity Development Service at the Tavistock Clinic in London could not continue to prescribe puberty blocking drugs to children under 16 experiencing gender dysphoria. The judge wrote:

> It is highly unlikely that a child aged 13 or under would be competent to give consent to the administration of puberty blockers. . . . It is doubtful that a child aged 14 or 15 could understand and weigh the long-term risks and consequences of the administration of puberty blockers.
>
> (Hunte, 2020)

While this was welcomed by some feminist groups, newspaper columnists, and others who argued it protected vulnerable children, it was also denounced heavily by others who argued it undermined children's rights to be consulted and to participate in decisions regarding their medical treatment. The debate and legal battles continue and in September 2021, the original ruling was overturned, and in the following year, in 2022, the Gender Identity Development Service was decentralised and relocated. There is still little agreement or middle ground. Both sides care passionately about children and young people's wellbeing but differ fundamentally in what they believe to be their best interests. These medical cases show, however, the difficulties and controversies involved in trying to balance children and young people's rights to protection and participation, while simultaneously trying to ensure children's best interests.

Researching 'with' and researching 'on' children and young people

The importance of children's participation is central to Childhood and Youth Studies as an academic field, and many researchers have looked at how children can play a more active role in research. They have argued that researchers in CYS need to go further than working 'on' children by going into schools or laboratories (which might suggest they are researching from a distance and that children are simply the objects of study and have no real participation in it) and instead research 'with' children or young people in more neutral or informal settings, like the home or the playground, and asking children directly about their lives and how they view the world. There is now a large body of literature on different methods of working with children, and one thing that unites much of this work is the insistence on learning about children's lives, as far as possible, from children themselves.

One example of how researchers have tried to ensure that children are listened to and acknowledged as experts in their own lives is the Mosaic approach, first pioneered by researchers Alison Clark and Peter Moss in the late 1990s. This was conceived as a research approach 'with' children which ensured that even the youngest children truly participated in research. Clark and Moss set out a framework for listening to younger children and incorporating their views into policy, especially policy relating to the early childhood services they accessed. In order to do this, they used various techniques, including short, informal interviews, followed up several months later; giving children single-use cameras to take photographs of things which were important to them; encouraging child-led tours of the nursery during which children would point out places that were important to them; nursery mapping where children drew the nursery as they saw it; and close observation of children.

Through these methods, Clark and Moss built up a picture of the ways that children experienced their lives in the nursery. They learned about children's favourite places, where children could go for privacy, and the places where they liked to play with their friends. For example, 3-year-old Gaby was given a disposable camera and asked to photograph 'important things'. Almost every photo she took was of another child or children. She took the researcher around the nursery, explaining that she currently ate lunch in the conservatory but went on to say, 'I can't wait to be big', because this meant she could eat in the Orange Room with the older children. She also talked about the activities she most liked and about the role of adults (Clark, 2005). According to Clark and Moss, listening to young children in this systematic way enabled everyone, including both parents and staff, to understand more about what life feels like for young children and what they value which, in turn, enabled changes to be made which reflected children's concerns and preferences.

Key points

- Children's rights are set out in the United Nations Convention on the Rights of the Child (UNCRC).
- The rights in the UNCRC are usually grouped into the rights concerning protection, provision, and participation.
- Participation rights have been controversial, especially in health care, because they can clash with adults' perceptions of children's rights of protection and provision and have to be balanced against them.

- Working 'with' children rather than 'on' them aims to ensure that they are properly listened to and can participate in research.

Conclusion

This chapter briefly introduced you to some of the main ideas that are central to contemporary Childhood and Youth Studies. Firstly, it discussed the growth and importance of the study of childhood and youth in the 21st century and explored how this relatively new subject area can help us understand and improve children and young people's lives in contemporary societies. Secondly, it argued that childhood can be usefully understood as social construction and that children's lives are affected by social expectations and beliefs about childhood. Thirdly, it described how CYS acts as an umbrella term which includes other subfields, such as Early Childhood, Youth Studies, or Disabled Children's Childhood Studies. Finally, it recognised that children are the bearers of rights and that children have rights to protection, provision, and participation, although the latter have sometimes proved difficult or controversial to implement.

References

Clark, A. (2005) 'Ways of seeing: using the mosaic approach to listen to young children's perspectives', in A. Clark, A. T. Kjørholt, and P. Moss (eds.) *Beyond Listening: Children's Perspectives on Early Childhood Services*. Bristol: Policy Press, pp. 29–49.

Cornock, M., and Montgomery, H. (2014) 'Children's rights since Margaret Thatcher', in S. Wagg and J. Pilcher (eds.) *Thatcher's Grandchildren*. Basingstoke: Palgrave Macmillan, pp. 160–178.

Curran, T., and Runswick-Cole, K. (eds.) (2013) *Disabled Children's Childhood Studies. Critical Approaches in a Global Context*. London: Palgrave Macmillan.

Hendry, J. (1986/2017) 'Peer pressure and kindergartens in Japan', in J. Hendry (ed.) *An Anthropological Lifetime in Japan: The Writings of Joy Hendry*. Leiden: Brill, pp. 164–176.

Hunte, B. (2020) 'Puberty blockers: parents' warning as ruling challenged', *BBC News*, Available at: www.bbc.co.uk/news/education-55369784 (Accessed 22nd March 2021).

Kusserow, A. (2004) *American Individualisms: Child Rearing and Social Class in Three Neighborhoods*. New York: Palgrave Macmillan.

Lansdown, G. (1994) 'Children's rights', in B. Mayall (ed.) *Children's Childhoods: Observed and Experienced*. London: The Falmer Press, pp. 33–44.

Montgomery, H. (2003) 'Intervening in children's lives', in H. Montgomery, R. Burr, and M. Woodhead (eds.) *Changing Childhoods: Global and Local*. Chichester: John Wiley, pp. 187–232.

Spock, B. (1946) *Baby and Child Care* (1st ed.). New York: Pocket Books.

United Nations (1989) *Convention on the Rights of the Child*. Available at: https://www.ohchr.org/en/instruments-mechanisms/instruments/convention-rights-child.

2 The psychology of childhood and youth

Mimi Tatlow-Golden

Introducing psychology

Psychology is the science of mind and behaviour, an academic discipline and profes-sional practice that aims to understand, describe, and explain how people think, feel, and behave. It also aims to apply this knowledge to achieve the best outcomes for children and young people and the worlds in which they grow, eat, play, learn, and socialise.

To do so, psychologists study many domains of life spanning the social, the biologi-cal, and more. Many people think first of mental health when they think of psychology, and mental health is an important field of psychological inquiry (explored in more detail in Chapter 6), but it is certainly not the only one. Psychology spans domains across the social and natural sciences, and one way of representing the aspects of life psychology covers is shown in the five pillars in Figure 2.1: developmental, biological, cognitive, social/personality, and mental/physical health.

Developmental psychology is shown on the left of Figure 2.1. Developmental psy-chologists examine how human life changes over time. Whereas earlier conceptualisa-tions assumed development was complete on reaching adulthood, developmental science now understands that change occurs over the whole lifetime (Baltes, 1979) – as people learn new skills and change in response to life events, such as childbirth, new roles and relationships, bereavement, mental or physical illness and recovery, and more. The definition of childhood and youth itself has also extended beyond the age of 18 years to encompass the early 20s, a very active time of development (see Chapters 13 and 14). It is also understood that pre-birth development (both genetic and environmental) can play out in childhood and youth.

When focusing on childhood and youth, developmental psychology addresses chil-dren and young people's change over time and the factors that influence this. However, not only development but all the domains of psychology shown in Figure 2.1 are relevant to childhood and youth. Looking at the other pillars, *biological* psychology examines bodily processes that affect development, as well as sensation, human con-sciousness (our awareness of ourselves, our thoughts, and feelings), and includes neu-ropsychology, a branch of biological psychology considering the impact of brain function, the nervous system, and hormones, among others.

Cognitive psychology, or the psychology of thinking, spans perception, memory, cognition, and intelligence and aims to understand how children and young people

DOI: 10.4324/9781003358855-3

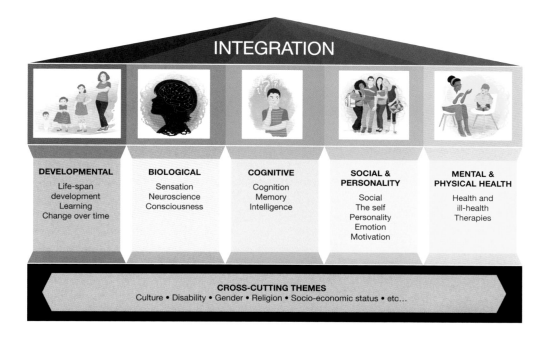

Figure 2.1 The key pillars of psychological inquiry. *Adapted from*: Gurung et al. (2016).

Figure 2.2 Development spans all of life, from babyhood to old age.

process information and learn. *Social and personality* psychology includes the study of emotion and motivation, individual differences in personality, the self, and social processes in human groups and societies and, therefore, explains individual feelings and differences, and how we function in groups. *Mental and physical health* psychology examines variations in human wellbeing. Finally, at the base of the diagram, you can see *cross-cutting themes*. These refer to the many individual, social, cultural, and other diversities that are also crucial features of childhood and youth, including (among others) age, gender, gender identity, sexual orientation, ethnicity/race, culture, national origin, religion, disability status, language, and socioeconomic status. You have learned about some cultural and social differences in childhoods in Chapter 1 and will learn about many more in the coming chapters. In addition to these, ethics are important, as psychological research and practice is always bound by ethical principles similar to the injunction in medicine: 'first, do no harm'.

These pillars indicate the ways that psychologists generally research children and young people's lives and development, as if they consisted of separate topic areas – as indeed we do in this Reader. Yet it may well have occurred to you that none of these aspects of human experience takes place in isolation. Whether considering children and young people's families, schooling, early relationships, bodies, physical development, or mental health, these many psychological domains need to be understood as co-existing in the same person, influencing one another to create behaviour, experience, and change over time. As an example, we might consider a child who is struggling to make progress at school. How can we understand this? It might make logical sense to assess their overall ability to concentrate, or to process information, perhaps their reading ability, their 'intelligence', or capacity to learn and adapt (but with cautions – see later in the chapter). Although understanding these *cognitive* psychological factors can be vital, there might be other factors affecting the child's school learning. These might include, for example, their *social-emotional abilities*: are they able to understand their own emotional states and regulate them? Can they form positive relationships with peers and with teachers? Or perhaps their *mental health*: are they experiencing anxiety that impedes their ability to learn?

As the previous example suggests, multiple psychological factors might be found 'within' any given individual. However, psychological factors are also found in the environment around them. For example, psychological research has shown that attitudes and expectations held by others, such as teachers, can affect children's capacity to learn. Such attitudes might be about gender: do teachers believe that boys are inherently better at maths and girls better at reading? If so, research shows they may implicitly (or even explicitly) teach differently, based on this. (Later on, in Chapter 8, you will learn how teachers' beliefs about disability change the way they respond to and teach disabled children.) Equally, teachers' attitudes about social groups can affect children's ability to learn. Teachers' beliefs about ability and gender, social class, ethnicity, or race have been shown to affect how they teach and support children, and you will learn more about this in Chapter 7. Similarly, attitudes held by parents and the wider community can be relevant – for example, whether school-based learning is valued or not – and can influence children's own attitudes to school. Furthermore, external factors that may seem quite distant, such as economic inequalities in society, can have a profound effect on children's capacity to learn: for example, when children come to school hungry, this affects their ability to process information and to concentrate. Overall, therefore, the psychology of childhood and youth is a web of interconnecting factors, and when learning about any one of them, it is important to bear other potential influences in mind.

Key points

- Psychology consists of many different domains spanning mind, brain, and behaviour.
- Developmental psychology is a key area of psychological study of childhood and youth.
- Developmentalists of childhood and youth study the age range from pre-birth to the early 20s.
- The psychology of childhood and youth is a web of interconnecting factors that interact with one another.

Figure 2.3 A psychologist takes notes as she watches a child play with colourful blocks.

Many different kinds of psychologists

Psychology addresses many facets of life and so child and adolescent psychologists are found in many settings. In the UK, these career pathways require an under-graduate (or equivalent) psychology degree recognised by the British Psychological Society before further training can be undertaken. Other pathways that draw on psychological insights, but do not necessarily require psychological training, might include youth work, social work, nursing, teaching, teaching assistant, and mentoring, among others.

In the box, you can read about some of the roles professional psychologists perform.

Different psychologists and where we might find them

Clinical psychologist

Clinical psychologists in the UK and Ireland are key players on the multi-dimensional teams that make up *Child and Adolescent Mental Health Services* (generally referred to as CAMHS). They have completed postgraduate training that equips them for health services work. They can carry out tests to diagnose children's difficulties and provide psychotherapeutic, behavioural, or other kinds of support. In general, psychologists cannot prescribe medication however – that is the responsibility of a psychiatrist (a medical doctor who has qualified for mental health work, as discussed in Chapter 6), although this varies globally, as, for example, in some states in the USA where psychologists have prescribing rights.

Educational psychologist

Educational psychologists usually work for Local Authorities in the UK (although they can work privately) and support children and young people's access to education across a range of settings, including schools and home. They address barriers that may prevent a child engaging in education and making progress in their learning (e.g., learning disabilities; physical and sensory needs; social, emotional, and behavioural needs; language and communication needs; and more).

Forensic psychologist

Forensic psychologists work in the legal and criminal justice system in many roles including giving advice, guidance and support for courts, witnesses, evidence, and juries; carrying out offender management and treatment; and understanding criminal behaviour and forensic mental health. Roles may relate to children as trial witnesses, or on Youth Offending Teams.

Hospitals and health care

Psychological support is an important feature of holistic health care. Clinical psychologists and others, such as play therapists, work with in- and outpatients supporting children and young people having treatment, or coping with pain, bereavement, unwell relatives, and more.

Research psychologist

Research psychologists, usually in universities and often collaborating with practitioners, generate knowledge about children and young people applied by all these professionals.

Development involves change over time – and children may know more than adults

From infancy to adulthood, children change dramatically – not just physically from baby to adult but psychologically as well. They acquire language. They develop the ability to think and reason, to understand what others know and what others are think-ing. They also learn social skills, how to form and sustain friendships and other rela-tionships, and how to moderate their emotions and much more.

In many ways, therefore, development consists of a progression and growth through childhood and youth towards greater capacities and competence. However, this doesn't necessarily take place in an ordered pace over time. Some complex compe-tences only come on stream very late, as you will learn in Chapters 13 and 14. For example, *executive function* – the complex ability to manage certain behaviours, stay focused, resist temptation, and deal with the unexpected via self-control, focus, memory, and cognitive flexibility – only fully matures in the early 20s. This is probably due to the late maturation of the prefrontal cortex (Diamond, 2013), the front part of the brain's frontal lobe, which is involved in planning and controlling behaviours. Yet *language*, another highly complex, specifically human competence, develops astonish-ingly early. Children hear sounds of the language around them while in the womb and vocalise from birth. In just five years, they go from these basic vocalisations to bab-bling, to speaking words, to coordinating conversation and dialogue, to the expressive ability to tell stories, name emotions, and even tell jokes and lies, and describe the past and imagine the future (Ibbotson, 2022).

Despite the many clear gains typically made from infancy through to adulthood, development is better characterized as an ebb and flow of capacity and change, as it involves not only gains but losses too. For example, from birth, infants have about 100 billion brain cells (about 15% more than adults) and are cognitively prepared to learn to hear and speak any language. However, after about one to two years, children have focused on the language(s) and culture around them, through a selective 'sculpting' process (that might be characterized as 'use it or lose it') in which the most relevant brain circuits are strengthened, while others weaken and die. Their ability to distin-guish other sounds then rapidly diminishes, and learning new languages becomes progressively more difficult – a substantial developmental loss. As another example, in early-to-mid-childhood, a cognitive gain brings potential social-emotional losses. Young children have unrealistically grand ideas about their abilities – a cognitive lim-itation. As they develop the cognitive capacity to perspective-take, they gain the insight that others may be faster, stronger, or smarter than they are. This leads to greater realism but also a loss of their earlier boundless self-confidence, which can then result in lower self-esteem (Harter, 2012). You will learn more about self and self-esteem in Chapter 4 and about gains and losses in adolescence in Chapter 13.

Depicting development as ever-growing gains can also lead to the false conclusion that adults are necessarily more competent than children. This widespread view is one we encounter as researchers working with children and young people. 'What's the point in asking children?' people often ask us. 'Wouldn't you be better off just asking their parents?' or even 'Why bother? Children don't tell the truth anyway'. And yet chil-dren are routinely better than adults at certain things, sometimes due to develop-mental factors and sometimes due to their experience. One example is that children are better than adults when learning about cause-and-effect relationships. They are less biased by prior assumptions and pay more attention to current evidence (Lucas *et al.*, 2014). Another example is in family migration, where children become more competent in the new language than their parents, as they still have the capacity to learn languages more easily compared to adults. Indeed, where parents have not been able to learn the language, children often become social and cultural 'brokers', acting as translators and helping parents with administrative, medical, and other personal or complex interactions – gaining competence in all these tasks, too, through their experience with them (Cline, Crafter and Prokopiou, 2014). Finally, children are by definition expert in their own lives and experiences, knowing many things adults do not – an expertise which they may not always choose to share with adults, sometimes protecting their parents and other adults from knowledge children believe could cause them worry (Valentine, 1997).

Not only do development and competence involve complex processes but they also take place within complex contexts. Many accounts of the psychology of childhood and youth indicate that learning, growth, understanding, or resilience are internal, individual characteristics. Yet every child's life unfolds in the contexts they live in. This back-and-forth nature of children's experiences and development can be imagined when thinking about how a nurturing family, learning, or other environment may either support optimal development or hinder it. An example involves 'school readiness' research and policy, which focuses on identifying whether young children are 'ready' for transitioning

Dandelions and orchids: Children's characteristics interact with environments

What does it take for a child or young person to thrive? The question of how we can support children to do their best is of perennial interest. One body of research that has become known as the 'dandelion-orchid' studies shows a very interesting interaction between children's individual characteristics and the environments they are in. Researchers found that some children are more sensitive not just to challenging circumstances but also to positive ones. 'Dandelions' is the descriptor that has been applied to up to a third of children who can thrive and do well despite living in tough environments (like the sturdy dandelion plant that can grow and flower just about anywhere). In contrast, 'orchids', also about a third of children, are more sensitive to their settings and only do well in the right environment. Interestingly, whereas 'orchids' respond very strongly to positive environments and flourish in them, 'dandelion' types are not particularly affected by them.

Still, more recent research has proposed there may be a middle group as well – the sturdy medium, representing up to half of children who consistently do reasonably well. One researcher even extends the floral metaphor and refers to these as the 'tulips' – flowers less delicate than orchids but not as robust as dandelions (Pluess *et al.*, 2018).

Figure 2.4 Robust dandelions can flower in almost any place, whereas more delicate orchids need the right conditions to flower and flourish.

How this interaction between children's *nature* (their individual characteristics) and *nurture* (the environments they are raised in) plays out – and the implications for their resilience – can be seen in an example of a school-based anti-bullying intervention trialled with over 2,000 children in 13 schools in Italy (Nocentini, Menesini and Pluess, 2018). This intervention's activities and supports were effective overall in the schools, but notably, boys who scored high on environmental sensitivity benefited most, reporting being bullied less and fewer negative psychological symptoms, while boys who scored low on sensitivity were not affected by the intervention.

to formal schooling (see more about this in Chapter 3). Yet equally pertinent questions are also: how ready is the *school* for the children that are about to arrive? Does the school have the resources and knowledge to support children and their learning? And do adults know what skills children think are needed to be ready? Indeed, adult assessments of 'school readiness' only partially consider what children say is important for starting school, often leaving out crucial issues such as making friends, bullying, toilet use, school-family relationships, and more (O'Farrelly *et al.*, 2019).

The importance of the environment and how it interacts with children's individual characteristics is illustrated with research on children's differential sensitivity.

Finally, a reminder that as you read in the 'Introduction' and Chapter 1 and will return to in Chapter 5, another key feature of children and young people's environments is *culture*. Remember that much of psychology's data gathering has taken place in the global North, more frequently in cities, with middle-class urban participants. Of course, this reflects only a small proportion of the world. Although this is starting to change, the slow rate of progress on this issue means that one should assume that most psychological theories and conclusions are based on this research with urban, middle-class people in the global North.

Key points

- Development involves not only gains but losses too.
- Children may be more competent than adults.
- Children and young people are differentially sensitive to their contexts.
- Culture is a crucial feature of childhood development, yet most psychological research is limited to studies of urban, middle-class participants in the global North.

Psychology and its methods

To understand human behaviour, much (though not all) of psychology constructs itself as a science. In doing so, it seeks to study humans systematically, to achieve findings that are thought to be as unbiased as possible by using *quantitative*, scientific methods that require devising ways to *measure* children and young people's thoughts, feelings, experiences, and behaviours. Quantitative psychological evidence carries great weight in policy arenas, such as health and education, where spending decisions are made that materially affect children's lives.

The 'scientific method': Using quantitative research in psychology

Key principles governing the scientific method as it is applied in psychology are that research is systematic, replicable (can be repeated and get the same or similar results), ethical, and objective. To achieve these goals, psychological research asks questions about features of human life – whether anxiety, depression, language ability, learning, intelligence, self-esteem, or anything else. These features are measured to produce data, that are then statistically analysed to identify whether a relationship or a difference between them is due to chance – or due to a factor of interest. Examples of statistical analyses are the following:

- *Correlation*: Are the findings related to one another? For example, depression and anxiety often co-occur, so they can be said to be *correlated*. Note that being statistically related doesn't necessarily mean that one *causes* the other.
- *Difference*: Are groups, when measured, found to be statistically different? For example, are there gender differences in prevalence of depression or anxiety?
- *Experiments*: Can a causal effect be shown? In psychological experiments, a researcher specifies a hypothesis and tests it by manipulating one variable and measuring another. For example, a researcher might develop a new anxiety-reduction programme for teens, carrying out an experiment to measure its effect and predicting (hypothesising) it will be more effective than treatment as usual. Participants due to receive the new treatment or treatment as usual would be divided into two similar groups. Measuring anxiety levels before and after the treatments in both groups allows the hypothesis to be tested, to see if the new treatment was more effective at reducing anxiety.

There are many ways in which psychological research can create valuable knowledge about children and young people. In this Reader, you will learn about many psychological studies exploring correlations (whether things are linked to one another), group differences, and experiments. You will find that psychology has added to our knowledge about many important features of childhood and youth, including the effects of different kinds of family life, early parenting, cultural expectations in growing up, racism, brain development, mental health, and much more.

However, caution is also warranted. According to research principles, experiments need to 'isolate' variables (e.g., anxiety versus depression) to measure them separately, but as you have learned, there are many complex interactions of the many features of human life, such as anxiety, that are not generally experienced in isolation. Furthermore, human life is not experienced in measurable units, meaning we should be cautious about over-reliance on quantitative studies that measure behaviour. Where children and young people are concerned, measurement accuracy can be even more of an issue, as many 'scales' or surveys have been created by adults, and research shows that children and young people's priorities are not necessarily represented. You read about this above regarding school readiness; you will learn more in Chapter 4 on the issue of self-concept.

Quantitative research methods underlie much psychological research. A smaller, but no less important, strand of psychological research is *qualitative*: research that does not seek to measure human behaviour but rather to understand how it is experienced. It does so, for example, by carrying out interviews and using many creative and visual methods to achieve rich descriptions and deeper understandings of children and young people's lives. For example, if psychologists wanted to understand anxiety, *quantitative* researchers might seek to measure how much anxiety a child is experiencing (on a scale of 'none' to 'severe') and compare the effectiveness of different interventions designed to reduce anxiety, whereas *qualitative* researchers might aim to understand the nature of children's experiences of anxiety and how they describe it affecting them. Combining both approaches is known as *mixed methods research*, and this provides a more holistic view of children and young people's lives.

Understanding psychological research methods is important, because methods are key to identifying the evidence that academic research creates, including its strengths and limitations. Two key issues of concern about psychological research have come to light in the 21st century. These have caused psychologists to engage in long-overdue self-examination, questioning aspects of their activities and evidence base.

First, a 'replication crisis' has been developing in psychology (and other sciences). This refers to when the tests and experiments that generate psychological evidence cannot be replicated (i.e., they are repeated but do not produce the same findings). This has resulted in a closer examination of the rigour of methods used in psychology as well as other sciences, and the principles that aim to ensure only high-quality research gets published. Second, it has become more widely accepted that psychology was used in the services of many oppressive and discriminatory activities in the 20th century. The US-based American Psychological Association (APA), for example, adopted a resolution in 2021, expressing 'profound regret and deep remorse' for long-term failures, and concluded that the APA had

> failed in its role leading the discipline of psychology, was complicit in contributing to systemic inequities, and hurt many through racism, racial discrimination, and denigration of people of color, thereby falling short on its mission to benefit society and improve lives.
>
> (APA, 2021)

Psychology can be used to discriminate – or to shine a light on discrimination

Psychology has a history of contributing to stereotyping and inequalities. Psychological methods and measures have been used to classify children negatively in many countries, providing justifications for prejudice and stigma. One example in the UK was in the 1960s and 1970s when children from the Caribbean were misclassified as 'educationally subnormal' in British schools. This was driven in part by widespread racist attitudes and was underpinned with inappropriate psychological measures – for example, expecting the children to perform well using English vocabulary they were unfamiliar with. They were removed from mainstream education and sent to 'special schools' where they received little or no education. In response, the British Psychological Society pledged in 2020 to 'challenge structural racism and remove the barriers that affect . . . the profession and children and young people Educational Psychologists work with' (BPS, 2021).

This reckoning for psychology is essential. At the same time, it's important to know that psychological research also *generates* evidence that prejudice and discrimination exist and can refute claims on which discrimination is based. For example, in the realm of gender, 46 meta-analyses of psychological gender difference studies (which analyse many studies to see if they come up with the same results) have shown that 78% of the gender differences found were very small or close to zero, supporting the 'gender similarities hypothesis' that males and females are similar on most psychological variables (Hyde, 2014). Further psychological research is able to explain why societies frequently emphasise the differences between genders and how children learn about these, despite the many similarities between females and males.

Throughout this Reader, you will learn more about psychological studies that have shown how prejudice and discrimination can develop and what kinds of evidence underlie them.

The failures the APA specified included ignoring opportunities in research and practice to identify and address poverty, racism, and other inequities, and defining and studying aspects of psychology – such as intelligence, health, and human capability – in ways that harmed communities of colour.

It is important, therefore, to bear in mind two key things. Psychological research can have great explanatory power, helping us to grasp development in childhood and youth and showing us about the impact of, and identifying ways to ameliorate, mental health; prejudice and discrimination; social, economic, and educational inequities; and more. Yet as major psychological associations now also recognise, psychology as a scientific practice can fail to meet its own goals of objectivity and accuracy, and psychology would be a better science if it acknowledged these limitations more openly, as achieving context-free 'scientific' objectivity in studies of human life is not possible.

At the heart of any scientific methodology, including psychology, lies scrutiny and debate, and this indicates a strength, rather than a weakness, of the discipline. Many questions need to be asked when considering the credibility of psychological research claims. Are measures of children and young people's experiences accurate enough? Can a study's findings be 'replicated' (i.e., confirmed when other scientists repeat the studies)? Have the cultural factors and other social and environmental factors affecting any measure or experiment been considered appropriately? Asking these and other questions leads psychologists to argue, re-evaluate, and critique what data actually *mean*.

As an example, let us consider the classic 'marshmallow' test of children's self-control.

The marshmallow test: What research about waiting for a treat tells us about children – and about psychology

The marshmallow test is a famous laboratory test devised by psychologist Walter Mischel at Stanford University in California in the 1960s (technically, it is known as the 'delay-of-gratification paradigm'; Mischel *et al.*, 2011). It measures how long pre-schoolers can tolerate sitting in front of a sweet treat (such as a marshmallow) without eating it, while alone in a room, if they are promised they will get two if they wait until the researcher returns. Many entertaining filmed versions of this study can be viewed online. Although it may seem cute and possibly self-evident, we can draw many insights about psychology and how its impact has unfolded from this study.

Figure 2.5 In the 'marshmallow test', a young child sits alone in a room, trying to resist eating a marshmallow (or other sweet treat) until the researcher returns.

Having originally carried out the test with 4-year-old participants in the late 1960s and early 1970s, in the Stanford University lab, in 1988, Mischel and colleagues published a study that caused a sensation in child development and education. They had managed to follow up with some of the original participants once they had completed school, and the researchers asked how their lives were progressing. Mischel and his team reported that those who, as pre-schoolers, had been able to delay gratification waiting for a second marshmallow were more likely to report better adolescent social-emotional functioning and to have higher test scores for university entry. The researchers, therefore, hypothesized that early self-control led to later life successes. From this, they articulated a theory that *teaching self-control* to young children would improve their later outcomes (see Mischel *et al.*, 2011).

Since the 1990s, this morally intuitive idea – that children will benefit in life if they apply willpower and self-control – has been picked up by the media, policy makers, and school authorities (particularly in the United States). There have even been TED Talks. Claims were made that delayed gratification training would improve children's life success, it was implemented in many schools, and parents whose pre-schoolers 'failed' informal versions of the marshmallow test found themselves fearing for their children's futures.

And yet, has it just been hype? There have been criticisms of the study from the outset. The first study was carried out with an extremely narrow social sample: White middle-class children from a very privileged cohort: the Stanford University nursery. Furthermore, the follow-up findings relied on a very small subset of participants: just 185 of the original 653 participants could be contacted, and of these, only 35–48 children had completed the marshmallow test itself (Watts *et al.*, 2018). Indeed, subsequent major studies were later to show that *the 'marshmallow test' as a test of early self-control does not predict later outcomes*. Another longer-term follow-up of the original study when the original participants were in their 40s, and a much larger-scale replication study with a more diverse sample, have shown that claims of the delayed gratification paradigm are not borne out, with implications for psychology and educational policy and practice. Yet, the 'marshmallow test' studies have still yielded interesting findings. Here's what they tell us:

The long-term follow-up: A follow-up with the original participants, now in their late 40s, Daniel Benjamin *et al.* (2020) examined educational qualifications, health and financial planning, income, and debt. There was no relationship between these mid-life outcomes and pre-schooler delayed gratification on the marshmallow test. This suggests that findings focused on self-control do not apply throughout life. Indeed, further analyses suggest that a marshmallow test may be picking up on more general cognitive and behavioural issues rather than self-control specifically.

The replication: In 2018, a large-scale replication and extension of Mischel and colleagues' studies was published, with 918 child participants in the US and with greater diversity than the first study (although not fully nationally representative) (Watts *et al.*, 2018). The children took the 'test' at age 4 1/2 years, and many other factors were measured, including academic achievement, cognitive function, parent-reported child behaviour and temperament, plus observations of children's home environments.

When children who ate the marshmallow at age 4 were compared with children who waited for the second one, there were very few statistically significant links to outcomes at age 15 years. This analysis suggests that Mischel's findings do not apply beyond the original study.

Interestingly, a second study used these same data and applied different statistical analyses (Michaelson and Munakata, 2020). They agreed with Watts and colleagues that personal self-control did not influence later outcomes. However, they established links between early *social support* and later life, and so they proposed further investigation of the idea that it is a child's early environment that affects their later outcomes.

'Marshmallow' variations

Further interesting variations on the marshmallow test have explored aspects of psychology by asking different research questions:

Are adults reliable? The marshmallow test was adapted for an experiment in which researchers mimicked unreliable and reliable environments, by dividing children into two groups (Kidd, Palmeri and Haslin, 2013). Researchers gave children crayons to draw with and some stickers. They promised extra crayons and more stickers when the researcher left the room – but half of the children never received these. Next, the marshmallow test was carried out, and the children who had experienced the 'unreliable researcher' who hadn't fulfilled their promise were more likely to eat the first marshmallow. This showed that these young children made a rapid, realistic assessment of whether an adult could be trusted to keep a promise. From this, psychologists have hypothesised that in the original marshmallow test, at least some children who eat the marshmallow do so as an expression of their own life experience that adults don't always keep their promises, rather than because they are unable to exert self-control.

Does children's cultural upbringing affect their ability to delay gratification? Psychologist Bettina Lamm and colleagues (2017) sought to assess the impact of children's cultural experience. They compared children of Nso farmers in Cameroon (Africa) with urban German middle-classes on the 'marshmallow test' (using different sweet treats popular in each culture). They found that the Cameroonian children were significantly better at this task. They ascribed this to differing cultural parenting practices and goals: in Cameroon, even small children are expected to exercise substantial self-control.

How well do children cooperate? Researchers RebeccaKoomen, Sebastian Gruneisen and Esther Hermann (2020) gave the 'marshmallow test' to 5- and 6-year-old children in pairs who didn't know one another, *both* of whom needed to wait if they were to get the extra treat (in this case, a cookie). The researchers found that children cooperated to ensure both got the additional cookie. This is evidence of early development of the ability to work together to achieve shared goals; as it was found in two diverse cultures, Kenya and Germany, it may be a general ability in young children across cultures.

In sum, what have 50 years of marshmallow tests shown us? They have *not* confirmed the first theory that delayed gratification early in life is a personal characteristic that predicts a wide range of later life success. Here, psychology's mistake was corrected by critical evaluation of original research and by follow-up research that suggests the long-term impact may be more related to social and cultural factors. The insights that the mistake may have been based on having too narrow a group of parti-cipants or on focusing too narrowly on individual self-control as a single explanation are very important. Interestingly, the ongoing variants of marshmallow tests show psychology working effectively as a science: setting up hypotheses, testing these, and continuing to explore them further. It's a useful warning to be wary of hyped-up, simple 'right/wrong' stories in psychology and a good example of how psychology can be self-correcting – even if it can take many years for this to happen.

Overall, therefore, marshmallow studies help us to understand some characteris-tics, pitfalls, and potential of psychology, including child/developmental psychology. They alert us to the need to be cautious about assuming that psychological laboratory tests and experimental findings can readily transfer to real-life settings, such as educa-tion, home, and elsewhere – particularly if they are not carried out with representative groups of participants. They remind us of the importance of contexts, cultures, and children's experience. They also remind us to treat intuitively 'obvious' concepts with caution and to be particularly sceptical about simple-seeming explanations of child development and wellbeing.

Finally, there is a very important side note to take away from psychological studies. You will encounter many studies in this Reader that sum up children's outcomes in scenarios in the home, family, friends, school, mental health services, and more. It is essential to remember that these studies *are not predictive for individuals*. They collate data for groups of children and young people, and they report on statistical averages, or overall group tendencies. Any child or young person experiences a complex inter-action of factors – their differential sensitivities and characteristics, the home and other environments they are in, and the experiences they are yet to have – all of which will influence how their lives unfold (Baldwin *et al.*, 2021). It's essential to bear this in mind as you read, particularly when thinking about your own childhood, your children, or children you know.

Key points

- Quantitative psychology applies the scientific method, translating human experi-ence and behaviour into measurable units and applying statistical analyses to identify effects, group differences, and relationships.
- Qualitative psychology explores experience by analysing words, visuals, and other forms of human expression to identify the meanings associated with these.
- Psychology has a history of studying urban, wealthy White children in the global North and of assuming these are a universal 'norm', leading to lack of under-standing of the range of human experience and discrimination against other social groups. As a discipline, psychology is now seeking to remedy this.
- The 'marshmallow test' findings claimed early self-control is linked to later life outcomes, but this has not been replicated nor confirmed in longer-term studies.
- 'Marshmallow test' study variations (all quantitative studies) show that experience, environment, and culture can all affect how children behave.

Conclusion

Psychology is a wide-ranging field that seeks to apply the scientific method to explaining human minds, brains, and behaviour. In many countries around the world, psychological explanations have become the dominant way of interpreting childhood and youth, and indeed, it could be argued that the UNCRC (see Chapter 1) is informed by simple psychological ideas of development, such as the idea that children have 'evolving capacities' that align with their chronological age. The psychology of childhood and youth, understandably, focuses on growth over time, yet in fact, as you have learned in this chapter, psychological research also shows that change across childhood and adolescence is more complex and is affected by many interacting factors. Furthermore, psychology itself has begun to actively question the accuracy of its methods more widely. Psychological explanations can easily lend themselves to assuming that there is a one 'best' way of being, of growing, and of supporting children's optimal development. Yet culturally informed approaches to psychology can provide powerful correctives. Research in psychology, when it is well-designed, contextually and culturally thoughtful, and carefully interpreted, has many insights to offer on how children and young people think, feel, learn, and grow – and how we can create the conditions for them to do well.

References

APA (2021) *Apology to People of Color for APA's Role in Promoting, Perpetuating, and Failing to Challenge Racism, Racial Discrimination, and Human Hierarchy in U.S.* Available at: www.apa.org/about/policy/racism-apology (Accessed 12nd June 2022).

Baldwin, J. *et al.* (2021) 'Population vs individual prediction of poor health from results of adverse childhood experiences screening', *JAMA Pediatrics*, 175(4), pp. 385–393 doi:10.1001/jamapediatrics.2020.5602.

Baltes, P. B. (1979) 'Life-span developmental psychology', in P. B. Baltes and O. G. Brim Jr. (eds.) *Life-span Development and Behavior* (Vol. 2). New York: Academic Press, pp. 256–281.

Benjamin, D. J. *et al.* (2020) 'Predicting mid-life capital formation with pre-school delay of gratification and life-course measures of self-regulation', *Journal of Economic Behavior and Organization*, 179, pp. 743–756.

British Psychological Society (BPS) (2021) *DECP Response to BBC Documentary 'Subnormal: A British Scandal' and the Role of Educational Psychologists.* Available at: www.bps.org.uk/news-and-policy/decp-response-bbc-documentary-subnormal-british-scandal-and-role-educational (Accessed 10th June 2022).

Cline, T., Crafter, S., and Prokopiou, E. (2014) 'Child language brokering in schools: a discussion of selected findings from a survey of teachers and ex-students', *Educational and Child Psychology*, 31(2), pp. 34–45.

Diamond, A. (2013) 'Executive function', *Annual Review of Psychology*, 64, pp. 135–168.

Gurung, R. A. *et al.* (2016) 'Strengthening introductory psychology: a new model for teaching the introductory course', *American Psychologist*, 71(2), pp. 112–124.

Harter, S. (2012) *The Construction of the Self* (2nd ed.). New York: Guilford.

Hyde, J. S. (2014) 'Gender similarities and differences', *Annual Review of Psychology*, 65, pp. 373–398.

Ibbotson, P. (2022) *Language Acquisition. The Basics*. London: Routledge.

Kidd, C., Palmeri, H., and Haslin, R. A. (2013) 'Rational snacking: young children's decision-making on the marshmallow task is moderated by beliefs about environmental reliability', *Cognition*, 126, pp. 109–114.

Koomen, R., Gruneisen, S., and Hermann, E. (2020) 'Children delay gratification for cooperative ends', *Psychological Science*, 31(2), pp. 139–148.

Lamm, B. *et al.* (2017) 'Waiting for the second treat: developing culture-specific modes of self-regulation', *Child Development*, 89(3), pp. e261–e277.

Lucas, C. G., Bridgers, S., Griffiths, T. L., and Gopnik, A. (2014) 'When children are better (or at least more open-minded) learners than adults: developmental differences in learning the forms of causal relationships', *Cognition*, 131(2), pp. 284–299.

Michaelson, L. E., and Munakata, Y. (2020) 'Same data set, different conclusions: preschool delay of gratification predicts later behavioral outcomes in a preregistered study', *Psychological Science*, 31(2), pp. 193–201. doi:10.1177/0956797619896270.

Mischel, W. *et al.* (2011) 'Willpower' over the life span: decomposing self-regulation', *SCAN*, 6, pp. 252–256. doi:10.1093/scan/nsq081.

Nocentini, A., Menesini, E., and Pluess, M. (2018) 'The personality trait of environmental sensitivity predicts children's positive response to school-based antibullying intervention', *Clinical Psychological Science*, 6(6), pp. 848–859.

O'Farrelly, C., Booth, A., Tatlow-Golden, M., and Barker, B. (2019) 'Reconstructing readiness: young children's priorities for their early school adjustment', *Early Childhood Research Quarterly*, 50(2), pp. 3–16.

Pluess, M. *et al.* (2018) 'Environmental sensitivity in children: development of the highly sensitive child scale and identification of sensitivity groups', *Developmental Psychology*, 54(1), pp. 51–70.

Valentine, G. (1997) '"Oh yes I can." "Oh no you can't": children and parents' understandings of kids' competence to negotiate public space safely', *Antipode*, 29(1), pp. 65–89.

Watts, T. W. *et al.* (2018) 'Revisiting the marshmallow test: a conceptual replication investigating links between early delay of gratification and later outcomes', *Psychological Science*, 29(7), pp. 1159–1177.

3 Children's bodies

Victoria Cooper and Vicky Preece

Introduction

The very essence of being a child centres around the body. Recognised as smaller, often regarded as unfinished and in a process of developing, bodies mark the transitions from being a child to becoming an adult. Bodies are important in distinct ways and shape how children look, from the colour of their eyes, skin, and hair to their gait, sex, and mobility. How children develop and interact in their world is facilitated to some extent by the body. Children use their bodies to move, eat, communicate, learn, and connect to people, places, and things. Bodies are also monitored, primarily by adults, to gain greater understanding into how children mature this is often set against notions about what is considered a 'normal' way for a child's body to develop. Ideas about what is 'normal', however, can be contested, as introduced in Chapter 2, and this is illustrated in the ways in which different societies impose their own views on what children's bodies should look like and how they should behave.

By exploring how children experience their bodies, it is possible to gain a greater appreciation of how bodies, although primarily regarded as biological, are also social: they are perceived, evaluated, and often judged by the individual child and also by other people, and these judgements can impact children's lived experiences. Bodies are perceived according to deeply ingrained social and cultural values which may, for example, deem some bodies as too fat or too thin and some as too big or too small. Exploring bodies thus provides insight into how children understand and value their own bodies and those of others. It also reveals some of the power relations evident in how children's bodies are defined, categorised, and sometimes controlled according to their age, size, colour, and gender.

This chapter is structured to look firstly at how children's bodies are examined – considering. in what ways bodies are both biological and social. We then look at how bodies are used to categorise 'other' and potentially marginalise children. Finally, we consider how bodies are disciplined, using a case study example which illustrates how children's bodies are 'schooled' to conform to institutionalised, dominant, adult-imposed boundaries and rules.

DOI: 10.4324/9781003358855-4

Examined bodies

Children's bodies are a longstanding topic of academic and professional interest. They are weighed, measured, and examined by professionals and practitioners to monitor a child's development; checked by parents who may question if their child is developing in what might be considered the 'right' way and according to their age and stage of life; and studied by academics in an attempt to understand how bodies impact children and young people's experiences.

Children and young people's experience of the world can be substantially affected by their bodies. A child who is born with muscular dystrophy, for instance, who finds moving around their environment challenging by virtue of their disability, may experience their body in different ways to a child who can move with relative ease. Muscular dystrophy is a genetic condition that causes muscle weakness and decreases mobility, making everyday tasks difficult. There are other conditions which can affect children's bodies. A child born with the genetic condition cystic fibrosis, for example, produces thick and sticky mucus in the lungs which inhibits their respiratory, digestive, and reproductive systems and can cause poor growth, frequent lung infections, and shortness of breath and which can impact how a child plays and interacts with their

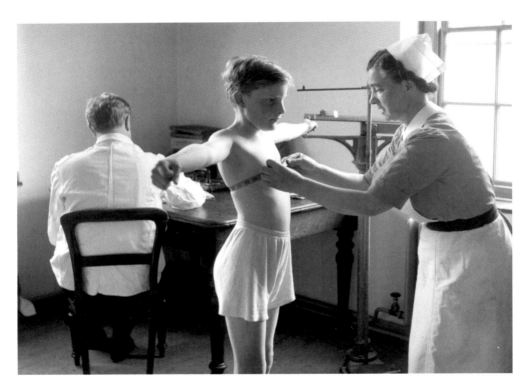

Figure 3.1 A photograph published in 1956 depicting a newcomer to the Royal Commercial Travellers School Pinner, Middlesex, being measured and weighted by the school nurse. Weighing and measuring children in school has recently returned as a practice in England.

environment. These examples illustrate how children's experiences of their bodies can be shaped to some extent by their biology, including hormonal and genetic influences. As the psychologist Willis F. Overton (2018, p. 2) suggests, the 'kind of body we have is a necessary precondition for having the kind of behaviours, experiences, and meanings that we have'.

Genes are the units by which traits are inherited within families and determine characteristics, such as eye, hair, and skin colour, gait, height, sex; and certain abilities. Genes are also responsible for a number of health conditions as the examples previously illustrate. There can be no denying that a child's biology – their genetic make-up – shapes some aspects of how they look, how they move, and may also impact their health, but it is important to also consider how the environment influences a child's development. Take for example a child born with cerebral palsy, who will experience challenges to their mobility and coordination. Cerebral palsy is a neurological condition caused before, during, or shortly after birth as a result of injury to the brain. It can occur for various reasons, such as genetic changes, which affect the development of the baby's brain but also including limited or interrupted oxygen supply to the baby's brain, a bleed within the baby's brain, a premature or difficult birth, or the mother catching an infection whilst pregnant. Cerebral palsy will unfold in the child's life, and their experience will depend on social and cultural attitudes to disability, access to therapeutic resources and supports, and different kinds of therapeutic approaches. These examples illustrate how biology can also be influenced by the environment.

Bodies are not solely biological

The sociologist Laura Fingerson (2006) argues that although humans are immersed in a world that has a bodily dimension, the body and bodily processes are not solely biological. With a focus on menstruation and specifically adolescent girls' and boys' (ages 13–19 years) experiences connected to this, Fingerson suggests that even though menstruation is a natural biological process, it is intimately tied to social life.

For some adolescent girls, menstruation can be a source of pain and discomfort, and many describe how it can also impact their mood, behaviour, and energy levels. Yet for many adolescent girls, menstruation can provide entry into a community where girls can share their experiences and where it marks their status as women. Rather than feeling discouraged by their lack of control over their bodies during menstruation, Fingerson's research reveals how adolescent girls respond by using their bodies as a source of power and agency in their interactions with other girls and with boys. Whilst boys might have the power in interactions when they teased or embarrassed girls about menstruation, girls also had significant sources of power as they used boys' and men's embarrassment about menstruation to achieve desired ends – such as getting out of gym class or urging boys to leave the conversation.

Largely taken as a 'female' issue, often considered taboo and not a focus of everyday conversation, Fingerson's research indicates how exploring experiences of and attitudes to menstruation can provide some important insights into the social aspect of bodies and bodily processes.

For many years, researchers spanning different disciplines have examined how child-hood experiences are determined by biology. Often referred to as *biological determinism*, this theory overlaps in many respects with debates about the origins of child develop-ment. Psychological research, for instance, has examined the impact of genes on a child's personality, 'IQ' (or so-called 'intelligence quotient'), and behavioural traits. Indeed, the extent to which a child's development is determined by biology – often described as *nature*, in contrast to being shaped by the environment, termed *nurture* – has been a longstanding focus for debate. The nature-nurture debate reflects a desire to better understand how and why some children appear more intelligent, anxious, or happy than others. Is this because they are born this way, or does it reflect how children are raised? Overton (2018) stressed the significance of biology in influencing children's experiences but also goes on to question how far these experiences and meanings are shaped by societies' views about how their bodies should look, move, and behave.

At its most extreme, *biological determinism* assumes that how children's bodies develop – albeit a changing process for the individual – is fairly predictable and is not influenced by the society in which children are raised. In some respects, this assump-tion is reflected in some of the language and expectations surrounding children's developing bodies for many years.

In the UK, *infant* is a term used to refer to children during the earliest stages of life who, as anthropologist David Lancy (2015, p. 545) describes, are 'helpless' and 'speech-less' and are perhaps most marked by their dependence on caregivers for survival. Other terms such as *toddler* describe the period through which many young children begin to explore their environment and develop a number of gross motor skills, includ-ing crawling and walking. The *middle years* of childhood are most notably aligned with increasing independence, as children mature and are often further associated, although not exclusively, with children's time spent at school or in education. Classi-fied by physical growth, *adolescence* is defined by pubertal changes in the body, including menstruation and the growth of facial and pubic hair (and you will read more about adolescence in Chapter 13). Often connected with the teenage years (although frequently beginning before them), adolescence is considered a transitional stage of development, both physically and emotionally, as children develop into adults.

This section demonstrates how researchers often place different emphasis on the relative importance of nature and nurture in understanding children's bodies and the impact that this can have upon their everyday lives. In more recent years, our under-standing of this debate has become more nuanced, illustrating the interconnection of bodies as biological and social. As Overton (2018, p. 2) argues, the development of the person cannot be understood purely in biological or socio-cultural terms. A person is just not a set of genes that causes behaviour nor is it an isolated culture that shapes who the person is. The development of behaviour emerges 'from the fully embodied person actively engaged in a sociocultural and physical world'.

Key points

- A child's genetic make-up determines their sex, hair, and eye colour as well as certain abilities and disabilities.
- While children's bodies are shaped by biology, their development is also social, reflecting the expectations placed on children by the society in which they are raised.
- The nature-and-nurture debate – when applied to childhood – examines the extent to which children's development is shaped by the interrelationships between biology and the environment and the society in which they are raised.

'Othered' bodies

As a primary site of identity, physical changes in the body across childhood and adolescence have a significant impact on how children or young people view themselves and their emerging identity and also influences how they are seen by others and their expectations of them. Bodies can be sites for concern for parents and carers, professionals, and also children. It is not only a concern for when they go 'wrong' but also when they appear not to be developing or behaving in ways considered 'normal' or when they look and act in ways which are regarded as different or 'other'.

Through comparing their bodies to others, children develop a sense of 'self' as well as a growing appreciation of the identity of others, often guided by markers of age, ethnicity, and gender (in Chapter 4, you will learn more about self and identities). Bodies are also a means through which children (and adults) make judgements and in which bodies become labelled as different, less than, or broken. This can be used as a way of 'othering' children – who may then become ostracised, bullied, and marginalised as a consequence.

Embodied experiences are a site of learning for children about what matters about the body in the social world. Through part of the socialisation process, children learn the importance of engaging in all kinds of *body work* which describes the different ways in which they manage and perhaps also change how their body is seen (James, 2013). This is amplified in children's contemporary lives and in social media, evidenced in a number of ways, such as sports that train up the body to become a particular physique and conform to ideals of health, different approaches to eating to try and control and contain the body, and how bodies are adorned and clothed to appear in a particular way often aligned to cultural definitions of beauty.

For early pioneering sociologists such as Charles Horton Cooley, understanding the social world highlights how children's bodies are not entirely physical in so far as they are seen, evaluated, and gauged according to deep-seated social and cultural ideas and expectations.

The looking glass self

Cooley (1902) coined the phrase 'the looking glass self' to describe the process through which children (and adults) develop a sense of 'self' from the reactions and behaviours of others around them. Cooley emphasised that the 'self' emerges not just from who children are in terms of how they look but also from how they are seen by others (and how they imagine they are seen) as well as how others relate to them (see also Chapter 4).

How we see others, for instance, may be influenced by their age, appearance, and behaviour. Stereotypes and assumptions, for example, of gender and known abilities and any observable disabilities may guide an expectation of how they may behave. Through verbal and non-verbal communication, we may add to our initial impression by evaluating how the person speaks and presents themselves, perhaps taking cues from their accent and assumptions about their cultural heritage and social status. This is a complex social process.

Figure 3.2 Young people taking a selfie.

In her research exploring children's perspectives and experiences of school, sociologist and anthropologist Allison James set out to understand the importance of the body as a way for children aged between 4 and 9 years to express their identity and sense of self. James (1993, p. 66) suggests that through noting and recognising 'differences between one body and another and through having their own bodies singled out, children learn to distinguish between anybody's body and their own and between normal and different bodies'. Through ethnographic research, she observed five characteristics of the body that had particular significance for the children she studied. These included height, shape, appearance, gender, and performance. She recounts how each of these characteristics influenced children's emerging identities and their interactions and relationships with others. Children typically focus on height and weight to mark social rank within particular groups:

> The relationship between concepts of body size and those of social identity may become critical for children whose bodies refuse to grow at an appropriate rate. By the ages of eight and nine-years-old height has become, quite literally, a quantifiable measure of social status and, consequently also of identity.
>
> (James, 1993, p. 113)

As a measure marking progress towards becoming an adult and obtaining a position of maturity, height affords children status and potential power (Fingerson, 2006). Alice Palmer carried out an ethnographic study exploring how children come to know and understand bodies. She suggests that many children look forward to growing taller, partly due to the social status conferred to those who are 'bigger' within their social groups, as a young boy Harry describes:

> I want to be taller because if anyone's mean to me I can say, 'Don't say that' . . . like at home . . . I wasn't very happy, well I was just having a bad morning this morning and everyone was in a bad mood and I'd like to be taller because it would make me more powerful.
>
> (Palmer, 2015, p. 81)

Being seen as 'big', however, is not always viewed positively by children. In her research exploring children's views on bodies, Palmer (2015) describes some children's concerns with being regarded as big or fat and being picked on as a consequence. She further describes how many engage in 'body work' in order to change the presentation of their body, their body's actions, as well as how their body looks, such as attempts to look thinner or taller, for example. It's important also to recognise that being taller for a young boy might be more highly valued than for a young girl. Similarly, ideas about height and weight are very much shaped by socio-cultural values.

Judgements about bodies are marked by assumptions made about their gender, their race, their ethnicity, their class, and their natural abilities (Weiss, 2013), as well as their age and perceived attractiveness. As a process of 'othering', children's bodies can be categorised as tall, small, thin, or fat and set apart as different in some way. Chapter 8 examines how the way in which people talk about and understand disabled children reflects implicit beliefs about the nature of difference and disability which goes on to affect how these children are treated. Take for example the experience of dwarfism.

In humans, dwarfism is typically classified when an adult is less than 4 ft 10 in inches in height, although the average adult height among people with dwarfism is 4 ft. There are many types of dwarfism, including *disproportionate dwarfism* which is characterised by either short limbs or a short torso. The most common and recognisable form of dwarfism in humans is the genetic disorder achondroplasia, whereby all the limbs are small. Growth hormone deficiency is responsible for many cases of dwarfism. Tharina Guse and Clare Harvey (2010) state that throughout history, persons with profound short stature have primarily been regarded in negative terms. Despite normal intelligence, children and young people globally experiencing dwarfism have been 'othered' in quite different ways. Seen as freaks, mythical creatures, and in possession of magical powers, dwarfs have been ridiculed and marginalised. Laura Backstrom (2012) describes how historically, dwarfs have been sought as entertainers and objects of curiosity due to their unusual stature, and in the 21st century, dwarf performers are still in demand. In 1990, dwarfism was classified as a disability, but there is some debate about whether such a label is appropriate.

Growing up with Dwarfism | The Mighty a blog written by Svea McNally (2017)

In my younger years, I was opposed to acknowledging my dwarfism. I was unaware that the reason I was being bullied in elementary school was because of my dwarfism; instead, I thought the bullying was sparked by my personality, academic abilities, or the fact that I wasn't as perfect as everyone else around me seemed to be. I started to realize that the people who were whispering, staring, and laughing at me were all doing it because I was a little person. It hurt. Badly. I cried myself to sleep some nights thinking of how I would never have real friends because of my dwarfism. I stopped being myself at school. I was so insecure that I started acting out just to get attention from others and validate my acceptance among my peers.

All of this changed in the past couple of years. I realized I shouldn't be complaining about my short stature, I should embrace it and strive for success and change. As I continue my love of advocacy for dwarfism, I am not going to come up with excuses. I'm trying to create steps toward a more accepting and inclusive world. As I got into older levels of my sports and school life, I have learned to stop using my dwarfism as an excuse. I play hockey, and when I skate, I have half the legs my opponents and teammates do. Take a single skating stride of my teammates, double that number, and your answer will be how many strides I take. I don't have a long stick either, so therefore I don't have a long reach. If I reach for a girl with the puck instead of skating to her, and she ends up skating around me, I can't have an excuse. If my coach asks me why I reached for it instead of skating towards it, I can't say that my dwarfism made my legs not move. That's impossible. I have the same mobility as others, I just have to put more work into it.

The importance of understanding how bodies impact childhood is particularly pertinent for understanding the experiences of disabled children, as both social constructions of the 'normal' child's body and the physicality of the body itself and how it is experienced are significant to the everyday lives of children (McLaughlin and Coleman-Fountain, 2014). According to Robert Kruse (2003), however, individuals with certain physical statures do not necessarily view themselves as disabled but more as bodily different. How they are seen, however, can profoundly impact their lives. There are multiple and interconnected ways in which bodies are seen, categorised, and 'othered' which influence the lives of children, and throughout this Reader, you will consider how children's bodies are differentiated and constructed by virtue of their gender, disabilities, and race and ethnicity.

Key points

- Children's bodies can be 'othered' by how they are seen by other people and by children themselves: categorized, and sometimes marginalized, as 'different', 'less than', and in some way, lacking.
- Conceptualisations of 'normal' bodies can be contested.

Disciplined bodies

Bodies can be weakened, become ill, or damaged, and children can put their bodies at risk. Bodies can be embarrassing; they can break social rules and can become the subject of concern over how they should be seen and how they should behave. As sites for concern, children's bodies are surveilled and monitored by adults built upon the premise that they require protection, safeguarding, and control – under the guise of what Valerie Steeves and Owain Jones (2010, p. 187) define as 'surveillance as care'. Analysis of how bodies are seemingly controlled by adults unveils the power dynamic between children and adults and where adults often wield most power.

Kate Cregan and Denise Cuthbert (2014) argue that young people's bodies are often sites for both concern and control. They describe, for example, how young people are viewed as capable and as having the right to choose how they manage, use, and place their own bodies – medically, sexually, and often in areas which pose risks. Yet in another sense, risks such as drug use and sexual encounters cause concern about the ways young people use their bodies. Palmer (2015, p. 25) argues that children's and young people's bodies are thus regulated and controlled through different media, including literature and music, as well as through adult-pupil interactions based on ideas about how children and young people should look, behave, and use their bodies. Through her research with school-age children, Palmer describes how these ideas begin during the early stages of education and schooling, where children's bodies are often required to be 'ordered, tidy, and neatly presented'.

Regulating the body begins at home with learning to eat, wash, dress, and use the toilet, but starting school is a time when the demands on the body become more prescribed. Being able to meet these demands successfully is necessary if children are to show they have become a 'good' school child (Preece, 2021). Schooling the body

Figure 3.3 School rules displayed using body parts.

involves learning to sit still in the correct position, how and when to speak or be silent, and how to regulate bodily functions, such as eating and going to the toilet at the correct times of the day.

School is thus a space where power is exerted over children. The UK and Ireland have among the youngest school-starting ages worldwide (Sharp, 2002). Although the statutory starting age is the term after children are five years old, the majority start school when they are four. Vicky Preece's (2021) research, which focused on children's lived experience of starting infant school in England, reveals that a key element for these 4-year-olds centred around the physicality of the experience and how bodies are schooled. The following case study extract illustrates these experiences and are taken from some of Preece's ethnographic field notes and observations that were carried out in the first few weeks of the children entering school.

Bodies being 'ready' for school

Schools communicate expectations about what it means for children to be ready for school to early years educators and parents who, as a result, spend time teaching children how their bodies need to move or not move – such as sitting still and lining up. Research reveals the centrality of the physical demands that need to be taught for children to be perceived as ready for school and for early years staff and parents to be seen as successful in preparing them. Parents speak about practising doing up buttons so that their children can manage their school uniform and about helping children to be independent in using the toilet. Parents often express concerns about their child's inability to sit still, as the following extract illustrates:

> And I think 'Oh gosh is he going to get into trouble and be upset because he's in trouble and I think is that going to stop him enjoying school as much'. . . . So I think that's the main thing, he's quite young and it's the sitting down and listening and is he going to get in trouble and then is he not going to like going.

Formal practices are introduced by early years practitioners working with 3- and 4-year-olds to 'ready' children for school, including learning to stop on the signal of a bell and lining up, sitting still, and using the toilet. Early years settings can feel judged by this.

> We've always got feedback from everyone that ummmm ours are good kids going up and they do know how to line up, they do know how to go to the toilet, wash their hands and all that so yeah and they do know how to sit on the carpet at certain times um so **yes** we do get good feedback that they are doing well sending them up.

Once in school, a large part of children's lived experience is focused on learning the physical requirements that school imposes on them. Children are explicitly taught how to position their bodies when sitting on the carpet in the classroom during times when the whole class gather together, where the rules are depicted with large pictures along the side of the space. The legs, hands, and lips are all specifically directed to do particular things, and this is observed closely by adults and corrected if necessary. The carpet thus represents a space where power is exerted through the combination of children, teaching staff, carpet, and chairs. Children are praised by the teaching staff for sitting in the cross-legged position with hands in lap, for example:

> 'You're sitting the smartest, well done'.
> 'Sit smartly'.
> 'Put your legs like this'.

As well as the physical requirements of sitting in particular ways for particular lengths of times, the children are also required to control their voices and language. In order to speak in a whole class situation, the carpet rule of 'Hands up and wait with lips closed' is taught and reinforced. One child, Cassandra, called out during her first carpet-time session and was reminded to put her hand up. She continued to struggle with this rule during carpet time on the second session of school.

> Cassandra starts chatting loudly about what she can see. Ms Brown says, 'We must use an inside voice in here'. Cassandra looks down and blushes. She looks over to me and slightly smiles, then looks at the teacher. Ms Brown reminds everyone not to talk on the carpet and Cassandra puts her fingers to her lips. Her body was affected by the interaction as she tried to conform to the image of a 'docile body' – made visible through her blushing and withdrawal of her gaze which suggested her embarrassment. This was further supported by looking over for reassurance. In addition, her finger to her lips suggests her determination to try to comply with these new rules.

As well as trying to stay quiet, children are required to talk at certain times and in certain ways. For example, taking the register – a twice-daily practice – employs the use of key phrases that need to be learnt and copied. First, the teacher speaks and signs, 'Good morning, children', before the whole class repeats in unison, 'Good morning, Ms. Brown. Good morning, Ms. White'. For some of the children, this is an uncomfortable experience.

Five of the children complied with this during the first session in school, however Olivia was too shy:
Olivia looks down at the floor when her name is called for the register. She hunches her shoulders and tilts her head. Ms Brown says, 'Practise tomorrow!' and moves on.

Managing the timing of bodily functions, particularly going to the toilet and eating, is also a significant part of learning the rhythm of the day, regulating impulses until the correct time. At lunchtime, for example, children are expected to go to the toilet before going to the hall and then staying in place until they have eaten, illustrated by clear instructions:

'Did you go to the toilet when you were asked?'
'You must go to the toilet before you go in the hall. You can't keep leaving!'

As well as controlling their urge to go to the toilet, children are required to learn to eat at specific times. Before the direct teaching begins, children are introduced to going to the toilet at playtime or during their free choosing sessions and to eating at snack time and lunchtimes. While many children are keen to be seen as 'good' school children, they do find ways to resist and subvert using their bodies, such as wriggling in their seats so as to appear in need of the toilet and so being granted permission to go or very politely asking permission from the teacher. Using 'evasive stealth tactics' identified by Michael Gallagher (2010, p. 270), children also manage to escape the surveillance of the teacher by escaping to the toilet.

During lunch and snack times, interactions between children and adults demonstrate the 'relational aspects of children's and adult's shared lives' (Hansen, Hansen and Kristensen, 2017, p. 238) as they negotiate how much food is to be eaten. Children exert their agency by stating their dislike of particular foods and the refusal to eat certain types of food.

> Although Cassandra did not want to eat her rice or peas and could have felt anxious about this, she appeared to reject . . . adults deciding what and how much she should eat. She did not appear concerned about conforming and instead informed Ms. White confidently. 'I don't want the rice. Peas make me sick'.

Practitioners will often use strategies as a way of negotiating with the child and encouraging them to eat, such as changing the size of the food mouthfuls and lessening the amount that would be acceptable to eat, exemplified by the following extract from field notes observing a practitioner, Ms. Brown, interacting with a young pupil, Jim, at lunchtime:

> Ms. Brown comes and asks him how he is getting on.
> Jim: I don't like the rice, or meatballs or the bread.
> Ms. Brown: Shall I cut the meatballs up smaller?
> He nods. She cuts it very small and mixes the rice with the tomato/onion mix.
> Ms. Brown: Is that better?
> Jim looks at it.
> Jim: I don't like the peas.
> Ms. Brown takes them out.
> Ms. Brown moves away at this point to help someone else. Jim takes a tiny mouthful then looks over at her. He sips his water again then takes another tiny mouthful followed by a sip of water. Between each mouthful he puts his fork down so that he can hold the cup with two hands. His movements are hurried. He takes another forkful, puts the fork down, takes a deep breath and looks out of the window. He takes another forkful and puts his fork down. He looks at me and seems worried. He is not smiling.

This 'surveillance as care' (Steeves and Jones, 2010, p. 187), whilst well intentioned, seeking to ensure that bodily requirements for food and drink are met, may result in a loss of autonomy for some children over their own bodily needs.

While many children, despite feeling uncomfortable, conform to the eating practices expected within school, other children exert their agency by refusing to conform and rebuffing attempts at coercion and negotiation.

Despite the extent to which adults can and do exert power to control bodies, which is often enacted through institutions, including school, children negotiate and manage their bodies in ways which allow them to exert their own agency.

Key points

- Children's bodies are disciplined and controlled in ways which highlight the complex power relations between children and adults.
- Schools are recognised as contexts and institutions where children's bodies can be disciplined and controlled.
- Despite adults wielding most power over children and their bodies, research indicates how children find ways to exert their own agency.

Conclusion

In this chapter, we have considered how children's bodies are both biological and social, and how the ways they are seen and understood has a significant impact upon children's lived experiences. In comparing themselves to others, children develop a sense of self, and in this chapter, we have examined how this process engenders the categorisation and potential 'othering' of children who may be ostracised and marginalised as a consequence. While children's bodies are surveilled and controlled within contexts such as school, this chapter has examined the manner in which children also resist and use their bodies to exert their individual agency.

References

Backstrom, L. (2012) 'From the freak show to the living room: cultural representations of dwarfism and obesity', *Sociological Forum*, 27(3), pp. 682–707.

Cooley, C. H. (1902) *Human Nature and the Social Order*. New York: Scribner.

Cregan, K., and Cuthbert, D. (2014) *Global Childhoods. Issues and Debates*. London, New Delhi and Los Angeles: Sage.

Fingerson, L. (2006) *Girls in Power: Gender, Body, and Menstruation in Adolescence*. Albany: SUNY Press.

Gallagher, M. (2010) 'Are schools panoptic?', *Surveillance and Society*, 7(3/4), pp. 262–272.

Guse, T., and Harvey, C. (2010) 'Growing up with a sibling with dwarfism: perceptions of adult no dwarf siblings', *Disability and Society*, 25(3), pp. 387–401.

Hansen, S. R., Hansen, M. W., and Kristensen, N. H. (2017) 'Striated agency and smooth regulation: kindergarten mealtime as an ambiguous space for the construction of child and adult relations', *Children's Geographies*, Routledge, 15(2), pp. 237–248.

James, A. (1993) *Childhood Identities: Self and Social Relationships in the Experience of the Child*. Edinburgh: Edinburgh University Press.

James, A. (2013) *Socialising Children*. Basingstoke: Palgrave Macmillan.

Kruse, R. J. (2003) 'Narrating intersections of gender and dwarfism', *The Canadian Geographer*, 4, pp. 495–508.

Lancy, D. F. (2015) *The Anthropology of Childhood: Cherubs, Chattel, Changelings* (2nd ed.). London: Cambridge University Press.

McLaughlin, J., and Coleman-Fountain, E. (2014) 'The unfinished body: the medical and social reshaping of disabled young bodies', *Social Science and Medicine*, 120, pp. 76–84.

McNally, S. (2017) 'How dwarfism has developed my maturity', *The Mighty* (themighty. com) (Accessed 10th March 2023).

Overton, W. F. (2018) 'Embodiment', in Marc H. Bornstein (ed.) *The Sage Encyclopaedia of Lifespan Human Development*. Thousand Oaks: Sage Publications.

Palmer, A. (2015) *Embodied Childhoods, an Ethnographic Study of How Children Come to Know about the Body*, unpublished thesis submitted to the University of Sheffield.

Preece, V. (2021) *Young Children's Bodies: Multiple Perspectives on the Embodied Experience of Starting School*, unpublished thesis submitted to The Open University.

Sharp, C. (2002) *School Starting Age: European Policy and Recent Research*, Paper presented at the Local Government Association Seminar 'when should our children start school?', LGA conference centre, London, November 1st, Slough, NFER.

Steeves, V., and Jones, O. (2010) 'Editorial: surveillance and children', *Surveillance and Society*, 7(3/4), pp. 187–191.

Weiss, G. (2013) *Body Images: Embodiment as Intercorporeality*. London: Routledge.

4 Making sense of the self

Mimi Tatlow-Golden

Introduction

The self is the core of who we are, and it is centrally important to our ability to function. It is shaped in childhood and youth by individual characteristics and development but also created in interactions with people, places, things, and culture(s). Yet – even to ourselves, and to those parents who may imagine they know everything about their children – the self is challenging to understand. This chapter will introduce you to developmental, social, and cultural aspects of the self. It first explains what self-concept and self-esteem are, why it's important to understand them, and what impact they can have on children and young people's lives. It then explores how caregivers' interactions with young children shape the self with potentially enduring effects. The final section explores young adolescents' views of the relationships and activities they find most important, identifying what psychological researchers get right when they aim to measure young people's self-esteem – and what they miss.

The self and why it matters

Much of the time, we function without stopping to consider that we have a self because it is so integrated into our experience of daily life. This can create the illusion that the self is a straightforward aspect of our existence. And yet the self consists of so many thoughts, feelings, experiences, and more, and it also contains contradictions that usually surprise people. For example, almost everyone, from childhood onwards, has a continuous sense that 'I've always been me', yet while this sense of 'me' is maintained, the self is in constant flux, as individuals change, grow, and learn, their minds and bodies develop, and they interact with others and the world around them. Another feature of the self that often surprises is that even though it is completely private and cannot be known by an outsider, it is created and develops largely through experiences and interactions with others. As the chapter will show, how children are cared for, the stories that carers tell children and others, and the expectations and assumptions of the culture(s) in which we live, can all shape the ideas and feelings children and young people have about themselves as well as the *kinds* of selves that they become.

The self-concept and self-esteem

Psychology and sociology both identify the self as having many different facets, and one of psychology's earliest theorists, William James, described these more than a

DOI: 10.4324/9781003358855-5

century ago in his classic text, *The Principles of Psychology* (1890/1907, Vol. 1, p. 330). Although a great deal of new research has been carried out since, these early conceptualisations still stand. James proposed that a key part of the self, which he described as the *Me-self*, is what we think about when we ask the question 'Who am I?'

This chapter concerns itself with the *Me-self*, also referred to as the *self-concept*. The self-concept is the image we hold of ourselves, as another classic US psychologist, Morris Rosenberg (1986), explained a hundred years after James. This image of ourselves matters. It is central to our ability to function in the world, as we need some insight into our qualities, characteristics, and identities. The self-concept, Rosenberg said, is:

> the most constant feature of the individual's experience and the most important basis for human action. Without some picture of what one is like – one's traits, statuses or other qualities – one is virtually immobilised.
>
> (Rosenberg, 1986, p. 124)

This self-concept, the 'picture of what one is like', is like a vast and detailed tapestry. Into it are woven a huge range of ideas and feelings about 'me'. Some are more important to the self; many are less so. Their importance varies across time and situations, as if a spotlight falls on one part of the tapestry and fades from others from moment to moment and in different times of life. This 'tapestry' of ideas and feelings about the self continues to be woven and added to through childhood, youth, and beyond.

The ideas and feelings that make up the self-concept create an overall sense of 'me', including identities (characteristics, relations, roles, and group memberships) that together define an individual (Oyserman, Elmore and Smith, 2012). What are all these ideas about the self that make up the tapestry of the self-concept? They include *individual characteristics*, whether physical (e.g., appearance or size), psychological, moral or spiritual values, or favoured activities (e.g., hobbies, talents, pastimes). They

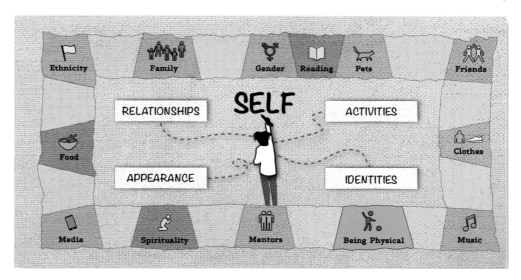

Figure 4.1 The 'Me-self' as a tapestry.

include group and collective *identities* that feel meaningful to 'who I am', such as gender, ethnic, class, national or regional identities, among others, as well as *relationships* with family and peers and others who are important. There may also be ideas about important material (or virtual) *things* that we feel reflect 'me' or are a part of 'me'. These days, often, this is a mobile phone, but it could be anything that feels meaningful: a bicycle, an item of clothing, a painting. Individuals' self-concepts also include 'who I am *now*', *past selves* ('how I was then'), and, importantly, as renowned self psychologist Hazel Rose Markus found, '*possible selves*' ('who I could be, or want to avoid being, in the future'), which are motivators for action (Markus and Nurius, 1986).

Note that 'self' and 'identity' are sometimes used interchangeably in general speech and indeed also in psychology and sociology (Oyserman, Elmore and Smith, 2012). This chapter uses 'self-concept' for the 'me' as a whole and 'identities' for the many aspects that contribute to the overall 'me' (or self-concept). We all have many identities, and these might include our relationships (e.g., 'parent') or group-based identities, such as 'Black' or 'Chinese' or 'Irish'.

People evaluate themselves in the self-concept aspects that feel important – and these self-evaluations are the source of their *self-esteem*. Self-esteem is an important facet of the self that can be conceptualised as the answer to 'How good am I?' (Schaffer, 2006). It is important to mental health, as low self-esteem is a feature of some mental health difficulties. The parts of the self-concept that contribute to self-esteem vary greatly from person to person, though they generally include meaningful close relationships, group or collective identities, activities, and abilities. Feeling competent and successful in these meaningful self-aspects is critically significant for self-esteem (Rosenberg, 1986).

How does this overall picture of 'me', the self-concept, develop? And what does it have to do with studying childhood and youth? The self-concept is shaped by internal factors, including cognitive development, and by external factors, such as culture and social settings. The developmental psychologist of the self Susan Harter explains that it begins to be formed in the very early years, arising from the interweaving of interactions with others (including the earliest caring relationships); engaging with the environment; cultural child-rearing practices and goals; individual characteristics and temperament; cognitive development; and progress in valued activities (Harter, 2012).

A developing self

This chapter focuses largely on the self as socially and culturally constructed. However, individual cognitive development is also important for the sense of self through childhood and youth, causing shifts in a person's view of themselves and others, shifts that can sometimes be quite destabilising – or a 'veritable mine-field' as Harter (2012, p. 14) characterises it.

Toddlers gain a sense of self as they develop agency, through control over actions they perform and positive emotions over these successes. However, they also gain cognitive insight that they are not omnipotent and that their carers, more separate than they realised, cannot be controlled, leading to frustration and anger. As toddlers learn language, they can label their self and they can be labelled by others, as 'good' or 'bad' – which can be a liability as well as a strength.

As you learned in Chapter 2, cognitive development in middle childhood leads to changes in how children can think about and view themselves and results in age-typical changes in self-concept and self-esteem (Harter, 2012). Greater cognitive capacity leads to being able to evaluate oneself, including in different domains, and assess one's abilities more accurately – a cognitive advance that can also lead to negative self-evaluations.

Later, through adolescence, as Chapter 13 will explain, cognitive abilities and the capacity for more abstract thinking lead to uneven gains that can lead to conflicting senses of self and its priorities. This can cause confusion (and frustration again) over what the individual feels is real and valued. Importantly, these various changes are by-products of cognitive change over time, and they typically settle as the developing self grows.

Later, this chapter will consider young people's own views of their 'favourite', most important activities and relationships (i.e., those contributing to self-concept and self-esteem) and contrast them with what adults focus on. First, however, we explore how early relationships contribute to forming the self. As Harter notes, self-esteem (self-evaluation) is not purely an individual characteristic; rather, it is co-constructed with those who care for children in their early years:

> The self, as a social construction, develops within the crucible of interpersonal relationships with caregivers. One outcome is that the child comes to adopt the opinions that significant others are perceived to hold toward the self. These reflected appraisals come to define one's sense of self as a person. Through an internalisation process, the child comes to own these evaluations as his/her own judgments about the self.
>
> (Harter, 2012, pp. 11–12)

Thus, children's earliest caring relationships can shape their sense of self and self-esteem. The next section considers care in the early years. The psychological theory of attachment proposes how early caregiving can affect aspects of the self over the life-span, and cultural psychological research into family storytelling shows how this can shape selves differently across cultures.

Key points

- The self-concept, the image we hold of ourselves, is central to our ability to function in the world, as we need insight into our qualities, characteristics, and identities.

- The self-concept is like a tapestry with many features: individual characteristics, group and collective identities, relationships, things (past selves and 'possible selves' among others). It also includes self-esteem – how we evaluate ourselves in the aspects of the self-concept that are important to us.
- The self-concept changes with cognitive and emotional development over time.

Attachment and children's early sense of self

One of the most famous psychological theories, attachment theory, describes how children and their carer(s) in the first two years of life form a relationship that can affect wellbeing and development through childhood and beyond. Attachment theory and some of its assumptions have been supported in tens of thousands of psychological research studies. There are, however, also limits to its application, and importantly, as you read, remember (as discussed in Chapter 2) that quantitative psychological research reports on statistically *average* findings across groups of children. It cannot determine any single individual's experience, as children and young people have many different trajectories.

Attachment: the theory and the 'Strange Situation'

Attachment theory was created in the mid-20th century by child psychiatrist John Bowlby and psychologist Mary Ainsworth (Bretherton, 1992). Bowlby made observations of children who had been deprived contact with their mothers and combined these with insights from developmental psychology, psychoanalysis, and animal studies to propose a theory that babies and infants have an evolutionary need not just for food but also for tactile and social contact with a consistent caregiver, which he described as the mother or 'permanent mother substitute' (Bowlby, 1969). Attachment theory hypothesised that, from this relationship, infants developed an 'internal working model' of the self as valued or unworthy based on their caregivers' affection and responsiveness, which affected their ongoing self-image, self-esteem, and hence, their later behaviour (Bretherton, 1992).

Having carried out observational research in Uganda (near Kampala) and the US (Baltimore), Ainsworth then devised a method, the 'Strange Situation' protocol, that allowed this theory to be tested. Ainsworth created a 20-minute structured observational protocol for a mother with a 1-year-old child in an unfamiliar setting, similar to a waiting room, with seats and toys. A sequence of eight events takes place involving a stranger entering the room, the mother briefly leaving, and the mother returning to the child. The child's behaviours are observed, including responses to the stranger and reunion with the mother. From these brief laboratory-based observations, Ainsworth and others inferred that infants were either 'securely' attached, or 'insecurely' attached in one of three different ways. Ainsworth concluded that the attachment figure's *sensitivity* is crucial for a secure attachment relationship and that the attachment figure provides a "secure base" from which an infant can explore the world (Bretherton, 1992). Since then, tens of thousands of studies have replicated these findings and links to later cognitive, emotional, and behavioural outcomes in children, and research shows brief interventions with carers that support sensitive caregiving enhance attach-ment security (Bakermans-Kranenburg, van IJzendoorn and Juffer, 2003). However, questions about 'sensitive' caregiving are considered further in the next section.

Attachment was a radical child-centred theory that foregrounded children's needs for consistent care; it revolutionised thinking about young children's and carers' rela-tionships and how neglect, deprivation, separation, and bereavement affect them (Bretherton, 1992). It led to important changes in thinking about childcare. At the time, childcare manuals in the global North discouraged parents from soothing crying infants, recommending strict feeding schedules and leaving babies to cry. Medical staff, prioritising hospital routines over children's emotional needs, did not permit parents to be present when children were admitted. Furthermore, attachment theory resonated widely as it was developed shortly after the Second World War, when mil-lions of young children had been traumatically separated from their families.

Yet attachment theory also overgeneralised, making universal claims that have been challenged. It led to an excessive focus on a brief laboratory procedure, on mothers as the only carers, on defining optimal care as 'sensitive', and on interpretations that 'insecure' attachment necessarily leads to poor later outcomes.

Some perils of attachment theory

Attachment theory is generally presented in psychological texts as universal, an account of an evolutionary human need that applies to any culture or time. Yet although young children certainly need attentive care to survive and thrive, its uni-versal claims were challenged from the outset (Vicedo, 2017), as across cultures and over time, caregivers' early interactions with young children, and conceptualisations of what is healthy for development, vary substantially.

Not just mothers but many others

Attachment theory assumes that a single caregiver-infant relationship is focal to well-being. Although Bowlby had acknowledged the primary carer might not be the child's mother, he and others consistently used 'mother' as shorthand. This probably reflected prevailing post-war conditions in the global North (e.g., in the UK, women's employment rates dropped from a wartime high of 80%, to below 35% in 1951). Soci-ologists Viola Klein and Alva Myrdal declared in 1956 that 'it is no exaggeration to say that the cleavage between the worlds of job and home is . . . more complete than it ever was in the past' (1956, Ch. 3). Yet caring practices vary hugely: in 150 societies, only 3% had mother-exclusive care (Weisner and Gallimore, 1977). Cultural psycholo-gist Heidi Keller (2018) notes that caregiving networks may or may not include special roles for mothers or grandmothers but that 'often, however, children are the most significant caregivers of infants' (p. 11416). Furthermore, fathers' roles in childhood have been neglected in developmental and social research (Fitzgerald, 2022; Smyth and Russell, 2021), although Keller (2018) notes that across the world, fathers often do not play a role in early infancy. Cultural assumptions, amplified by attachment theory, that consistent care should only be provided by the mother have led to rigid gendered childcare roles in many parts of the world. You will learn more about how different kinds of families can support children and young people's wellbeing in Chapter 5.

Beyond 'sensitive' parenting – and attachment itself

Further limitations of attachment theory are differences in what constitutes ideal parenting and how important 'sensitive' care is. Netherlands-based psychologist Judi Mesman and colleagues (2016) wanted to identify caring behaviours mothers identified as 'ideal'. They spoke with 751 mothers in 26 cultural groups across 15 countries (11 of which were not Western, industrialized countries) and found that mothers in rural areas, or with lower incomes, or with more children, rated sensitivity as less important, suggesting that survival and meeting basic needs matter more. Notably, of the 26 cultural groups, mothers in seven groups did not rate *shows enjoyment of child* in their top-20 caring behaviours, and in six groups, they did not rate *being cheerful* in the top-20. Yet in many countries, parents and researchers consider being upbeat with small children and showing enjoyment of the young child to be central to 'sensitive' care.

However, almost every cultural group cited in the top-20 behaviours a mix of what psychologists classify as emotional warmth and sensitivity: *seeking contact* with the child, *showing affection by touching*, *showing the child they are happy with them*, *encouraging trying new things*, and *interrupting dangerous activities*. This shows important commonalities across cultures of valuing tactile warmth, exploration, and safety. It also points us to the need to consider carefully how psychologists define the behaviours and attitudes they are measuring.

Furthermore, carer-child relationships are a complex mix beyond attachment as psychiatrist and attachment researcher Michael Rutter noted (1995), and psychologists have pointed to less frequently researched features, such as connectedness, intimacy, the balance of control, humour, and shared positive emotions. Also, it is crucial to remember that, due to children's developmental flexibility, a lack of secure attachment can be improved later in childhood or beyond. Indeed, even the effects of quite serious neglect can be greatly improved with care, as Rutter's studies of Romanian children show; they had been placed in group homes as babies, and Rutter assessed them at adoption and across the years afterwards. Finally, longitudinal research shows that relationships with family members such as siblings can protect wellbeing regardless of attachment to the primary carer (Gass, Jenkins and Dunn, 2007).

'Good-enough' parenting: Why perfect is not good

Although early childhood care is crucial for development and wellbeing, a focus on 'sensitive' parenting and secure attachment has led some to conclude that motherly perfection, and constant availability, is required for children to thrive. A helpful corrective was provided by Donald Winnicott, an English paediatrician and psychoanalyst, a contemporary of Bowlby's who worked thoughtfully with children and parents and whose writings have been very influential. Winnicott explained that a 'good-enough', but not perfect, mother was essential for child wellbeing, as a young child needs to learn that their carer is a separate and imperfect being:

> The good-enough mother . . . starts off with an almost complete adaptation to her infant's needs, and as time proceeds she adapts less and less completely, gradually, according to the infant's growing ability to deal with her failure. Her failure to adapt to every need of the child helps them adapt to external realities.
>
> (Winnicott, 1953, p. 95)

In this way, the good-enough mother (or other carer) gives the child the space, over time, to learn that their every need cannot be fulfilled and that even though every child deserves nurturing care, learning to tolerate frustration, and to know that the self can survive it, is also an essential task of childhood.

Selves are created differently across cultures

Many developmental tasks that young children need to master are universal, and these include how to behave and be accepted within one's community and culture. In different cultures, however, social constructions of childhood mean that cultural beliefs and goals for children's social development can vary, as you learned in Chapter 1 and will continue to learn throughout this Reader. As parenting goals influence their care practices, young children have their early universal needs met in culture-specific ways, and this 'lays the ground for gradually diverging developmental pathways' (Keller and Kärtner, 2013, p. 63).

One of the ways in which cultural beliefs and goals are transmitted in the family is through storytelling. With children as young as two years, researchers have shown that parents' stories are themselves shaped by particular cultural goals. This, in turn, has the capacity to create different kinds of selves.

A story every 15 minutes: Creating culturally congruent selves

In Taiwan and the United States, cultural developmental psychologists Heidi Fung, Peggy Miller, Todd Sandel, and Chung-Hui Liang (Miller *et al.*, 2001) studied the stories that parents and other relatives told their 2-1/2-year-old toddlers. The researchers observed middle-class family interactions in Taipei (Taiwan) and a suburb near Chicago (United States), assigning a Taiwanese researcher to work with the Taiwan families and a US researcher to the Chicago families to ensure they would be alert to the underlying meanings of the inter-actions they observed.

The researchers carried out detailed comparisons of the storytelling narratives and practices in both cultures. They found both cultures engage in spontaneous storytelling about what the young child has experienced and done as part of everyday family life and that it happens with notably similar frequency – about every 15 minutes. Families also adopted similar modes of storytelling across cultures, a 'co-narration' in which family members and the child jointly told stories about the toddler's past experiences and behaviours and also about the parents when they had been young children.

Beyond these similarities, however, there were striking divergences in the *content* of the stories told in the two cultures about children and parents, divergences that mirrored one another. The Taipei families emphasised the toddlers' misdeeds and told these stories directly and firmly in front of others, often trying to extract confessions from children and sometimes shaming them (although also with non-verbal cues signalling humour). They also suppressed stories of parents' childhood transgressions. In contrast, the Euro-American families in the Chicago suburbs skipped over young children's misdeeds, or ensured to present the child in a positive light despite a misdeed. They focused instead in their storytelling on children's achievements, and in contrast to the Taipei parents, they told funny stories about parents being naughty when they were little.

Heidi Fung concluded that:

> compared to their American counterparts, Taiwanese families are much more likely to use storytelling to impart moral and social standards and to treat children's past transgressions as a didactic resource. Euro-American families, on the other hand, tend to downplay the child's misdeeds and to treat stories as a medium of entertainment and affirmation . . . Although American care-givers consider invocation of the child's misdeeds as potentially damaging to her well-being, they frequently report their own misdeeds for fun and for strengthening the connection between them and their children. To Taiwanese caregivers, in contrast, the adults' past transgressions are seen as potentially undermining parental authority and diverting the child from the narrow right path, and therefore should not be divulged to the young child.
>
> (Fung, 2011, p. 107)

Importantly, Fung distinguishes between the self-goals that the two cultures believe children need to be prepared for, with US parents aiming for overwhelm-ingly positive self-evaluations and seeking always to promote their child's self-esteem, while Taiwanese parents use a particular form of protective or constructive shame in their stories, aiming to protect their children from the greater shame of being judged negatively by others and believing that children must learn early about ways to become a 'better self'.

The contrasting examples in the box show that in these middle-class Taiwanese families, a 'good' child is viewed as one who is oriented to the needs of the group and shows deference, and this is encouraged by the use of what might be described as constructive shame. In contrast, in the US European middle-class families, children are encouraged to be confident, self-assured, and evidently cheerful. These values reflect deep-seated cultural differences not just between these two settings but also across the world. Although there are many nuanced differences between and within countries, psychologists have found that some cultures have more individualistic (or autonomy-focused) 'me' goals, whereas other cultures have more group-oriented, collective (or relatedness-focused) 'us' goals. From these differing early child-rearing values and goals in different cultures, selves with different priorities are created.

Two philosophical phrases from two different cultures can illustrate the differences between these ways of thinking. One is the phrase '*I think; therefore, I am*' with which the 17th-century French philosopher and scientist Rene Descartes located selfhood in the cognitions in an individual's mind. This constructs the self as a rational, bounded, autonomous individual, whose own thoughts create the self. It can be contrasted with the phrase '*A person is a person through other persons*', a rendering of the 'Ubuntu' philosophy found in multiple cultures in southern Africa (Ewuoso and Hall, 2019). This recognises the fundamental paradox of human existence: that to be a fully realised self, we cannot simply exist alone but must also be interconnected with others – or as Markus summed it up: 'You can't be a self by yourself'.

These phrases encapsulate differing cultural approaches to the idea of what it is to be a self. Psychological research has characterised these as reflecting two types of cultures: *individualistic* or *independent* versus *collective* or *interdependent* (Markus and Kitayama, 2010). Broadly, global North countries are more independent-oriented whereas self-concept in many other cultures is more interdependent. It is important to note, however, that there are exceptions to this, as, for example, Japan and Korea are highly industrialised and developed democratic societies that are also more interdependent (though to different degrees), and there are also differences across Western Europe; for example, data suggest that Spain is more relatedness focused than Germany.

The contrasting support in storytelling described in the box previously, for (constructive) shame in Taiwan versus overt self-esteem in the US, shows how self values are partly created in children's earliest years as a reflection of cultural values and the social construction of childhood. It is important to note that this does not mean that self-esteem is necessarily lower in cultures more focused on interdependence goals. Rather, it means that self-esteem (i.e., valuing the self in meaningful domains) is experienced differently, for example, by fitting in with the group and deferring to others rather than by seeking to stand out from it and 'be the best'.

Lost in translation: Migration and forming a new self

When she was 13 years old, in 1959, Eva Hoffman (then Ewa Wydra) left Cracow in Poland with her parents and sister for a new life in North America without any knowledge of English. Her vivid memoir, *Lost in Translation* (Hoffman, 1989), offers a powerful example of how moving across cultures during childhood requires a reshaping of the self and a reckoning with the self left behind. 'Every immigrant', she was later to say, 'becomes a kind of amateur anthropologist' (Brown, 2001), needing to decode the new culture they have arrived in and also needing to learn to understand her own parents who are now detached from their origins. Hoffman describes her teenage transformation into a new North American self as a process of both losing and gaining identities, which form part of the self-concept or 'me'. She notices how people react when she is demonstrative and voluble in the Jewish-Polish way typical to her family origins, and this is a reminder that selves are constructed in relationship with the culture around us:

> My mother says I'm becoming 'English'. This hurts me, because I know she means I'm becoming cold. I'm no colder than I've ever been, but I'm learning to become less demonstrative . . . perhaps my mother is right . . . after a while, emotion follows action . . . I'm more careful about what I say, how loud I laugh, whether I give vent to grief. The storminess of emotion prevailing in our family is in excess of the normal here, and the unwritten rules for the normal have their osmotic effect.
>
> Hoffman (1989, p. 147)

Hoffman highlights the challenges migrants face and the adaptability of the self in childhood and youth. Underlining how multiple identities make up every self-concept, Jamaican-British sociologist and cultural theorist Stuart Hall stresses the conflicts we all experience as:

> within us are contradictory identities, pulling in different directions, so that our identifications are continually being shifted around. If we feel that we have a unified identity from birth to death, it is only because we construct a comforting story or 'narrative of the self' about ourselves.
>
> (Hall, 1992, p. 227)

Importantly, shifts in identities affecting the self can be encountered throughout childhood and youth not just when moving country but also with smaller migrations whether it is to a different school, new town, new region, or elsewhere.

Key points

- Attachment is a key theory of early childhood development that explains how early care affects the child's sense of self.
- There are many different cultural patterns to early care, and the most common globally is care by older children.

- After early care, 'good-enough', rather than perfect, parenting is essential so children can learn to tolerate frustration.
- Storytelling in the toddler years develops a first sense of a culturally congruent self.

Understanding children and young people's self-concept

In developmental psychology, childhood has typically been documented by adults, based on the assumption that adults have more insight and understanding than children. Adults often ask parents or teachers when they want to find out about children's lives. However, this approach to understanding and researching children and young people's experiences has been challenged by researchers who believe that children themselves are experts in their experiences, lives, and selves (Greene and Hill, 2005). Indeed, children's views of their lives, priorities, and themselves often differ from adults' (Crivello, Camfield and Woodhead, 2009).

Psychological researchers have explored and measured children and young people's self-concept and self-esteem for over 50 years, using questionnaires largely devised by adults. These questionnaires focus on performance in school, team sports, and peer popularity as well as behaviours, appearance, and overall self-evaluations. As this is quite a restrictive view of the self, to understand the self-concept factors that are most important to children and young people, I consulted 625 10–13-year-olds across the greater Dublin region and in different types of schools (Irish- and English-language, and in wealthier and poorer communities). I asked them to share their most important activities and relationships and the meanings they associated with these (Tatlow-Golden and Guerin, 2017; Guerin and Tatlow-Golden, 2019). They drew and wrote about themselves, completed 'Identity Pies', took part in 110 individual interviews, and completed standardised self-concept questionnaires used in psychological research.

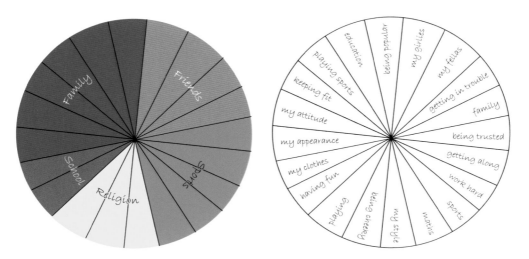

Figure 4.2 Example of young people's 'Identity Pies'.

Young people favoured over 150 activities, some organised and adult-led, others peer-based or more solitary. Their most favoured active selves involved being physically active not just in team sports but also in many other ways, such as individual sports or informal peer-led games and activities; being creative in multiple modes, including music, drama, drawing, writing, and more; using media for personal entertainment, gameplay, social networking, and learning; and being social with friends, family, and pets. The *meanings* they associated with these active selves included social connection with friends, family, and pets; experiencing challenge in favoured activities and improving their skills; and having fun. For example, an 11-year-old girl liked a fashion game website because she communicated with all her school friends on it: 'everyone's on it and we can chat to each other and it's fun'. And an 11-year-old boy found improving at soccer satisfying: 'I've really got to like it 'cause I'm getting better all the time'.

Where their most important social relationships were concerned, young people cited family first – including extended family and family members far away, as well as pets – and also friends. The *meanings* that young people associated with these relationships – unlike the psychological measures that adults have developed – did

Some of my friends from school play on my team (boy, 11)

I love basketball because it is my favourite sport (girl, 12)

I like to play football it cool. When I was about 8 I started play and I was play nice... I'm legend on football I love football (boy, 11)

Figure 4.3 Young people's views of some of their most important active selves.

not focus on peer popularity or on excellence but rather on a sense of being cared for emotionally and practically by family and friends, caring for younger relatives and pets, having fun, sharing activities and interests (including talking) with friends and family, liking and loving people, and sometimes fighting with friends and siblings.

Sometimes I love to play listening to music (girl, 12)

I am skipping with my friends in my back garden and we are having lots of fun together (girl, 10)

I am good at drawing cartoons and skateboarding and football (boy, 12)

I am having real fun (boy, 11)

Figure 4.3 Young people's views of some of their most important active selves.

Interestingly, although gendered trends were evident in some activities, with boys citing team-based physical activity and media-related activities more, and girls naming hobbies, non-team physical, creative activities, and pets more, there were almost no gender differences in the *meanings* young people associated with their active and social selves. Boys and girls valued their chosen activities and people for broadly similar reasons – such as being social in their physical activities and being cared for emotionally by family and friends. For example, an 11-year-old girl described her friends as salient because 'they care about me! They just make me happy!', while similarly, a 10-year-old boy described his family as cheering him up: 'like whenever I'm sad, they make me happy'. A 12-year-old boy valued his father's positive view of him and his faith in him: 'he gives me hope that I can do better and . . . [that] I'm good'.

My big cousin. He is really <u>fun</u> and I love him more than anything or anyone else in the world. (Boy, 11)

I drew my granny. She is my favourite person because she loves <u>me</u> and I love her
(Girl, 11)

This is my nephew and to my left is his sister (Boy, 12)

My mam my dad my <u>anty</u> my dog and my nanny and my cat (girl, 12)

Figure 4.4 Young people's views of some of their most important social selves.

And a 12-year-old girl appreciated her mum and dad because 'they tell me what's, like, the right thing to do, and they help me decide what to do'.

What can this study tell us about children's selves? Young people, in their drawings, interviews, and also their analyses of their peers' Identity Pie charts, focused on a wide and subtle range of features that they identified as most important to their self-concept. This suggests that psychological self-concept researchers' methods take a limited view of what's important to young people and what contributes to their self-concept and self-esteem. Adult-designed measures focus on school-based, performance-based, and athletic-related values, behaviours, appearance, and peer popularity. Yet young people noted a wide range of relationships beyond peers, identifying family members, including extended families and pets. Their peers were important but for friendship rather than popularity. Furthermore, the meaning they associated with activities differed from self-concept questionnaires which ask about comparative ability; instead, they valued *progression* in the activities that mattered to them whether computer games, playing a musical instrument, or sport. For example, they might say, 'I'm not the best at volleyball, but I'm getting better all the time'.

Finally, into these tapestries of young people's self-concept and meanings were threaded consistent references to fun. Although fun is often invoked as a component of a good childhood, it is rare to see it being taken seriously by adults as a feature of children and young people's selves. Overall, therefore, when psychological researchers use existing adult-devised methods to study young people's self-concept, they will underestimate the role of relational, caring, and self-development features of young people's selves as well as the role played by fun in their lives and experiences.

Key points

- Psychological researchers measure children and young people's self-esteem with questionnaires focusing on a limited set of aspects of the self-concept.
- Research with children and young people shows that they have important self-concept aspects and meanings that are not reflected in these psychological measures.
- Adults underestimate the importance to children of self-improvement and relationality in these measures and the role of fun for children's sense of self.

Conclusion

William James described the self as psychology's 'most puzzling puzzle' at the end of the 19th century, and it is still puzzled over by researchers in the 21st century. Yet by observing children and parents and listening carefully to children and young people, researchers have learned a great deal about how self-concept and self-esteem are shaped by children and young people's experiences and how in turn they shape their experiences, learning, behaviour, and development. A common thread in this chapter has been that children and young people's selves, although individual and deeply personal, are socially constructed. Selves are experienced differently by every individual and change over time with development, but all are shaped by relationships, settings, and cultures.

References

Bakermans-Kranenburg, M.-J., van IJzendoorn, M. H., and Juffer, F. (2003) 'Less is more: meta-analyses of sensitivity and attachment interventions in early childhood', *Psychological Bulletin*, 129(2), pp. 195–215.

Bowlby, J. (1969) *Attachment and Loss: Attachment*. New York: Basic Books.

Bretherton, I. (1992) 'The origins of attachment theory: John Bowlby and Mary Ainsworth', *Developmental Psychology*, 28(5), pp. 759–775.

Brown, A. (2001) 'Hoffman's tale', *The Guardian* [online]. Available at: www.theguardian.com/books/2001/apr/28/internationaleducationnews.socialsciences (Accessed 24th November 2022).

Crivello, G., Camfield, L., and Woodhead, M. (2009) 'How can children tell us about their wellbeing? Exploring the potential of participatory research approaches within Young Lives', *Social Indicators Research*, 90, pp. 51–72.

Ewuoso, C., and Hall, S. (2019) 'Core aspects of Ubuntu: a systematic review', *South African Journal of Bioethics Law*, 12(2), pp. 93–103.

Fitzgerald, H. E. (2022) 'Family systems and relationships: dyadic and triadic contexts in-the-moment and over time', *Early Childhood Research Quarterly*, 60, pp. 334–335.

Fung, H. (2011) 'Cultural psychological perspectives on social development in childhood', in P. K.

Smith and C. H. Hart (eds.) *The Wiley-Blackwell Handbook of Childhood Social Development* (2nd ed.). Oxford: Blackwell, pp. 100–118.

Gass, K., Jenkins, J., and Dunn, J. (2007) 'Are sibling relationships protective? A longitudinal study', *Journal of Child Psychology and Psychiatry*, 48(2), pp. 167–175.

Greene, S., and Hill, M. (2005) 'Researching children's experience: methods and methodological issues', in S. Greene and D. Hogan (eds.) *Researching Children's Experience. Methods and Approaches*. London: Sage, pp. 1–21.

Guerin, S., and Tatlow-Golden, M. (2019) 'How valid are measures of children's self-concept/self-esteem? Factors and content validity in three widely used scales', *Child Indicators Research*, 12, pp. 1507–1528.

Hall, S. (1992) 'The question of cultural identity', in T. McGrew, S. Hall and D. Held (eds.) *Modernity and Its Futures*. Cambridge: Polity Press, pp. 273–326.

Harter, S. (2012) *The Construction of the Self* (2nd ed.). New York: Guildford Press.

Hoffman, E. (1989) *Lost in Translation: A Life in a New Language*. London: Penguin Books.

James, W. (1890/1907) *The Principles of Psychology*. London: Macmillan.

Keller, H. (2018) 'Universality claim of attachment theory: children's socioemotional development across cultures', *PNAS Proceedings of the National Academy of Science*, 115(45), pp. 11414–11419.

Keller, H., and Kärtner, J. (2013) 'Development. The cultural solution of universal developmental tasks', in M. J. Gelfand, C.-Y. Chiu and Y.-Y. Hong (eds.) *Advances in Culture and Psychology* (Vol. 3). Oxford: Oxford University Press, pp. 63–116.

Klein, V., and Myrdal, A. (1956) *Women's Two Roles*. Oxford: Routledge.

Markus, H. R., and Kitayama, S. (2010) 'Cultures and selves: a cycle of mutual constitution', *Perspectives on Psychological Science*, 5(4), pp. 420–430.

Markus, H. R., and Nurius, P. (1986) 'Possible selves', *American Psychologist*, 41(9), pp. 954–969.

Mesman, J. *et al.* (2016) 'Is the ideal mother a sensitive mother? Beliefs about early childhood parenting in mothers across the globe', *International Journal of Behavioral Development*, 40(5), pp. 385–397.

Miller, P. J., Sandel, T. L., Liang, C.-H., and Fung, H. (2001) 'Narrating transgressions in Longwood: the discourses, meanings, and paradoxes of an American socializing practice', *Ethos*, 29(2), pp. 159–186.

Oyserman, D., Elmore, K., and Smith, G. (2012) 'Self, self-concept, and identity', in M. R. Leary and J. P. Tangney (eds.) *Handbook of Self and Identity* (2nd ed.). New York: The Guilford Press, pp. 69–104.

Rosenberg, M. (1986) 'Self-concept from middle childhood through adolescence', in J. Suls and A. G. Greenwald (eds.) *Psychological Perspectives on the Self* (Vol. 3). New York: Lawrence Erlbaum, pp. 107–136.

Rutter, M. (1995) 'Clinical implications of attachment concepts: retrospect and prospect', *Journal of Child Psychology and Psychiatry*, 36(4), pp. 549–571.

Schaffer, H. R. (2006) *Key Concepts in Developmental Psychology*. London: Sage.

Smyth, E., and Russell, H. (2021) *Fathers and children from infancy to middle childhood*. Research Series 130. Dublin: Economic and Social Research Institute Ireland.

Tatlow-Golden, M., and Guerin, S. (2017) 'Who I am: the meaning of children's most valued activities and relationships, and implications for self-concept research', *Journal of Early Adolescence*, 37(2), pp. 236–266.

Vicedo, M. (2017) 'Putting attachment in its place: disciplinary and cultural contexts', *European Journal of Developmental Psychology*, 14, pp. 684–699.

Weisner, T. S., and Gallimore, R. (1977) 'My brother's keeper: child and sibling caretaking', *Currents in Anthropology*, 18, pp. 169–190.

Winnicott, D. (1953) 'Transitional objects and transitional phenomena', *International Journal of Psychoanalysis*, 34, pp. 89–97.

5 Diverse families

Michael Boampong

The family – an introduction

The word family seems simple, yet it contains many complexities; everyone has an idea of what 'family' is, but these ideas can vary considerably across and within communities, countries, and cultures. 'Family' is also inherently contradictory: families are private spaces away from public life and the outside world but are also profoundly public in the sense that society and policy imagine them in particular ways and expect people to behave accordingly.

Psychologists, sociologists, anthropologists, and historians have looked at different family forms, how they influence children's lives, and whether there are universal patterns across time or place. This chapter will begin by considering various meanings of the word family before turning to focus on children's views. It will also look at how different family forms and parenting practices emerge in response to changes in contemporary societies. To explore this in depth, the chapter will focus on transnational families: those with members separated from each other some or most of the time, especially overseas, considering how parents and children maintain their family across geographical borders.

Defining and doing family

Most children live in families – an exception being children who are living in some kinds of care, or 'looked-after' children – and yet the word family holds different meanings for different people. The concept of family is enmeshed in social and personal ideas about what families should do, how they should behave, and who counts as a family member. Parenting and caring practices are shaped by culture and circumstance, and children have always grown up in both 'blood'-related and other families. Families usually give emotional and material care and provide an environment where children are socialised and raised to maturity, and ideally, children will experience family life as a caring and loving space.

The family can involve many shapes, sizes, and forms. Many people may first think of a 'nuclear' family: a married, heterosexual couple, who live with their biological children in one household and operate as a single economic unit. But there are many other family forms, such as extended families; male, female, or child-headed families;

DOI: 10.4324/9781003358855-6

gay and lesbian families; co-resident, blended, or stepfamilies; and 'kinship care', where members of the family other than parents care for children – such as older siblings, aunts and uncles, or grandparents. About 2% of the world's population in the Middle East, sub-Saharan Africa, and Asia live in polygamous households (Kramer, 2020), where communal family living may involve a husband, co-wives, children, and other relations in one household with significant decisions made by the patriarch, meaning that dozens of people in a household can share a house, land, and food.

Extended family or large family structures are common in the global South and some European countries, and these can promote interdependence and collective responsibility towards the welfare and socialisation of household members through the transmission of culture, provision of care, and risk sharing. For instance, research has shown that in Ghana and the Philippines, some children of migrants are cared for by extended family members rather than their parents, and likewise, the provision of support and care is not restricted to parents, even when they are present (Parreñas, 2005; Boampong, 2020). In some cases, grandparents provide day-to-day child-rearing and pass on childcare practices, and siblings, aunts, and uncles may provide financial support for children's educational needs, thereby reducing the risk of falling into poverty. More widely, grandparents are considered vital in supporting grandchildren who have experienced parental separation or family transitions (Rigg and Pryor, 2007). In the UK, the 2001 census shows that 173,000 children live in informal kinship care (Selwyn and Nandy, 2014). In Uganda, Ghana, and other matrilineal societies (in which ancestry is traced through maternal, not paternal, lines), a woman's brother plays a crucial role in providing financial support for her children's education and wellbeing (Evans, 2012). These practices reflect socio-cultural norms in many parts of the world that taking care of a child is not the sole responsibility of biological parents but a shared one (this will be discussed further in the final section of the chapter). Families are also heavily influenced by economic factors, and the search for better opportunities and lives for their children is a major factor in many people's migration and family experiences.

In the global North, the nuclear family still retains – especially for policy makers and politicians – symbolic, ideological significance as the 'gold standard' of family life. Deviations from this norm have been stigmatised, with single mothers portrayed as feckless benefit scroungers or gay parents and their children once referred to as being in 'a pretended family relationship' (according to the controversial Section 28 of the Local Government Act 1988 in the UK, which banned the 'promotion' of homosexuality in schools and which was not repealed until 2003). Such attitudes are often heavily racialised, with 'Black families', especially those headed by single mothers, provoking particular anxiety in public policy. In the UK in 2007, the then–Home Secretary Jack Straw led a campaign highlighting absent fathers, particularly those in Black communities. He was quoted as saying:

> As we know – lads need dads. Of course, they need their mums as well, but there is a particular point in teenagers' development, of young men, where fathers are very important and they are more likely to be absent in the case of the Afro-Caribbean.
>
> (Faircloth, 2014, p. 184)

This view persists as a stereotype, even though the evidence for fathers' ethnicity and their presence and involvement with children is much more mixed (Reynolds, 2009). It pathologises diverse families and sees social problems as originating in certain family forms or ethnic groups while ignoring wider social issues of racism, poverty, and social exclusion. It suggests that the make-up of the family is more important than the caring and nurturing that goes on within it, and it ignores how single mothers rarely raise their children in isolation but rather are often supported by their relations, other potential male role models, and the wider community.

Children, families, and the importance of 'one good adult'

Social attitudes often hold that children will experience worse outcomes in single parent, divorced, or other family constellations that diverge from the two-parent nuclear family 'ideal'. Earlier 20th-century psychological studies also regularly reported more frequent behavioural and emotional difficulties in children in non-nuclear families.

Yet more carefully designed research has long since shown that there is a very wide range of outcomes associated with diverse family formats, and the *reasons* for negative effects found in research studies appear to be more complex than social norms imagine (Deater-Deckard and Dunn, 1999). Indeed, children's behaviour problems, rather than being a result of non-nuclear family arrangements, are often the result of financial hardship, unstable parent employment, or parental conflict (Formby, Hardy and Simpson, 2021).

Recently, psychologist Susan Golombok and colleagues compared children in two-parent families, with those in families where mothers are single by choice, and found their emotional and behavioural difficulties did not differ (Golombok *et al.*, 2021). They conclude that having two parents is not required for children to flourish and that family *structure* is less important than family *relationship quality*.

The significance of the quality of care in a child or young person's life was identified in the large scale My World Surveys 1 and 2, the 'National Study of Youth Mental Health in Ireland' (Dooley *et al.*, 2019). With over 14,000 young people (12–25 years) in Survey 1 and over 19,000 in Survey 2, it was found that 'one good adult' in a young person's life positively affected their mental health and improved their self-belief, confidence, coping skills, and confidence about the future. For example, adolescents who reported having very high support from a person they identified as 'one good adult' were much less likely to experience depression. In 2019, 76% of adolescents reported having a special adult in their lives in times of need. This 'one good adult' was often a parent, but 35% reported it to be a member of the extended family, such as a grandparent, and others identified non-family members, such as a coach or teacher.

Rather than being concerned, therefore, with the *structure or arrangement* of a family, research indicates that it makes more sense to be concerned with the *relationships* and *interactions* within it. One way to do this is to identify the qualities people associate with effective family relationships and how to maintain a supportive family environment. Sociologist David Morgan (1996) uses the term 'doing family' to make the point that families are formed through everyday activities, relationships, and interactions. These are processes within and outside households, and people 'do family' in different ways. Some 'do family' through infrequent visits, such as parents separated from their children, or family members visiting extended family relations, such as grandparents. 'Doing family' also involves emotional and material practices of sending items, including gifts, so people know you are thinking about them, creating a sense of family closeness. Contact at special times, such as phone calls on birthdays, at times of bereavement, on Father's Day or Mother's Day, can promote affective bonds among kin and non-kin relations (Boampong, 2019).

The notion of 'doing family' underscores the fluidity of families: 'family represents a quality rather than a thing' (Morgan, 1996, p. 186). It draws attention to everyday experiences, activities, plans, memories, and meanings attached to place and actions. For instance, family rituals, such as a daily gathering for prayers or a meal, may not only be an essential practice but also permits sharing of family values, discussing issues, and nurturing children's social and cultural identities (Mason and Tipper, 2008) – and also support children's language, emotional, and social skill development (Spagnola and Fiese, 2007). In some cultures, children refer to non-related adults as auntie or uncle at home, school, or elsewhere to express a sense of respect and 'doing family' in practice. In my research with children in Ghana, children not only had friendships with peers at church but also had close relationships with youth and women leaders, whom they referred to as their 'church father or mother'. In these various ways, family can be created less by biological relationship than by what we do and who we trust.

Key points

- Families are diverse, and there is no one ideal family type.
- The nuclear family is imagined as the dominant model in the global North but is only one type of family among others.
- It is more important to think about what families do and how they nurture and support children than what shape they take.

What do children think about family?

Early research exploring children's ideas of family came from psychologist Jean Piaget (1928), who looked at children's definitions of family at different ages. Before the age of five years, children tended to see family simply as the people they lived with. This was mirrored in 20th-century sociological work which, like Piaget, found that more abstract ideas of what family means and what families do start to become important to children in middle to late childhood. Sociologist Virginia Morrow (1998) interviewed 183 children between 8 and 14 years in two parts of England – a rural area and a large town with a population of British Muslims originating from Pakistan – asking them directly how they understood their families and what they valued in their parents. She found that, as Piaget suggested, the idea that family are who you live with largely held true for younger children, and from eight or nine, what families do became more important than who lives where, and the view that family members provide mutual love and care took on greater significance. 10-year-old James, for example, defined family as 'a group of people who love you. Families are for loving you and for being kind to you' (Morrow, 1998, p. 25).

Similarly, sociologists Carol Smart, Bren Neale and Amanda Wade (2001) asked older children about their families. They found children were much less concerned with family forms, the structure of the household, or the gender or number of adults than they were about being raised within families with good relationships where adults provide love, warmth, and security. 12-year-old Claudia, for example, said:

> A family isn't really like blood relatives, it's just people who love each other. . . . If I didn't love my mum or I didn't love my dad then, by law, they'd be a member of my family but you wouldn't really feel like a family, 'cos I mean it doesn't matter if you're rich or poor, or if you live on the streets, as long as you love each other. Of course you're going to have arguments and stuff, but if you love each other it doesn't really matter, does it, what arrangements you're in?
>
> (Smart, Neale and Wade, 2001, p. 42)

Smart and colleagues identified three aspects of family relationships which children value differently at different ages: *residence* (who lives where and with whom), *family roles* (what family members do for each other), and the *quality* of relationships (love, care, support, respect, and nurturing that children feel within the home). Similarly, in New Zealand, psychologists Stacey Anyan and Jan Pryor (2002) found that regardless of gender, age, and ethnicity, children cited emotional connections with a broad range of people that did not reflect biological connections, the nuclear family, or legal factors (marriage or other ties). With Andrea Rigg, Jan Pryor (Rigg and Pryor, 2007) further found that just 2% of 111 children's definitions of family cited parents' relationship status, with most (78%) citing emotional reasons, such as 'Family is people who care for and love you and are there for you' (New Zealand Maori girl, 10). Researchers elsewhere have also found that children are flexible about what constitutes family and include many people in their descriptions, including relatives both living and dead, members of other households, and even animals; for example, in Ireland, participants aged 10–13 regularly drew cousins, extended family members, and pets as members of their 'family' unit (Tatlow-Golden and Guerin 2017).

The persistent nature of interpretations of family defined through love, support, and time given can be seen in the Independent Family Review by the Children's Commissioner for England (2022). This reports that government data is failing to keep up with family trends for single parents, blended families, and other diverse family structures; yet children and families themselves continue to define family as 'loving and strong relationships, through practical and emotional support, and through a life spent together' (p. 7). As an example, a six-year-old boy said:

> The purpose of family is to love us. They give us all the love we need. They provide everything that we need. They look after us and help us to grow. They care for us and if we are upset, they look after us. They make sure that we go to school every day.
>
> (Children's Commissioner, 2022, p. 26)

It must be remembered that whereas many children may be talking about their experiences, others may be describing a cultural ideal. There are many children who grow up without this kind of help, care, or love, and families can be a great source of unhappiness. Studying UK secondary school children's perceptions of who and what makes them happy, Cordelia Sutton (2018, p. 108) explored these ambivalences about family life. She asked 40 young teenagers to draw a happiness map with themselves at the centre and then to draw concentric circles in which they showed activities, people, and things that made them happy. While family scored very highly as something that made them happy, several young people modified this, writing that only a happy or a calm family did so. Paige wrote, 'Family and friends – I love my friends and family but sometimes they cause me sadness', while Sharina wrote, 'My family but only when we're not arguing or no one's angry'. Another child spoke of 'a negative aura around your family sometimes' (Holly). Sometimes children feel pressure to 'do' happy even if they do not feel like it, as it is what their parents expected of them, and in this way, some ways of 'doing' family can be burdensome rather than supportive for children.

As an example of how the quality of care influences how children and young people construct 'family', consider this statement by 16-year-old Ama, who lives in Ghana, about Geraldine, a Ghanaian immigrant based in London, who is a single parent and a social worker (Boampong, 2020). When Geraldine visited Ghana several years earlier, Ama met her, through Ama's auntie. Ama describes how, even though they are not related and on different continents, Geraldine provides parental-style care for her, at a distance from London. Ama experiences Geraldine's distance-based support as being more caring than that of her biological mother, explaining how Geraldine is engaged in 'doing family':

> Geraldine is also my mother, but she is more caring than my biological mother. She takes care of me like her own child, keeps in touch every day, offers advice, asks me if I have eaten and how I am doing. Sometimes she sends me money for school . . . I also send her text messages to encourage her every morning.

Ama proactively uses various tools, including language, as a way of 'doing family', even though she does not live with Geraldine, and she is not a 'blood' relation. She sends motivational messages to Geraldine every morning. She updates her WhatsApp profile picture and status to that of Geraldine or Stella (Geraldine's daughter, whom

Figure 5.1 An example of a new family formation.

she has never met) regularly and for special occasions, including on Mother's Day, with messages such as 'sweet mother' and 'best four sisters', as seen in Figure 5.1. Ama refers to Geraldine as her *mother* because of the things Geraldine does for her and the relationship they have, even though they are not biologically related.

This example indicates both children's competence in forming 'new' family relations and also the fluidity of 'family', where family structures can change over the life course. Children and young people can be resourceful in seeking and receiving care from others if their immediate relations are unable to provide it, and adults may be willing to provide family-style care to young people for whom this is lacking, thus 'doing' family in various ways.

As the final section of the chapter will show, children's family ties may involve moving between multiple households. Children can form family-like networks with adults to secure support for education, apprenticeship, and food amid the rising cost of education and everyday life in countries within Africa and Asia, where cultural norms encourage contact among cousins, uncles, aunties, friends, and siblings (Mason and Tipper, 2008).

Siblings

Much of the work in both sociology and psychology on definitions of family, and on what families do, concentrates on relationships between adults and children. This, however, overlooks sibling relationships which are an important aspect of many children's experiences of family, important in their development and often some of the longest relationships of their lives. In many parts of the world, children spend much of their time with, and under the charge of, their older siblings, who play a central role in their lives. Many children, especially girls (including in the global North), are expected to look after, or at least keep an eye on, much younger siblings while their mothers do the housework or go out to work. While this active sibling oversight may have faded in some communities, it is still prevalent, and certainly, siblings remain highly significant.

The variety of sibling relationships is great, but in general, they are characterised by a strength and depth of emotion whether positive, negative, or ambivalent. Older siblings are often fundamental in socialising younger ones (and being socialised by them) and, through each other, learn how to cooperate, empathise, and play. Such proximity also means, of course, that siblings learn from an early age exactly which 'buttons to press' and how to rile each other; this contrast of love and antagonism is one of the defining features of much of the literature.

Psychologists have found that sibling teasing begins early in the second year of life, increasing rapidly from then on. Teasing demonstrates considerable understanding of the other child, showing that children's ability to understand others' minds, motivations, and sensitivities beings very early in life and can be beneficial. Psychologist Judy Dunn (2002, p. 231) argues that 'children who have engaged in frequent shared pretend play with an older sibling, and talked about mental states (knowing, remembering, thinking, believing, and so on) with a sibling are, over time, especially successful on the standard assessments of understanding emotions and mental states'. In Morrow's study described earlier, 11-year-old Callum summed this up succinctly: 'My little sister is important to me because I can sometimes trust her. She does get very annoying, though' (1998, p. 31).

Despite reservations, children often value the shared time and experiences of childhood, as with their siblings, they can 'be themselves' and don't have to put up pretence or be on their best behaviour. Sociologist Samantha Punch (2008, p. 338) has called this children's 'backstage behaviour' – the things they get up to when no one is watching and when they don't feel judged.

> [I] get pizza in my face, ice cream. . . . They (brothers) seem to think it's OK to have the door open when they're having a shower and when Elliot's doing the toilet like. . . . But like with my friends I wouldn't do that in front of them 'cos I don't know them like as well as that.
>
> (Henrietta, 11, oldest)

Children report feeling accepted 'warts and all' by their siblings and, in return, accept their brothers' and sisters' foibles and failings:

> if you try to take your anger out on your friends then they'd think you're, like 'oh no he hates me or something' but they (siblings) know I hate them some-times but I don't really hate them, you just say you do but you don't.
>
> (Craig, 11, middle child)

Key points

- Children are flexible about what constitutes family; their definitions include living and dead relatives, non-relatives, and even pets as family members.
- Children usually care more about love and care than they do about biological relat-edness or family formations.
- Siblings are an important part of a child's family, and these relationships provide evidence of very early understanding of others' minds and motivations.

Transnational families

During the Covid pandemic starting in 2020, new ways of 'doing' family and maintain-ing family ties developed quickly. Travel and social restrictions in most countries physically separated families. Meetings with parents, grandparents, siblings, and friends became harder or impossible, so many families found new ways of continuing and developing relationships, including depending on internet-based technologies, such as social media, to stay connected emotionally and socially. Even if they did not live together or could not see each other, people found ways to show distant love and care.

For many other families, however, long-distance relationships, and even long-distance parenting, were not new. Researchers have examined transnational families – families who live in different countries but who create and retain a 'sense of collective welfare and unity, in short "familyhood", even across national borders' (Bryceson and Vuorela, 2002, p. 18). This may involve parents who work overseas or children sent to other people to be rasied. Researchers have examined how adults can parent children from a different country, identifying caregiving arrangements, money/goods exchange, communication between children and parents, maintenance of cultural practices, and children's identity formation across borders (Parreñas, 2005; Coe, 2013).

As some countries continued to maintain Covid-related travel restrictions and physical distancing measures, migrants and non-migrant separated families had to organise care from a distance. Migration does not necessarily imply travel across borders, and many people migrate within their own country and region, for example, in order to secure work to support family members. Those who are unable to meet physically may feel guilty not being there for their children. Gendered care practices can be further reinforced, or changed, depending on who moves and who is unable to move (Brandhorst, Baldassar and Wilding, 2020).

In 2020, 281 million migrants were living outside their country of birth; this number includes 35.5 million children under 18 years, some of whom are refugees fleeing conflict and persecution in their home countries (UNICEF, 2021). Poverty, unemployment, and poor access to health, childcare, and education mean that many families or family members choose, or are forced, to migrate, becoming scattered or distributed and forming transnational families. Parents often move to meet rising aspirations, redress inequalities in access to education and work, and achieve a better life for themselves and their children (Parreñas, 2005; Coe, 2013). When parents move, the host countries' restrictive immigration policies or the nature of the parent's job can mean their children do not join them immediately – or ever. The family's relationships are stretched across borders with children in one country and their parent(s) in another.

Yet even though the external circumstances have changed, families can remain strong, and parents and children find new ways to communicate with each other. Women from central America, who work as maids in the USA, or those from the Philippines or Indonesia, who work as nannies in the Middle East or elsewhere in Asia or as nurses in European countries, do not cease nurturing their children or being very heavily involved in their lives. Research has shown how migrant working women call home daily, use Skype and WhatsApp to see their children, and in some cases, keep Skype on all day while they clean and housekeep and help their children with their homework while getting on with their day job thousands of miles away (Madianou and Miller, 2011). These studies of transnational families challenge dominant constructions of the good family that suggest that to be a 'good mother' or 'good child' requires a nuclear family or even physical co-presence.

Case study: Afia – Growing up in a migrant family and caregiving arrangements

Afia is a 7-year-old girl and only child to a single mother, who now works as a nurse. Afia was born in London, and her mother, who was born in Ghana, worked as a security guard, earning a low income. She found it was nearly impossible to support herself and Afia financially. She decided to arrange for a friend's mother to take care of Afia in Ghana, when Afia was 6 months old, and Afia lived in Ghana until she was three years old.

While they were separated, with Afia in Ghana and her mother in London, Afia's mother tried to maintain family closeness with her daughter through audio and video phone calls and by sending money and toys from London. She was able to visit Afia at least once a year in Ghana. Afia now describes her attitude whenever her mother joined her in Ghana: 'I will be her baby whenever she is in Ghana. I sometimes cry and want her to carry me even though I have grown. I would want to go everywhere with her'. Though her primary caregiver was present, Afia pre-ferred her returned mother to perform caring duties, thus building a physical parent-child relationship during visits. In this way, she sought to catch up on lost childhood moments and formed an attachment with her migrant parent.

Afia now lives in London with her mother and when asked what she likes about her mother, she said:

> since I came back to London, mum does a lot for me. She cooks and takes care of me when I am not well. She cleans my room and comes to school meetings. My father should be doing something right? My mum is doing what my dad should be doing.

Afia's mother is no longer a security guard and is now working as a nurse, so she goes to work early and comes home late. Afia enjoys ballet, music, and going to the park with her mother or a family friend who stays with them. Afia's school provides local authority–funded care, picking her up from home at 7 am for 'Breakfast Club' and keeping her in 'After-school Club' until her mother arrives home from work at 6 pm. Afia's mother then supervises Afia's homework and goes to bed. Even though they are now in the same country, Afia's mother still feels she does not have enough time to spend with her child as a mother. Cur-rently, Afia's mother has decided to move out of London due to rising rent, meaning another internal migration for Afia and her mother. Afia is sad she will be leaving London and notes: 'I wish I could be in London because I can see my friends at my school' (Boampong, 2020).

In this short account, we see that, while navigating time and financial constraints, Afia's mother cares for her, ensures she is well looked after, and responsibly and con-sciously chooses people (relatives and non-relatives) to perform what it means to be a mother – that is, 'cooking, engaging with the child's school, discipline, language and cultural awareness, reading bed-time stories, and essential child-rearing activities', all of which Afia's mother felt she was unable to accomplish on her own in London without affordable child care (Boampong, 2019, p. 206). While the idea of being separated for nearly three years from one's very young child might sound unimaginably difficult to some parents from the global North, it is important to note a long cultural tradition of child 'circulation' that exists in Ghana and in other parts of West Africa (and other parts of the world), where children are sent away to different parts of the country to be raised and educated by members of the extended family. This circulation of children is part of wider cultural beliefs about the relative roles and responsibilities of parents and the wider community. Children are collectively raised, and the concept of motherhood and caring responsibilities is inclusive and elastic and allows for many different people to participate in 'doing family', carrying out different aspects of nurturing, socialising, and educating children which would, elsewhere, be done solely by parents. Wealthier relatives may contribute to their school fees. Grandmothers or older siblings may feed children daily, socialise them, teach them to read, or instil cultural values, while their mother is many miles away.

The impacts of migration and separation on the parent-child relationship are complex, and there are no straightforward answers. Children's experiences depend on several factors, including the availability and nature of alternative caregiving, who moves and who stays, level of interaction (i.e., visits and communication), the duration and the age of separation from parent(s), poverty, and other resource constraints. Studying 48 children of Caribbean migrants, psychologists Andrea Smith, Richard Lalonde, and Simone Johnson (2004) argued that lengthy physical separation due to parental migration 'can potentially disrupt parent-child bonding' and lead to children's low self-esteem and skipping school at least once (pp. 116–117). Similarly, children of rural-urban migrant parents living in China often experience emotional challenges, including anxiety and depression (Zhang, 2015). Research in the Philippines, Lesotho, and Ghana suggests that amid parental migration or loss of parents, extended family (e.g., uncles, cousins, aunts, and grandparents) provide care and emotional support for children or redistribute roles, such as care for younger siblings, cleaning, and cooking to older children or siblings (Ansell and van Blerk, 2004; Parreñas, 2005; Boampong, 2020). When Filipino parents maintain regular communication with their children through telephone calls, it may reduce loneliness among left-behind children, although sociologist Rhacel Salazar Parreñas (2008) observed gendered differences in communication by migrant parents: Filipino fathers abroad, as compared to mothers, rarely communicated with their children at home.

While children sent to their parents' origin countries or those left behind often accept transnational care arrangements planned by their parents, some exercise control in choosing whom to stay with. Mercy (15 years, Ghana) was born in London, but due to her parent's inability to combine work and childcare, at 7 months old, she was sent to Ghana for foster care by her maternal grandmother. In later years, when her grandmother had to travel away for a week, the grandmother planned to entrust Mercy's care to her uncle. Mercy, however, chose differently:

My grandmother travelled to the village, and I went to my elder sister's (Portia, 26 years) house for some time because I was the only child in the house and wanted to be with my sister and my niece. I came back after a week when my grandmother returned. Going there was my decision.

Mercy resisted her grandmother's plan and went to live with her sister, whom she preferred, as she 'encourages' and 'advises' her on school assignments. Though her grandmother was her primary caregiver, Mercy considered her sister necessary to her education (Boampong, 2020).

Key points

- Transnational families are those where parents care and nurture across geographical boundaries and borders.
- There is a long history of children being moved between family members in West Africa, other parts of Africa and Asia, and in many other countries.
- Research on the outcomes for children are mixed, but most parents work hard to provide or arrange for care for their children wherever they live, doing their best to ensure they are looked after responsibly within their families.

Conclusion

Children across the world grow up in a variety of family types and structures. Some are prized in their own context while treated with suspicion in others, but as this chapter has argued, it is more helpful, and indeed more in line with children's own views, to see family in terms of what it *does*, rather than its structure. Unarguably, children need love, care, and physical and emotional nurturance as they grow up, and this usually happens within families, but the structure of these families and who is physically present or absent is of much less importance. Looking at the diversity of families shows us how parents, whatever the external constraints or the internal make-up of the family, continue to love, care, and nurture their children. Sometimes this may take the form of delegating certain aspects of parenting to others while continuing to be a good parent by providing and nurturing from afar. What is important to remember, however, is that there are wide variations in families and in child-rearing practices across the globe, as well as different understandings of family relationships, and that what is 'natural' and 'normal' in a certain country may not be so in other parts of the world.

References

Ansell, N., and Blerk, L. Van (2004) 'Children's migration as a household/family strategy: coping with AIDS in Lesotho and Malawi', *Journal of Southern African Studies*, 30(3), pp. 673–690.

Anyan, S. E., and Pryor, J. (2002) 'What is in a family? Adolescent perceptions', *Children and Society*, 16(5), pp. 306–317.

Boampong, M. (2019) 'Transnational practices and children's local lives in times of economic crisis, intersectionality and difference in childhood and youth: global perspectives', in Nadia

Von Benzon and Catherine Wilkinson (eds.) *Intersectionality and Difference in Childhood and Youth: Global Perspectives*. London: Routledge, pp. 198–212.

Boampong, M. (2020) *Growing Up in Times of Crisis : Negotiating Economic Constraints and Opportunities in Transnational Families*. Birkbeck: University of London. Available at: http://bbkthe ses.da.ulcc.ac.uk/462/.

Brandhorst, R., Baldassar, L., and Wilding, R. (2020) 'Introduction to the special issue: "transnational family care 'on hold'? Intergenerational relationships and obligations in the context of immobility regimes"', *Journal of Intergenerational Relationships*, 18(3), pp. 261–280.

Bryceson, D. F., and Vuorela, U. (2002) *The Transnational Family: New European Frontiers and Global Networks*. Oxford and New York: Berg.

Children's Commissioner (2022) 'London: children's commissioner. Family and its protective effect', *Part 1 of the Independent Family Review*. Available at: www.childrenscommissioner.gov. uk/wp-content/uploads/2022/08/cc-family-and-its-protective-effect-part-1-of-the-independ ent-family-review.pdf.

Coe, C. (2013) *The Scattered Family : Parenting, African Migrants, and Global Inequality*. Chicago, IL: University of Chicago Press.

Deater-Deckard, K., and Dunn, J. (1999) 'Multiple risks and adjustment in young children growing up in different family structures: the case of separation and lone parenthood', *Journal of Child Psychology and Psychiatry*, 40(5), pp. 809–819.

Dooley, B., O'Connor, C., Fitzgerald, A., and O'Reilly, A. 2019. *My World Survey 2. The National Study of Youth Mental Health in Ireland*. Dublin: Jigsaw and University College Dublin. Available at: www.myworldsurvey.ie/full-report (Accessed 7th May 2022).

Dunn, J. (2002) 'Sibling relationships', in P. K. Smith and C. H. Hart (eds.) *Blackwell Handbook of Childhood Social Development*. Oxford: Blackwell, pp. 223–237.

Evans, R. (2012) 'Sibling caringscapes: time-space practices of caring within youth-headed households in Tanzania and Uganda', *Geoforum*, 43(4), pp. 824–835.

Faircloth, C. (2014) 'Intensive fatherhood? The (un)involved dad', in E. Lee, J. Bristow, C. Faircloth and J. Macvarish (eds.) *Parenting Culture Studies*. London: Palgrave Macmillan.

Formby, E., Hardy, C., and Simpson, D. (2021) 'The role of family structure and socioeconomic status in children's behavior problems: a longitudinal analysis', *Journal of Family Psychology*, 35(1), pp. 30–40.

Golombok, S., Zadeh, S., Freeman, T., Lysons, J., and Foley, S. (2021) 'Single mothers by choice: parenting and child adjustment in middle childhood', *Journal of Family Psychology*, 35(2), pp. 192–202.

Kramer, S. (2020) 'Polygamy is rare around the world and mostly confined to a few regions', *Pew Research Center* [online]. Available at: www.pewresearch.org/fact-tank/2020/12/07/polyg amy-is-rare-around-the-world-and-mostly-confined-to-a-few-regions/ (Accessed 22nd November 2022).

Madianou, M., and Miller, D. (2011) 'Mobile phone parenting: reconfiguring relationships between Filipina migrant mothers and their left-behind children', *New Media and Society*, 13(3), pp. 457–470.

Mason, J., and Tipper, B. (2008) 'Being related: how children define and create kinship', *Childhood*, 15(4), pp. 441–460.

Morgan, D. (1996) *Family Connections: An Introduction to Family Studies*. Cambridge: Polity Press.

Morrow, V. (1998) *Understanding Families. Children's Perspectives*. London: National Children's Bureau.

Parreñas, R. S. (2005) *Children of Global Migration: Transnational Families and Gendered Woes*. Stanford, CA: Stanford University Press (Muslim minorities). Available at: http://library.soas.ac. uk/Record/b2069319.

Parreñas, R. S. (2008) 'Transnational fathering: gendered conflicts, distant disciplining and emotional gaps', *Journal of Ethnic and Migration Studies*, 34(7), pp. 1057–1072. doi:10.1080/ 1369183080223 0356.

Piaget, J. (1928) *Judgment and Reasoning in the Child*. London: Kegan Paul.

Punch, S. (2008) '"You can do nasty things to your brothers and sisters without a reason": siblings' backstage behaviour', *Children and Society*, 22(5), pp. 333–344.

Reynolds, T. (2009) 'Exploring the absent/present dilemma: Black fathers, family relationships, and social capital in Britain', *The ANNALS of the American Academy of Political and Social Science*, 624(1), pp. 12–28.

Rigg, A., and Pryor, J. (2007) 'Children's perceptions of families: what do they really think?', *Children and Society*, 21(1), pp. 17–30.

Selwyn, J., and Nandy, S. (2014) 'Kinship care in the UK: using census data to estimate the extent of formal and informal care by relatives', *Child & Family Social Work*, 19(1), pp. 44–54.

Smart, C., Neale, B., and Wade, A. (2001) *The Changing Experience of Childhood. Families and Divorce*. Cambridge: Polity Press.

Smith, A., Lalonde, R. N., and Johnson, S. (2004) 'Serial migration and its implications for the parent-child relationship: a retrospective analysis of the experiences of the children of Caribbean immigrants', *Cultural Diversity and Ethnic Minority Psychology*, 10(2), pp. 107–122.

Spagnola, M., and Fiese, B. (2007) 'Family routines and rituals. A context for development in the lives of young children', *Infants & Young Children*, 20(4), pp. 284–299.

Sutton, Cordelia (2018) *What Counts as Happiness for Young People in the Second Decade of the 21st Century? An Exploration*, PhD thesis, The Open University. Available at: http://oro.open.ac.uk/view/person/cs25749.html.

Tatlow-Golden, M., and Guerin, S. (2017) 'Who I am: the meaning of children's most valued activities and relationships, and implications for self-concept research', *Journal of Early Adolescence*, 37(2), pp. 236–266.

UNICEF. (2021) *Uncertain Pathways: How Gender Shapes the Experiences of Children on the Move*. New York: United Nations Children's Fund.

Zhang, N. (2015) 'Home divided, home reconstructed: children in rural – urban migration in contemporary China', *Children's Geographies*, 13(4), pp. 381–397.

6 Young people's mental health

Victoria Cooper

Introduction

What is mental health? The terms mental health and mental illness are commonly used and might also appear to be well understood, yet looking more closely reveals ambiguity and raises many questions, such as the following: What separates being mentally well and ill? Who decides? And is there even such a thing as 'normal' mental health?

Mental ill health can manifest in different ways and, generally speaking, becomes problematic when it interferes with some aspect of everyday living, including the ability to learn, feel, express, and manage a range of positive and negative emotions; the ability to form and maintain good relationships with others; and the ability to manage change and uncertainty (Mental Health Foundation, 2020).

This chapter looks at different understandings – also defined as 'models' – about the origins and treatments of mental illness. While experiences of mental illness have been well documented in adults, much less is known about young people's experiences, and yet understanding these is essential in informing the development of appropriate support. In many respects, this reflects the power that adults wield over young people and the way in which models of mental health have been constructed by adults.

The lived experiences of young people will underpin this chapter which will begin by exploring distinctions between 'mental health' and 'mental ill health' before looking in more detail at the different models that explain and treat mental illness.

When does 'mental health' become 'mental ill health'?

Mental ill health and mental health are concepts often thought of as distinct. Yet differentiating between feeling mentally well and ill is not always clear cut, and young people experiencing difficulties disclose feeling confused as they struggle to make sense of how they feel.

> It's kind of confusing. You know that something's wrong and you try and progress on things, but it's kind of hard when you know there is something going on in your mind or wherever else.
>
> (Interviewee 1, cited in McCann, Lubman and Clark, 2012, p. 337)

DOI: 10.4324/9781003358855-7

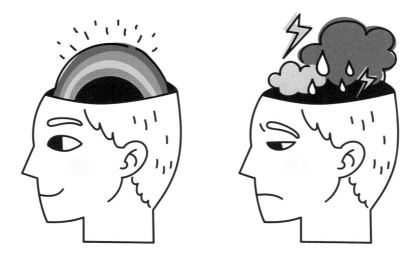

Figure 6.1 Young people can experience fluctuations in their mental health.

Much like ill health generally, experiences of mental illness may be brief, they may come and go, or they may endure for longer. Many young people may experience mental illness following major life events, including bereavement, physical illness and hospitalisation, or in response to adverse experiences, including abuse, bullying, prejudice, violence, and domestic upheaval. Young people may also experience a combination of mental health challenges.

> I started suffering from really bad social Anxiety as well as symptoms of Depression. Since then I have been diagnosed with Depression, Anxiety, Social Anxiety, Dissociative Identity Disorder and PTSD. It was a long process for anybody to actually come to terms with the fact that I do suffer from quite severe mental health and it's not an easy thing.
>
> (Dexter, YMCA, 2016, p. 33)

The diagram in the next section, produced by the UK Centre for Mental Health, shows a spectrum in which there is no clear dividing line between the transition from a sense of wellbeing – a situation where a young person is coping well with life's challenges – to points where they struggle or become unwell.

It may then be more helpful to think about mental health and mental ill health as 'porous' states through which young people can come and go (Stewart-Brown, 2015),

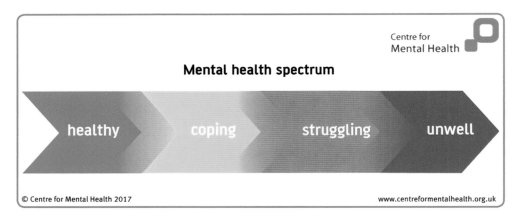

Figure 6.2 A spectrum of mental health.

much like a continuum where instead of being on one side or the other, individuals are at varying points and can move forwards and backwards in relation to life events (Coppock and Hopton, 2000).

Recognising that a young person is struggling may not be easy. Many young people may attempt to hide how they are feeling, often for various reasons, including the stigma and feelings of guilt and shame associated with mental illness. One young person, Seren, describes how she didn't realise she had mental health problems:

> I think it was my mum. She noticed, you know, the side-effects of an Eating Disorder like sunken eyes. I started to look like really unhealthy, I wasn't eating at all. I wasn't sleeping.
>
> (Seren, YMCA, 2016, p. 23)

As Seren describes, parents and carers may notice changes in their child's behaviour, typically citing withdrawal from family and friends, or changes to sleeping and eating patterns, as an initial sign that their child is struggling to cope. Young people describe withdrawal as a coping mechanism, but one that may cause further problems.

> When I was in like Year 7 and Year 8, I basically just flipped out of nowhere and then went really quiet for a few months. It felt very lonely I have to admit. It also affected me further on because Year 7 and 8 are obviously important for making mates and everything. I just stayed quiet and kept to myself. I generally kept myself to myself just because I thought it was a better way of dealing with things and sorting my own things out.
>
> (Adam, 17, YMCA, 2016, p. 22)

Diagnosing mental ill health

Mental illnesses are typically (but not exclusively) assessed and diagnosed by psychiatrists in the UK (a medical doctor who specialises in the branch of medicine focused on the diagnosis and treatment of mental health problems) and in some countries, also by psychologists and general practitioners (GPs). In the UK, GPs may also diagnose and prescribe medication, but they primarily refer young people for assessment and treatment. Many other practitioners may also be involved in referring young people for help if they are concerned about their mental health. This might include educational practitioners, social workers, mentors, youth workers, and nurses.

The Diagnostic and Statistical Manual of Mental Disorders (DSM) – which is the official list of mental illnesses recognised by the American Psychiatric Association – describes a variety of mental health problems and lists their symptoms. It is commonly used around the world for diagnosis, although other diagnostic tools are also used. The DSM builds upon the idea that mental illnesses are universal and can be defined by symptoms and assigned to a category. Some of the most common psychiatric diagnoses young people globally receive include emotional disorders (anxiety and depression), with an increase in self-harming behaviours and rates of suicide amongst young adults (WHO, n.d.).

First produced in 1952, the DSM has been developed and updated many times, and analysis reveals how these developments reflect changing ideas about what counts as a mental illness – and what doesn't (Cooper, 2014), showing how mental health can also be socially constructed. Academics, professionals, and lobbying groups continue to campaign to include certain classifications in the DSM, such as post-traumatic stress disorder (PTSD, which was included in 1980), whilst others campaign for the right for some diagnoses to be removed. Homosexuality was defined as a mental illness in the 20th century in Western cultures but was removed from the DSM in 1973.

Young people's lived experiences of mental illness reveal the challenges to wanting so desperately to feel what many describe as 'normal'.

> Well sometimes you get like thoughts of, why can't I be like other people?
> (Interviewee 5, McCann, Lubman
> and Clark, 2012, p. 337)

But ideas about normality can be very subjective and open to interpretation.

> How quiet do you have to be before you can be called withdrawn? How angry is aggressive? How sudden is impulsive? How unusual is delusional? How excited is manic? How miserable is depressed? The answers to all these questions are to be found not in some special measuring skill imparted during psychiatric training, but in the psychiatrists' and lay people's shared beliefs about how 'normal' people should behave.
> (Johnstone, 2000, p. 219)

However, the idea that mental illnesses are universal in their expression has been challenged, with criticism of mental health professionals who fail to acknowledge individual and cultural differences (Marsella and Yamada, 2000). American psychiatrist and anthropologist Arthur Kleinman, who writes predominately about adult mental health but whose views apply equally to the consideration of young people, has called for a much closer consideration of the relationship between culture and mental health. His research highlighted how culture can shape individual experiences of symptoms, the words and expressions used to report them, and decisions made by professionals about support treatment needed (Kleinman, 1977).

Culturally sensitive research

One example of the need for more culturally sensitive research and professional practices in the field of mental health is in the Chinese use of compound terms involving the heart (*xin*) to describe psychological distress, including *xinhuang* (heart panic), *xinjing* (heart dread/frightened), *xinfan* (heart vexed), *xintong* (heart pain), and *xinyi* (heart dysphoric/depressed/clutched/compressed), in which emotional distress could be felt inside or over the heart. Kleinman has argued that Chinese or East Asian patients are more likely to express mental distress as somatised – in which it is felt and experienced as an ailment of the body.

Exploring the lived experiences of depression amongst contemporary Chinese in Guangzhou, researchers Dominic Lee, Joan Kleinman and Arthur Kleinman (2007) found that not all depressive experiences could be put into words, and many of the research participants reported that they were extremely distressed but found it very difficult to articulate their psychological pain which was typically described in physical rather than emotional terms.

> My eyes are tired but my brain is active . . . That [emotional] pain is so unbearable. Very painful! Very painful! [hen xinku! hen xinku!]
>
> (Case 1, cited in Lee, Kleinman and Kleinman, 2007, p. 4)

Experiences and symptoms of mental ill health can be described in different ways and reflect distinct cultural understandings. So a young person from the UK who describes hearing voices might be considered to be displaying signs of mental illness, while among the Tungus in Northeast China who practice shamanism, it might be a sign of the start of a shamanic vocation.

Research also indicates that mental health professionals draw upon their own cultural ideas and values when making a mental health diagnosis. In the now-classic text *Aliens and Alienists*: *Ethnic Minorities and Psychiatry* (1982), the authors Roland Littlewood (an anthropological psychiatrist) and Maurice Lipsedge (a consultant psychiatrist) use a number of case studies to examine the racist bias in theories about mental health. They question how mental illness can be examined without the bias of *ethnocentrism*. Ethnocentrism is the process through which a person applies their own culture, race, or ethnicity as a frame of reference to understand and judge another person, without taking consideration of that person's own culture and values. The challenges inherent in applying universal standards and concepts to understand the lives of children and young people were introduced in Chapter 2 and Chapter 4 of this Reader, and you will learn more about them in Chapter 10 and elsewhere. These issues are important when considering all aspects of psychology, including mental illnesses and how they are understood, as they may be experienced differently throughout the world.

Key points

- There is no clear-cut distinction between 'mental health' and 'mental ill health'.
- The DSM has built upon ideas about universal categories of mental illnesses which can be contested.
- Cultural differences are evident in how mental health problems are experienced and expressed, highlighting the importance of cultural sensitivity in diagnosis and social constructions of mental health.

Different ways of understanding mental illness

Inevitably, there are differences of opinion about mental health and how mental illness should be treated. These are informed by longstanding debates as to the origins of mental illness as related to *nature* (in so far as mental illness can be explained by biology) or *nurture* (which explains how mental illness is shaped by social and cultural factors). Here, we look at three dominant discourses: the *biomedical*, *psychological*, and *social* models.

Young people and parents as well as professionals may orientate to one particular explanation, although as we discuss later in this chapter, many combine explanations to consider the myriad of interacting biological, psychological, social, and cultural factors which influence mental health. The aim here is not to polarise views or to suggest that one model provides a more effective explanation than another but to consider the different values and beliefs that are underpinned in each.

Biomedical model

The biomedical model evolved from medicine. It is a way of thinking based on diagnosing symptoms and problems within an individual, for example, chicken pox, high blood pressure, or a sprained ankle. The biomedical discourse refers to a model of mental health primarily based on biological origins, and it has been criticised for overlooking psychological, social, and cultural factors.

This model emerged in Europe and America during the 18th and 19th century, where the emphasis was mainly on how mental ill health is understood as biological and often hereditary. Treatment at this time largely involved medical intervention or institutionalisation. The limited accounts of young people's mental illness in the UK during this period focused mainly on issues such as seizures, sleep disturbances,

Figure 6.3 Entrance sign to a Victorian mental hospital.

stuttering, epilepsy, and failure to learn (Rey *et al.*, 2015). Young people experiencing mental illness were typically ostracised, often ridiculed, and many were placed in institutions away from their parents/carers and family and often in settings where children, young people, and adults were treated together.

While ideas about what counts as a mental illness and the treatments for them have changed considerably over the last century, the idea that mental health can be understood as biological in origin remains strong.

Where mental illnesses are assumed to be biological in origin, the biomedical model suggests that mental illnesses are universal in how they are experienced and can be allocated to a category or label defining the illness. You will recall the widespread use of the DSM introduced in the previous section which outlines universal categories of mental illnesses used for diagnosis and treatment. The biomedical model has continued to develop globally and underpins mental health services in the UK, America, and Europe, during which time the use of psychiatric medication has become widespread. Debates still ensue about the relative merits or dangers of using psychiatric medication for the treatment of mental illness (see LeFrancois, 2021), and despite its continued prevalence, the biological model faces criticism for applying a reductionist view of mental health – whereby mental illness is reduced to a series of biological symptoms which overlook how mental health is shaped by biological, psychological, social, and cultural factors.

Aside from the many criticisms, the biomedical model has made many advances in our understanding of the biological basis of mood, thinking, and behaviour and has developed many effective treatments to support particular conditions. If we take the example of depression, research within the biomedical model has looked at how depression affects specific areas of the brain, including the hippocampus and prefrontal cortex (Toates, 2011). It is important also to note how the considerable neurological and hormonal changes experienced during adolescence mark this as a particularly vulnerable period of development and is linked to the onset and development of mental illness for some people (this is discussed further in Chapter 13).

Despite many of the developments it has made in recognising and treating the mental health of young people, the biomedical model has come under scrutiny for promoting a 'deficit model', where young people experiencing mental illness are cast as 'abnormal' or 'broken' without addressing how thoughts, emotions, and behaviours can be supported to change and how young people can build on their own skills and strengths, including networks of support, often without medical intervention. Also, the biomedical model often underestimates the biological impact of non-medical interventions (see LeFrancois, 2021).

Research indicates that when discussing mental health and particularly mental illness, there are rarely definitive right or wrong answers but differences of opinion and different ways of understanding mental health. For some young people, framing their mental health problem as an illness – with a designated category – is seen as empowering, as this provides explanations that help them to better understand how and why they are feeling as they do.

> the fact that they understood me and . . . they understood what I was going through helped me . . . it was nice that I had someone who recognised what my illness, – and actually made me feel much better about it, made me feel like I was a normal person for it.
>
> (Lucy, cited in Martin and Atkinson, 2020, p. 140)

While for other young people, mental health labels can feel restricting.

> For mental health, they try to put you in a box like 'psycho', or 'freak' . . . they see 'depression', or 'anxiety' . . . and they stop looking at 'you' The label is with them . . . They don't actually look at you as a person.
>
> (Brandon, cited in Liegghio, 2016, p. 111)

Not only do some young people feel that the label of mental illness overshadows them as a person, but it may also contribute to social exclusion. A diagnosis can also lead many to internalise labels which can then become self-perpetuating (Timimi, 2010). Furthermore, the biomedical discourse locates the power for diagnosis and treatment within the hands of 'experts' within different medical professions and overlooks the insider knowledge and expertise of young people themselves. More recently, young people in some countries, such as the UK, are increasingly likely to seek to de-stigmatise mental health difficulties by declaring them openly.

Scholars draw attention to how the lived experiences of young people have been overlooked with the tendency to view young people's mental health through world-views about normality as well as the dominant beliefs of adults who exert power over young people (LeFrançois, 2021). In her research exploring young people's perspectives, child and family mental health therapist and social work researcher Maria Liegghio (2016, p. 121) describes how for young people it is not necessarily the mental illness that is impairing but rather the perceptions of others enacted on the young person that render them 'abnormal, incompetent, and too young to know any better'. Furthermore, she describes how many young people frame their mental illness as reflecting obstacles that they can overcome and which may reflect difficult life events but which are exacerbated by the reactions of other people, such as parents, teachers, and social workers.

Key points

- There are different models or discourses for understanding mental health.
- The biomedical model draws upon biological factors to explain mental health, typically uses medical intervention for treatment, and is still widely used as a way of understanding mental illness.
- The biomedical model is critiqued for locating mental health problems within the individual and emphasising limitations rather than strengths.
- Young people's lived experiences of mental illness have been overlooked and yet provide important insights.

Psychological model

Rather than understanding mental illness as being determined solely by biology, a psychological model focuses on how the mind works and the effect of this on a young person's thoughts, feelings, and subsequent behaviour. A psychological model aims to understand how people's past and present behaviour and experiences are linked, and how particular patterns of thinking and behaviour can both alleviate or exacerbate mental distress (May, Cooke and Cotton, 2008). This model builds upon the assumption that experiences of, for example, depression and/or anxiety, and feeling overwhelmed by strong emotions, reflect the way that a young person perceives or makes sense of different life experiences.

There are different psychological approaches to support a young person (often termed therapy), each reflecting different practitioners' beliefs about the best way problems can be addressed. Psychotherapy and counselling are used widely with young people to encourage

> **Psychotherapy** describes the use of psychological methods, particularly using talking therapies, such as one-to-one counselling with a psychotherapist – to help a person change behaviour and overcome challenging thoughts and feelings.

them to express how they feel and to consider different ways in which they can manage their emotions. The widespread use of cognitive behavioural therapy (CBT) in current UK mental health services, for instance, is underpinned by a psychological model and the belief that individuals can be supported to think differently about their feelings and emotions and learn to manage them with or without the support of medicines.

The research report *I am whole* (YMCA, 2016) documents how a significant number of young people appreciate the opportunity to talk and express how they feel, finding counselling useful, but also recognise the significant value of peer support and being able to discuss their feelings with other young people who share similar experiences.

In their research exploring young people's experiences of depression, Terence McCann, Dan Lubman and Eileen Clark (2012) found that young people cope with their experiences in different ways and that many deal with their mental illness by engaging in unhelpful behaviours, including alcohol and drug abuse which may aggravate their difficulties.

> because of being depressed I have made really stupid choices, and done some stuff that's given me a really bad reputation. I started having sex with heaps [lots] of different people, and drugs and alcohol were even worse. And then the depression came . . . at the start of this year, I hit rock bottom.
>
> (Interviewee 23, p. 338, McCann, Lubman and Clark, 2012)

The psychological model encourages young people to consider different ways in which they can process complex feelings and recognises the skills and strengths that young people can draw upon in learning to develop self-reliant behaviours. Assuming a strengths-based approach, the psychological model represents a shift from a somewhat deficit model of 'illness', to one which focuses more on 'wellness'.

Children and young people's coping skills

Lois Murphy was one of the first psychologists to carry out research during the 1970s which systematically examined children and young people's coping skills and their capacity to adapt to different challenges. Through observations in different family circumstances, Murphy and her colleague Alice Moriarty (Murphy and Moriarty, 1976) proposed that the ability to cope with difficult circumstances owes much to past experiences, particularly young people's success and failures in adapting and dealing (or not) with early stressful events. Rather than being fixed at birth, *resilience*, which defines a person's capacity to manage and bounce back from difficult experiences, is a skill that can be taught and nurtured.

Although the psychological model has proved highly successful in using talking therapies and CBT to support anxiety and depression, it is far less successful in the treatment of more challenging mental health problems, including psychosis and bipolar disorder. The psychological model has also been critiqued for placing too much emphasis on the individual resilience of the young person. As a social worker and researcher studying the psychological and social aspects of resilience, Michael Ungar (2011; Ungar, Ghazinour and Jorg Richter, 2013, and with Ross *et al.*, 2020) argues that while promoting and nurturing resilience is vital for helping young people develop skills in emotion regulation, it places the onus, or responsibility, for wellness on the young person without fully addressing the much broader social inequities that render many young people at risk of mental illness. Support for resilience, for instance, focuses on the value of nurturing families, supportive schools, and access to role models, caring adults/professionals, and often therapeutic interventions which are not readily accessible for so many young people. Although changes to thinking and feeling are clearly very helpful for many young people, it is also important to consider how changes to society and the environment are necessary.

Key points

- The psychological model looks at how mental health problems originate in patterns of thinking, feeling, and behaving.
- Resilience is a life skill that can be taught and can support young people's mental health.
- The psychological model has been critiqued for placing too much emphasis on how a young person can change their thinking and behaviour without also addressing broader social obstacles which may also impact mental health.

Social model

This model largely evolved in response to inadequacies within the biomedical model. The social model views mental illness as being a consequence of how young people are viewed and treated in society, rather than as determined by biology.

Described as 'the society as patient', psychologist Anthony Marsella (2011) suggests that rather than focusing predominately on the individual young person as having an illness, a social model looks to society and patterns of inequality, deprivation, and discrimination which impact mental health and may lead to mental health problems. This model typically avoids labelling a young person who experiences mental illness as abnormal or in some way deficient and looks more to the social factors, such as poverty, domestic unrest, family difficulties including discord, and poor relationships, as potential 'stressors' which can lead to distress. This model also considers the impact of early adverse experiences, such as abuse, neglect, and bereavement, as well as exposure to violence, on mental health. A social model has the capacity to challenge social inequalities and to look at ways in which policies and practices can be changed to provide the necessary infrastructure and support that young people need (Ungar, Ghazinour and Jorg Richter, 2013; Ross *et al.*, 2020).

This model is shaped by different ideas about what influences mental health and mental ill health. Where children and young people live, their domestic circumstances or caring relationships, their local neighbourhood and community, how they learn and their experience of education, relationships with friends, and their economic stability are just some of the influences that are recognised as significant. All sorts of relationships are important. In this Reader, you have already considered the impact of early attachments in Chapter 4 and diverse family and other relationships as well as the theory of 'one good adult' in Chapter 5. Later, you will focus on adolescence and young adulthood as well as relationships within families, neighbourhoods, communities, and cultures. Relationships take many forms and, as you learned in Chapter 4, the sense of self relies on many others including parents, carers, siblings, wider family as well as pets, and also relationships forged through social media. It is important then to question how mental health is understood as it changes throughout life and in relation to different social situations. As much as mental health is influenced by many factors, it is important to also note (as set out in the Reader 'Introduction' and in Chapter 1) how young people have *agency* and play a part in shaping their own experiences and sense of feeling well or ill.

For young people, the numerous challenges caused by mental illness may be aggravated by associated social consequences. Despite increasing awareness about mental illness, young people often feel stigmatised.

> I think the bad things would be the stigma associated with, because it's not something that you'd want to go and tell any of your friends that you have it, because you'd be perceived differently.
>
> (Interview 2, McCann, Lubman and Clark, 2012, p. 337)

One in three young people with a mental illness has experienced the negative impact of stigmatising behaviour which most often took place in school or at home (YMCA, 2016). The stigma of appearing weak and the guilt of not being able to cope can exacerbate young people's withdrawal and social isolation.

Stigma

The idea of stigma was first described by the American sociologist Erving Goffman (1963) as the cause of a 'spoiled identity'. Here, Goffman is describing how individuals are often seen as different in some way, by virtue of how they look, act, or behave and the impact that this can have upon how they feel and value themselves. Research exploring stigma associated with mental illness includes analysis of groups of individuals who are excluded, rejected, blamed, and devalued in some way and subject to prejudice.

The impact of stigma may be further heightened in relation to social constructions of identity linked to gender and race/ethnicity. Research carried out by Ulla Danielsson and colleagues in Sweden (2011), for example, found that stereotypical ideas and representations of masculinity influenced the extent to which young men felt able to

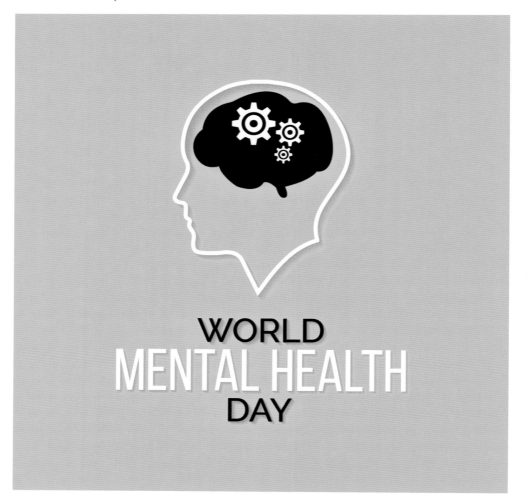

Figure 6.4 World Mental Health Day.

seek help. Similarly, researchers Darota Martin and Cathy Atkinson (2020) provide a detailed narrative of a young man's struggle to share his concerns about his own mental health and to seek help which he felt were constrained by his own ideas about 'being a bloke':

> I knew I needed help I just didn't know how to do it and I found straight up admitting my issue shameful so I couldn't do that'. it's quite hard to like . . . I guess part of it, you know, being a bloke and that, like you're meant to be like – you have this thing about being strong, you know, you've got to be successful and all that kind of thing and like, you know, you don't need help.
>
> Martin and Atkinson (2020, p. 139)

Research examining the stigma of mental illness amongst young people in the US suggests that ethnic minority youth compared with non-Latino White youth are less willing to talk about their mental health with their friends and peers (Corrigan *et al.*, 2016) which may impact their willingness to seek help (Lindsey, Joe and Nebbitt, 2010).

The stigma of mental illness is not confined to the individual sufferer but extends out to siblings and families. Families can face considerable stigma which includes rejection by peers, loss of social status within their neighbourhoods or peer groups, and 'contagion associations' whereby prejudices about a brother or sister were also attributed to siblings and family units (Sin, Moone and Harris, 2008). Various studies have examined stigma and how this is related to core beliefs, cultural values about mental illness, which connects to the work of Kleinman, and the emphasis on culture introduced in section 1. Researchers, for instance, have found that in Chinese culture, the stigma of mental illness is underpinned by conceptualisations of mental illness as 'evidence of weakness of character' and which may cause shame to the whole family which may result in families hiding or denying a relative's mental illness (Parker, Cheah and Roy (2001, p. 862). Similarly, Liegghio's (2017) research about family stigma connects emotional distress to the belief that people experiencing it are 'bad' with the idea that distress-related behaviours reflect a 'flawed' moral character and that siblings are implicated as members of 'flawed' families. Furthermore, Liegghio describes how, in seeking to manage social exclusion as an outcome of such stigma, young siblings attempt to conceal mental illness by hesitating to talk about a mental health issue and its effects.

Key points

- Rather than focus on the individual, the social model locates mental health problems within society.
- The social model looks at patterns of inequality, deprivation, and discrimination which impact mental health and at how society can be changed to support mental health.
- Despite increasing global awareness, the stigma of mental illness can be a barrier to young people sharing their experiences or seeking help which can be exacerbated by constructs of identity linked to gender and ethnicity.

Biopsychosocial model

While it is important to distinguish between different discourses and models for understanding mental illness, increasingly, researchers now use an interdisciplinary model which draws together biological (brain, genetics, and endocrine functioning), psychological (emotions and thinking), and social (diverse social experiences) explanations to form a *biopsychosocial model* (Black and Hoeft, 2015). This model is increasingly applied to health care contexts, where multidisciplinary professionals from different disciplines contribute to supporting a young person.

The biopsychosocial model blends learning from the biomedical, psychological, and social models and recognises how important it is to understand young people holistically – their lived experiences within families, communities, and cultures; their relationships, development, and learning; as well as their biological experiences.

Applications of the biopsychosocial model are reflected in contemporary discussions about young people's resilience, where resilience as a concept is defined as 'the process of harnessing biological, psychosocial, structural, and cultural resources to sustain wellbeing' (Panter-Brick and Leckman, 2013, p. 333). Recent neurological research also demonstrates the interactive nature of a young person's physiology, and particularly their brain development, with their environment. In Chapter 2, you learned about different sensitivities to negative life events and to psychological interventions, and psychologist Dustin Albert and colleagues (2015) have identified a specific gene variant amongst young people who appear highly sensitive to their environments and are particularly vulnerable to mental distress. Their research indicates that a young person's level of sensitivity to their environment is related to specific differences in their genes. Researchers Thomas Boyce and Bruce Ellis (2005) have also been studying how human genes influence young people's behaviour and particularly their reactions during stressful situations. They also suggest that to a large extent, genes predispose how sensitive young people are to stress during childhood. Yet rather than being fixed at birth, recent neurological research suggests a certain degree of adaptability – termed *neuroplasticity* which explains how an individual's neural pathways in the brain adapt and change throughout life in response to learning and external influences. Inferences from this research indicate the interactive relationship between a young person's biology and their environment and how important it is to foreground this interaction, rather than focusing on just one or the other when understanding and treating mental illness.

Key points

- The biopsychosocial model takes an interdisciplinary approach to understanding mental health and combines *biomedical*, *psychological*, and *social* models.
- Recent neurological research focuses on how social and psychological processes impact the extent to which biological predispositions for mental health problems manifest.
- *Neuroplasticity* describes the brain's ability to change and adapt (rather than being set during the early years of life).

Conclusion

This chapter has examined when 'mental health' is recognised as 'mental ill health' and has considered how distinctions are subject to interpretation and linked to social ideas about normality. Professionals and academics in the field of mental health recognise the range of factors that shape mental illness evident in increasing application of biopsychosocial models for diagnosis and support. Despite increasing awareness, many young people continue to feel stigmatised by their mental health problems, which, for many, presents a barrier to expressing their difficulties and seeking help.

References

Albert, D, Belsky, D. W., Crowley, D. M., Bates, J. E., Pettit, G. S., Lansford, J. E., Dick, D., and Dodge, K. A. (2015) 'Developmental mediation of genetic variation in response to the fast track prevention program', *Development and Psychopathology*, 27(1), pp. 81–95.

Black, J. M., and Hoeft, F. (2015) 'Utilizing biopsychosocial and strengths-based approaches within the field of child health: what we know and where we can grow', in E. L. Grigorenko (ed.) *The Global Context for New Directions for Child and Adolescent Development. New Directions for Child and Adolescent Development* (Vol. 147). San Francisco: Jossey-Bass, pp. 13–20.

Boyce, W. T., and Ellis, B. J. (2005) 'Biological sensitivity to context: I an evolutionary-developmental theory of the origins and functions of stress reactivity', *Developmental Psychopathology*, 17(2), pp. 271–301.

Cooper, R. (2014) *Diagnosing the Diagnostic and Statistical Manual of Mental Disorders* (5th ed.). London: Taylor and Francis.

Coppock, V., and Hopton, J. (2000) *Critical Perspectives on Mental Health*. London and New York: Routledge.

Corrigan, P. W., Kosyluk, K. A., Markowitz, F., Brown, R. L., Conlon, B., Rees, J., Rosenberg, J., Ellefson, S., and Al-Khouja, M. A. (2016) 'Mental illness stigma and disclosure in college students', *Journal of Mental Health*, 25(3), pp. 224–230.

Danielsson, U. E., Bengs, C., Samuelsson, E., and Johansson, E. E. (2011) '"My greatest dream is to be normal": the impact of gender on the depression narratives of young Swedish men and women', *Qualitative Health Research*, 21(5), pp. 612–624.

Goffman, E. (1963) *Stigma: Notes on the Management of Spoiled Identity*. New York: Simon and Schuster.

Johnstone, L. (2000) *Users and Abusers of Psychiatry: A Critical Look at Psychiatric Practice*. Abingdon: Routledge.

Kleinman, A. (1977) 'Depression, somatization and the "new cross-cultural psychiatry"', *Social Science and Medicine*, 11, pp. 3–10.

Lee, D. T. S., Kleinman, J., and Kleinman, A. (2007) 'Rethinking depression: an ethnographic study of the experiences of depression among Chinese', *Harvard Review of Psychiatry*, 15(1), pp. 1–8.

LeFrancois, B. (2021) 'Psychiatrising children', in V. Cooper and N. Holford (eds.) *Understanding Childhood and Youth*. Abingdon: Routledge, pp. 177–190.

Liegghio, M. (2016) 'Too young to be mad: disabling encounters with 'normal' from the perspectives of psychiatrized youth', *Intersectionalities: A Global Journal of Social Work Analysis, Research, Polity, and Practice*, 5(3), pp. 110–129.

Liegghio, M. (2017) 'Not a good person': family stigma of mental illness from the perspectives of young siblings', *Child and Family Social Work*, 22, pp. 1237–1245.

Lindsey, M. A., Joe, S., and Nebbitt, V. (2010) 'Family matters: the role of mental health stigma and social support on depressive symptoms and subsequent help seeking among African American boys', *The Journal of Black Psychology*, 36, pp. 458–482.

Littlewood, R., and Lipsedge, M. (1982) *Aliens and Alienists: Ethnic Minorities and Psychiatry*. Abingdon: Routledge.

Marsella, A. J. (2011) 'Twelve critical issues for mental health professionals working with ethno-culturally diverse populations', *Psychology International*, Twelve critical issues for mental health professionals working with ethno-culturally diverse populations (apa.org) (Accessed 10th September 2022).

Marsella, A. J., and Yamada, A. M. (2000) 'Culture and mental health: an introduction and overview of foundations, concepts and issues', in Israel Cuellar and Freddy A. Paniagua (eds.) *Handbook of Multicultural Mental Health. Assessment and Treatment of Diverse Populations*. London and New York: Academic Press.

Martin, D., and Atkinson, C. (2020) 'University students' accounts of living with depression', *Research in Post-Compulsory Education*, 25(2), pp. 127–148.

May, R., Cooke, A., and Cotton, A. (2008) 'Psychological approaches to mental health', in Theo Stickley and Thurstine Bassett (eds.) *Learning About Mental Health*. West Sussex: John Wiley & Sons, Incorporated.

McCann, T. V., Lubman, D. I., and Clark, E. (2012) 'The experience of young people with depression: a qualitative study', *Journal of Psychiatric and Mental Health Nursing*, 19, pp. 334–340.

Mental Health Foundation (2020) *What is Good Mental Health?* [Online]. Available at: www.mental-health.org.uk/your-mental-health/about-mental-health/what-good-mental-health (Accessed 29th January 202).

Murphy, L. B., and Moriarty, A. E. (1976) *Vulnerability, Coping and Growth: From Infancy to Adolescence*. New Haven: Yale University Press.

Panter-Brick, C., and Leckman, J. F. (2013) 'Editorial commentary: resilience in child development – interconnected pathways to wellbeing', *Journal of Child Psychology and Psychiatry*, 54(4), pp. 333–336.

Parker, G., Cheah, Y. C., and Roy, K. (2001) 'Do the Chinese somatize depression? A cross-cultural study', *Journal of Social Psychiatry Psychiatric Epidemiology*, 36(6), pp. 287–293.

Rey, J. M., Assumpção Jr, F., Bernad, C. A., Çuhadaroğlu, F. C., Evans, B., Fung, D., Harper, B., Loidreau, L., Ono, Y., Pūras, D., Remschmidt, H., Robertson, B., Rusakoskaya, O. A., and Schleime, K. (2015) *History of Child and Adolescent Psychiatry*. Available at: J.10-History-Child-Psychiatry-update-2018.pdf (iacapap.org) (Accessed 10th September 2022).

Ross, N., Gilbery, R., Torres, S., Dugas, K., Jefferies, P., McDonald, S., Savage, S., and Ungar, M. (2020) 'Adverse childhood experiences: assessing the impact on physical and psychosocial health in adulthood and the mitigating role of resilience', *Child Abuse and Neglect*, 103, pp. 1–8.

Sin, J., Moone, N., and Harris, P. (2008) 'Siblings of individuals with first-episode psychosis', *Journal of Psychosocial Nursing*, 46(6), pp. 33–40.

Stewart-Brown, S. L. (2015) 'Mental well-being: concepts and controversies in mental health policy and practice', in David Crepaz-Keay (ed.) *Mental Health Today . . . and Tomorrow: Exploring Current and Future Trends in Mental Health Care 2015*. Hove: Pavilion Publishing and Media Ltd.

Timimi, S. (2010) 'The McDonaldization of childhood: children's mental health in neo-liberal market cultures', *Transcultural Psychiatry*, 47(5), pp. 686–706.

Toates, F. M. (2011) *Biological Psychology*. London: Prentice Hall.

Ungar, M. (2011) 'The social ecology of resilience: addressing contextual and cultural ambiguity of a nascent construct', *American Journal of Orthopsychiatry: American Orthopsychiatric Association*, 81(1), pp. 1–17.

Ungar, M., Ghazinour, M., and Jorg Richter, J. (2013) 'Annual research review: what is resilience within the social ecology of human development', *Special Issue: Annual Research Review: Resilience in Child Development*, 54(4), pp. 348–366.

World Health Organisation (n.d.) *Mental Health of Adolescents*. World Health Organisation (who.int) (Accessed 10th March 2023).

YMCA (2016) *I Am Whole*. A report investigating the stigma faced by young people experiencing mental health difficulties, https://www.basw.co.uk/system/files/resources/basw_80811-6_0.pdf (Accessed 10th March 2023).

7 Education, schools, and learning

Amber Fensham-Smith

Introduction

Many people have views about what constitutes a 'good education', including parents, children, practitioners, policy makers, politicians, and researchers, all of whom have a vested interest in how children and young people learn. While most agree that education is important, not all agree on what, how, where, and when it should happen. Indeed, ideas about want counts as 'good' are widely debated. Although receiving an education is closely associated with going to school, learning can happen in a broader range of contexts, places, and spaces. A narrow view of education as a product of schooling, and as one that can be bought and consumed in a marketplace, precisely measured, and neatly ranked, seems to imply that learning itself is a one-way exchange and that children and young people and their social worlds do not matter. As this chapter will examine, receiving an education, in all its possible varieties, is not a neutral process.

This chapter will introduce some of the key perspectives that shape how the place, features of education, schooling, and learning in children and young people's lives are understood. Through the interdisciplinary lenses of psychology, philosophy, and sociology, it considers how education impacts on children and young people and their communities and its effects on inequalities.

A 'good' education?

The promise of formal education to transform children, their communities, and whole societies is now a worldwide project. The right to free and compulsory primary education is enshrined in the Universal Declaration of Human Rights and the United Nations Convention on the Rights of the Child (UNCRC, 1989) introduced in Chapter 1. While increasing access to and completing primary education is a priority for global organisations like the United Nations Educational, Scientific and Cultural Organisation (UNESCO, 2020), the accessibility of formal primary and secondary education varies across the world.

In the UK, education is compulsory, but formal schooling is not. As a signatory of the UNCRC (1989), the UK's devolved governments in its four nations play a role in ensuring that parents or caregivers can fulfil their duty to provide their child/ren with

DOI: 10.4324/9781003358855-8

Figure 7.1 As a global response to inequality, one of the 10 UN Sustainable Development Goals (SDG) includes ensuring inclusive, equitable and quality education for all by 2030.

an education. Almost all children in the UK receive their education at school, but a small number of families choose 'otherwise' via elective home education, or home-schooling as it is also known (Fensham-Smith, 2021).

In setting out parental duties to ensure children receive compulsory education, different pieces of legislation state that education should be both *suitable* and *efficient* for the age, ability, aptitude, and any additional learning needs a child may have. As an example, Section 7 of the 1996 Education Act (which applies to England and Wales) states the following:

The parent of every child of compulsory school age shall cause him to receive *efficient* full-time education *suitable*:

a) to his age, ability, and aptitude, and
b) to any special educational needs (in the case of a child who is in the area of a local authority in England) or additional learning needs (in the case of a child who is in the area of a local authority in Wales), he may have, either by regular attendance at school of otherwise.

Yet within these complex legal frameworks, there is no universal or agreed definition of what counts as a *suitable* and *efficient* education and, by extension, a 'good' education.

For children and young people, their parents, communities, and whole societies, education has multiple goals. Many centre on the assumption that receiving an education will transform learners and societies in positive ways. Some stakeholders argue that a good education should provide children and young people with specific skills, qualifications, or knowledge so they can access certain kinds of employment. A broader perspective suggests that education should aim to give young people cultural values that will enable them to lead fulfilling, independent lives, to participate in democracy, and to make autonomous and ethical choices (Biesta, 2019). Gaining a sense of self-confidence and belonging, and being able to express themselves freely, might be another key purpose (Fensham-Smith, 2021). There are many competing ideas about what should, or should not, count as a *suitable* and *efficient* education for children and young people or how, and indeed why, adults have built systems to educate them.

Fairness and education

From the ages of 5–16 years, most children and young people in the UK spend a significant proportion of their lives learning and socialising in a formal education setting. Being 'schooled', therefore, plays a prominent role in their experiences and in their social, emotional, and cognitive development. While the school-leaving age differs across the UK, this pathway is typically marked by a series of transitions that generally occurs at the ages as shown in Figure 7.2.

While the exact forms and types of education settings differ significantly across the four nations, several education reforms have produced what is now a highly complex and diverse collection, and the many forms of UK education settings include those shown in Figure 7.3.

There is considerable variation in how these settings are funded whether they are run by central government, local authorities, community groups, and/or charities. Some schools also differ in the extent to which they follow a national curriculum (a set of subjects and uniform standards for study and attainment within a formal programme

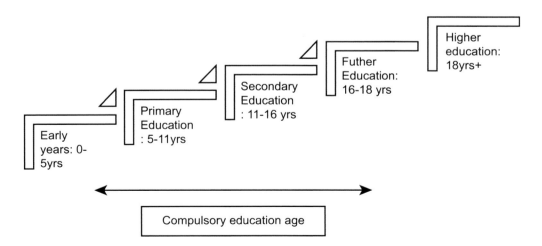

Figure 7.2 Key phases in UK education systems.

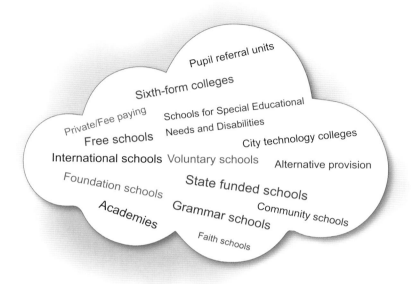

Figure 7.3 A word cloud showing the most common school types in the UK.

of study in state-funded primary and secondary schools), their 'ethos', and the degree to which entry criteria are based on selection (on the basis of gender, faith, or perceived ability) (e.g., grammar schools are selective in some of the four UK nations).

The increasing diversity of some school types, such as state-funded, faith-based schools, and the continued existence of fee-paying schools, continues to be a subject of debate among policy makers and educationalists (Ball, 2021), with contrasting perspectives about what counts as *fair* and how best to ensure that education promotes *equal opportunities for all* (Smith, 2018). These questions seem to raise even further questions rather than mutually agreed answers. Does fairness mean ensuring that all children and young people have access to the same modes of education? Here, there is a deeper philosophical debate: whether education is a *public good* for societies (like a National Health Service, but for learning) or a *private matter* (for individuals to personalise and manage in their homes and communities) (Ball, 2021).

As children and young people in the UK progress through formal schooling, standardised testing at various stages features heavily in their experiences. Words like *measurement, outcomes,* and *effectiveness* dominate when politicians, the media, and the public discuss what 'good' looks like. Educationalists, such as Gert Biesta (2020), are critical of what has become a narrow set of criteria, such as the numerical grades achieved in mathematics, science, and english as part of formal examinations in UK secondary schooling to judge the value of children and young people's achievements via education.

Key points

- What counts as a *suitable* and *efficient* and 'good' education is broad and debated.
- Education has many purposes, including to increase opportunities and to make societies fair and more equal. It can be considered as both a *private* and a *public* good.
- Systems of education across the four UK nations are diverse.

The rise of mass schooling: Intelligence, selection, and ability

To fully make sense of education systems in the present, sociologist Emile Durkheim suggested that we must examine the conditions of the past (Emirbayer, 1996). The lengthy journey towards the kinds of mass schooling visible in the global North today grew from social, economic, and political struggles. In this section, the birth of the modern school and some ideas which emerged from struggles about effective *learning*, *ability*, *intelligence* testing, and *selection* are discussed.

In the 17th century, prevailing views of children as immature and passive vessels, whose minds needed to be filled up with the 'correct' knowledge, influenced the belief that what and how children learn and were taught in schools needed to be carefully controlled (Aries, 1996). These views were mirrored in the various types and forms of schools that emerged in the UK and Western Europe between the 17th and 20th centuries. Many of these early schools were run by churches, a means to 'civilise' communities and to pass on the preferred norms, beliefs, and values of dominant, aristocratic White groups. School provision, access, and quality during this period was highly varied (Thomas, 2021).

In the UK, a national standard of schooling was established with the passing of the Elementary Education Act in 1870 in England and Wales (Chitty, 2014). In 1918, further Acts of Parliament saw the school-leaving age raised from 12 to 14 years, the abolition of fees in state elementary schools, and the basic inspection of nurseries and the school provision for children with additional learning needs. Though many ideas were put forward to further reform schools at the time, economic decline as the result of the 1920s Great Depression meant that plans for change were put on hold (Abbott, Rathbone and Whitehead, 2013).

In the early 20th century, John Dewey (1859–1952), an American philosopher and psychologist, argued that schools were dull and boring places that were not conducive to an open society (2016 [1916]). He argued that education should seek to promote a democratic society, and a good school, he reasoned, should be a place where all children could socialise together irrespective of their race, gender, social class, or religious beliefs. These ideas inspired what became known as the *progressive education movement*. Though stakeholder interest in progressive education approaches began to grow across wider Europe and North America, they didn't really feature in British schools until the 1960s (Thomas, 2021). Instead, very different ideas about children's minds had begun to capture the attention of policy makers and politicians.

In the late 19th century, psychology as a discipline began to grow. According to educationalist Clyde Chitty (2014), some psychologists were becoming increasingly

Figure 7.4 Boy's home industrial school, London, 1910. This school was created with the intention of separating 'destitute' boys not convicted of crime from the negative influences of the home. Corporal punishment, via use of the cane, for example, was used as means of disciplining children in all schools in England, Wales, and Scotland (banned in state-supported education in 1987).

interested in the development of the 'pseudo-science of "psychometry" – the precise measurement and testing of mental ability states and processes' (p. 65). At the time, it was believed that intelligence was a genetic and fixed trait, inherited at birth in the same way as eye colour or hair colour. Testing via psychometrics, therefore, aimed to provide the tools to accurately measure aspects of children's capacity (Bradbury, 2021). Alongside other social, economic, and political factors, ideas about intelligence measurement found their way into the design of another major educational reform in 1944, a three-tier approach to schooling known as the *tripartite system*.

Case study: The three-tier 'tripartite' system

The 1944 Butler Act introduced the entitlement to free schooling until the age of 15 in England and Wales. The Act also introduced the 11-plus, a psychometric test that assumed children's intelligence was innate and could be measured at age 11. On the basis of their performance in the 11-plus, children were segregated into one of three school types based on what were assumed to be their 'unique states of mind' (Boronski and Hassan, 2015): grammar schools, secondary modern schools, or technical schools.

However, in the 1950s and 1960s, mounting evidence from sociologists, psychologists, and educationalists pointed to the flawed nature of psychometric testing at age 11 as an indicator of future performance. Evidence also pointed to very few children from lower-income households being able to pass the 11-plus compared to those from wealthier families. There were also regional disparities in the allocation of grammar school places and further discrimination based on gender and race (Abbott, Rathbone and Whitehead, 2013).

Far from creating a fairer system, leading educationalist and campaigner Robin Pedley argued in the 1960s, psychometric testing could not satisfactorily distinguish between supposed 'natural talent' and that which had been learned, meaning that children whose parents could read and write had a significant advantage over those who didn't. The 1967 Plowden Report concluded that human intelligence was not solely innate, but rather, its development involved a mix of nature and nurture and that there was, therefore, no value in the tripartite system. In reality, very few children attended technical schools, and therefore, the tripartite system functioned more as a bipartite, or two-tier, selective education system (Abbott, Rathbone and Whitehead, 2013). In 1976, it was eventually replaced with the comprehensive education system: state-funded secondary schools without selection based on perceived aptitude.

Even though the tripartite system was replaced, with comprehensive schools becoming the most common form of secondary school throughout the UK, at the time of writing, 163 grammar schools remained in England and 69 in Northern Ireland (Rix and Ingham, 2021).

Early assumptions of proponents of psychometric testing were that intelligence was biologically determined. However, sociologist Alice Bradbury (2021) explains that research has since demonstrated that psychometric tests and measures of IQ (or 'intelligence quotient') are themselves socially constructed. What this means is that the way language and examples are used, in questions designed to assess verbal, non-verbal, abstract reasoning, and literacy skills, reflects the cultural values, attitudes, and knowledge of the groups who have designed them. Other critiques question whether the single concept of intelligence adequately covers the wide variety of skills, qualities, and capabilities that children and young people can learn (Bradbury, 2021). While the use of psychometric tests can support diagnosis of disabilities and enable access to specialist support, Bradbury argues that they have been predominately used as a political tool to oppress minoritised ethnic and lower socioeconomic social groups.

The social and historical baggage of intelligence testing has had a lasting impact on the ways in which practitioners and policy makers discuss children and young people's ability today (Bradbury, 2021). Words like 'gifted', 'talented', and 'special' educational needs imply certain hierarchies of knowledge (Rix and Ingham, 2021). Researchers

David Gillborn and Deborah Youdell (2001) argue that 'ability' is used by education stakeholders as a new kind of 'IQism' that serves the same purpose of segregation and exclusion as ideas about intelligence did in the 1940s–50s. This is most visible in practices including ability grouping, setting, and streaming children in classrooms.

In reviewing extensive research on the impact of education selection, Jonathan Rix and Nigel Ingham (2021) concluded that very little attention has been given to the long-term impacts of selection on the lived experiences and identities of children and young people, their families, and their communities. In one study exploring children's perceptions of ability grouping across primary schools in Ireland, researchers found that internal grouping in sets or streams affected how children came to see themselves as 'smarter' or 'not as brilliant' in relation to their peers (McGillicuddy and Devine, 2020). Children placed in 'high-ability' groups felt a sense of 'pride', 'happiness', and 'confidence', while those in 'lower-ability' groups felt a sense of 'shame', 'inferiority', and 'embarrassment'. As one child in the study explained: 'if you're in the lowest (group) they treat you like a low person or somebody who is kind of dumb (Sebastian, high-ability group)' (McGillicuddy and Devine, 2020, p. 566).

Measuring and categorising children's ability has influenced the perceived value and expansion of a one-size-fits-all standardised testing regime in the UK and similarly in Singapore and China, for example. As mass schooling has evolved around the world, Biesta (2019) highlights that a global education measurement industry has also grown to measure, track, compare, and rank the 'quality' of education systems.

In England and Wales, the idea of measuring, tracking, and ranking was taken further to encompass not just children but also schools via school league tables in another far-reaching set of reforms as part of the *1988 Education Reform Act* (England and Wales). In a speech in 1975, UK Conservative Prime Minister Margaret Thatcher argued that to increase equal opportunities, we should do the following:

> let our children grow tall, some taller than others if they have the ability in them to do so. Because we must build a society in which each citizen can develop his full potential, both for his own benefit and for the community as a whole.
>
> (Thatcher, 1975)

Marketisation is a broad term used to refer to a trend in education policy that emerged in the UK and beyond in the 1980s. It encompasses the notion that schools are set up and run like businesses in a marketplace. The assertion being that by encouraging competition, education standards improve and families have greater choice. Today, the principles and values of the marketisation of education are visible across a variety of education settings from early years education to higher education.

The political rationale was to raise standards by making schools more accountable and to give parents a greater degree of school choice (Chitty, 2014). In these marketised reforms, national testing was made compulsory at ages 7, 11, and 14; attempts were made to standardise the national curriculum; and school league tables were made visible to parents.

In the 1960s, educationalists like Robin Pedley had imagined a version of compre-hensive secondary education where children from all backgrounds could mix. Although comprehensive schools still dominate in the UK, sociologists argue that now another more hidden form of selection happens, based on postcode, as families with higher levels of income can use their resources to rent or buy houses in catchment areas of schools that are deemed to be 'good' based on their ranking in school league tables (Chitty, 2014). While the existence of multiple and varied forms of formal schooling implies all parents have agency in choosing a school for their child/ren, there are hidden forms of selection that can limit access to different families based on their social class, ethnicity, gender, and/or additional educational needs. This means that families with fewer resources cannot exercise the same degree of choice, and over time, formal education in the UK has become highly differentiated and unequal.

Key points

- The rise to mass schooling in the UK was a gradual and unequal process.
- Views of intelligence continue to influence how children and young people are grouped within and between schools based on perceived ability.
- School performance, choice, ranking, and measurement has affected how educa-tion is discussed, understood, and offered.

How children and young people learn

A narrow view of education as something that can be bought and consumed in a marketplace, precisely measured, and neatly ranked seems to imply that learning itself is a one-way exchange and that children and their social worlds do not matter. While schooling might represent a core feature in childhood, adolescence, and beyond, it will be shown that learning is active, rather than passive, and is not confined to formal education settings. This section explores key ideas about *what* children are taught (*curriculum*) and *how* they should be taught (*pedagogy*).

By the end of the 19th century, psychologists began to ask whether, rather than being empty vessels, children used a unique kind of 'internal architecture' that shaped their cognitive development differently from adults (Thomas, 2021). Dewey's (2016 [1916]) view of children as active learners laid the foundations for these new theories. Dewey saw children as 'natural scientists', who were curious and inquisitive. Instead of teaching children to regurgitate facts, education, he reasoned, should help children to become reflective, to answer back, and to be sceptical about what adults told them. The big question was that if children did have different ways of thinking from adults, how could practitioners adapt pedagogy to meet these individual needs and maximise the impact of learning in the classroom? In the 20th century, three contrasting per-spectives developed to address this (Thomas, 2021). These took different views on four key issues: whether children's learning is more active or passive; whether it requires interacting with the physical or the social and cultural environment;

whether it is determined by stages of biological development; and whether it needs support from adults and, if so, in what way.

Jean Piaget

In the 1920s, Swiss developmental psychologist Jean Piaget (1896–1980) con-ducted many observational experiments and found that children actively con-struct knowledge through their interactions with the world around them, rather than being passive recipients of a curriculum of 'facts'. Piaget suggested that, as a result of their environmental interactions, children pass through four different biologically determined stages of thinking from birth to adulthood:

1   The Sensorimotor Stage (birth–2 years): discover the difference between themselves and the environment using the senses and physical movement and learn that their actions can influence the world;
2   The Preoperational Stage (2–7 years): learn how to use words and symbols to represent things (but often see the world from their point of view);
3   The Concrete Operational Stage (7–11 years): start to use logic and reasoning; and
4   The Formal Operational Stage (12-plus years): acquire the skills of logical and more complex abstract reasoning.

An early concept children learn in the sensorimotor stage is *object permanence*. For example, if a ball rolls into some undergrowth, an infant will first think it has ceased to exist. However, with a combination of brain development and experi-ence interacting with objects, young children learn that physical objects that are out of view still exist – even if they cannot see them.

Piaget stressed that children must pass through each stage in this sequence to cope with the challenges of the next stage (Thomas, 2021).

Aspects of Piaget's theory of the development of children's thinking have been sup-ported by innumerable replications of his classic experiments with young children (you can see many examples on the internet). However, Piaget's theory has also been criti-cised. It is rather rigid, assuming that all children learn in the same way at the same time, not allowing for individual and cultural differences; it does not factor in how chil-dren can learn earlier than the proposed stages if information is relevant to them; and it assumes that children mostly learn by interacting with the environment alone, failing to factor in the influence of interactions with parents, teachers, or other children enough. The use of Piaget's theory has led, in education, to a focus on children's development as an individualised, biologically defined stage process in which there is a 'right' time to have acquired certain skills (consider the assumptions that underlie the idea of children's 'school readiness' as discussed in Chapters 2 and 3).

The core idea that children individually construct their learning by interacting with the world around them contrasts with alternative perspectives proposed by Lev Vygotsky and Jerome Bruner. Whilst they also focused on children's active involvement in their learning, they placed more emphasis on how children's internal worlds and learning are constructed through the use of social and cultural tools (e.g., language) and social relationships (e.g., with teachers, parents, and/or peers).

Lev Vygotsky, Russian psychologist (1896–1934)

Vygotsky highlighted the important impact of interactions between the child, their home, and their community upon learning. As children interact with and influence their own cultures, they in turn make new cultures. He emphasised the importance of play in children and young people's learning, especially in relation to the context of language and forming social connections. Rather than focusing on children existing in discrete biologically determined stages, instead, Vygotsky addressed the social influences within children's lives that gradually shape and reshape their development (Vygotsky, 1962).

Jerome Bruner, American psychologist (1915–2016)

In contrast to the Piagetian idea of distinct biologically primed, age-based stages of 'readiness', Bruner used the analogy of *scaffolding* to suggest that support and guidance allow children to progress their learning (Wood, Bruner and Ross, 1976; Bruner, 1997). This implies that it is the world around the child that must support their learning – not the child alone. In schools, methods of teaching build 'bridges' to help children to progress in gaining new skills and topics. Equally, scaffolding can facilitate learning beyond the classroom in parents' and children's own friendship groups and communities. Children can learn anything, it is argued, if the new task or activity builds on the skills and language (cultural tools) that they have already mastered (Thomas, 2021).

The theories developed by Vygotsky and Bruner have had a lasting impact on forms of pedagogy (methods of teaching) used in many places of formal education in parts of the world. They have also influenced the strategies and design of outreach and community programmes to support children and young people within wider community contexts (Kellet, 2010).

The 1970s saw the emergence of a contrasting psychological perspective from *behaviourists*. Psychologist B.F. Skinner described learning not as something that the child constructs themselves (whether in interaction with their environment or with their social and cultural worlds) but as a simplistic stimulus-response connection. Skinner suggested that everything, even learning language, could be 'fed' to the child in the most logical sequence after analysis by adults and division into tiny pieces. For example, if a child asked, 'What has caused the climate crisis?', according to Thomas (2021), the behaviourist teacher would prepare a pathway of analysis by dissection to the simplest units, for example, teaching in steps about the degree the planet has warmed, the countries that have experienced unusual weather patterns, and so on. Reflection, thought, and discussion about the influences of human behaviour on the causes of the climate crisis do not form a part of this process.

Behaviourism has fallen out of favour in more contemporary approaches to teaching and learning in the UK and many parts of the global North. However, traces are still visible in the UK in the way the national curriculum is divided up, measured, and tested, particularly in secondary education in England (Thomas, 2021). They also underpin 'whole school behaviour management' policies. These use the principles of *operant conditioning* which involves responding to specific behaviours through positive reinforcement (encouraging by rewarding) and sanctions (punishment after undesirable actions) as motivators for children to change. The extent to which these practices reflect intended behaviourist principles in teaching and learning, however, is debateable.

Isolation booths are a form of behaviour management (albeit highly controversial) where children are excluded from the classroom for disruptive behaviour to learn in isolation in a screened-off area. Isolation booths can negatively impact children's social and emotional wellbeing and mental health (Martin-Denham, 2020) and are often disproportionately applied to children with additional educational needs and to British children of Black Caribbean, Gypsy Traveller, and Roma cultural heritages, acting as gateway to permanent exclusion (Martin-Denham, 2020). Indeed, it is important to note that race/ethnicity, social class, and gender influence teachers' perceptions of a 'good' versus a 'poorly' behaved child (Deuchar and Bhopal, 2017). You will learn more about this in relation to race later and in Chapter 9.

Figure 7.5 Isolation booths are a form of behaviour management used in schools.

Key points

- Psychology gives us different ways to understand how children and young people learn as they interact with their social environments.
- Learning itself is not a solitary activity that is confined to a school, or dedicated educational organisation, it can happen between: children and parents, within families, other children, and in communities.

Reproducing inequalities?

Researchers have studied how the inner social fabric of modern schools can impact children's experiences of learning in both positive and negative ways via teacher-pupil relationships, friendships, and even in the material arrangement of classroom spaces and the uniforms that children are required to wear (as discussed in Chapter 3). Beyond these internal school factors, the wider world also has an impact. While access to schooling is often assumed to be a magic solution that will transform lives and communities, these systems do not exist in a vacuum. This final section will consider how, through their education, children and young people can acquire different resources, or what French sociologist Pierre Bourdieu (1930–2002) originally described as *forms of capital*.

As mass education systems have grown around the world, sociologists, psychologists, and economists have built theories to explain how education can affect children and young people's lives. Some explain the impact of schooling, education, and learning globally or in societies; some focus on the level of communities; and others describe the effects on individual's sense of self and identity to understand how education can be transformative in both positive and negative ways.

Bourdieu (1986) was interested in the ways in which societies reproduced social-class inequalities. He saw schooling as a key tool which allowed the privileged middle classes to gain an advantage in the labour market. Access to a good school is one of the ways in which the wealthiest families grow and increase a child's *cultural* and *social capital*. *Cultural capital* refers to the kinds of accumulated social assets that child might have, like their level of education, accent and language used, style of dress, and so on.

Social capital on the other hand refers to resources created through *networks of who you know* (Bourdieu, 1986). If you are sent to a fee-paying school for example, you are more likely to forge connections with others who are wealthy. Building these networks of who you know at school allows young people to make contacts who later offer work experience placements or other opportunities which can foster access to the labour market. The opportunities for wealthier groups to increase these kinds of resources through schooling is an example of the ways in which systems of education can both create, extend, and restrict opportunities for children in unequal ways (Siraj and Mayo, 2014). Different forms of *cultural* and *social capital* can, therefore, yield *economic capital* (income).

American critical race and media scholar Tara Yosso (2006) draws upon the work of Bourdieu to explain why the educational and social outcomes of marginalised young

Figure 7.6 Forms of cultural capital can include accents, dialects, and artefacts (e.g., clothes of the middle and upper classes that enable some children to gain an advantage through formal schooling and life more broadly). Wealthier groups can offer their children activities to extend their cultural capital via playing a musical instrument and/or visiting a museum.

people, with a particular focus on communities of colour, are significantly lower than those from White middle and upper classes. She argues that the beliefs, values, and cultural norms of historically powerful social groups define and influence what a *suitable* and *efficient* education is. This means that the ways in which we think and talk about educational outcomes can marginalise the values, cultures, beliefs, and norms of young people from historically oppressed and excluded social groups and can generate a 'deficit' model of education. This model assumes that 'students of colour' are 'at fault for poor academic performance because: (a) students enter school without the normative cultural knowledge and skills; and (b) parents neither value nor support their child's education' (p. 75). Within a deficit model, students of colour who possess different cultural knowledges and experiences, lack the social and cultural capital necessary to support their social mobility.

Therefore, stakeholders with an interest in children and young people's education should be looking for broader ways to acknowledge, recognise, and value a wider range of forms of capital that children can make when they interact with and learn in their own communities (Siraj and Mayo, 2014). This includes valuing the building of alternative and equally important forms of resources and challenging the oppressive systems and structures that have been historically built in the image of adults with the most power and the most privilege.

Key points

- More privileged groups in society hold social and cultural 'capital', and within education systems applying a deficit model, even if all children receive schooling, children from more advantaged groups have opportunities to benefit more.
- Exploring the multiple ways education and schooling can impact children and young people's lives requires different lenses and a variety of viewpoints on an individual, community, and societal level.

Conclusion

This chapter has explored some of the taken-for-granted assumptions about what education means, and how children and young people learn within and beyond the school systems that adults have created to educate them. It has discussed how ideas about children's development, perceived intelligence, ability, and selection have influenced how stakeholders talk about and imagine a 'good' education. It has also summarised three classic approaches to thinking about how children learn. As children and young people navigate through their lives, the feature, place, and influence of schooling is mediated by a range of other social influences and contexts. Learning is not isolated to the bricks and mortar of school building; it can happen in a variety of social contexts, with other children, parents, and in wider communities. Education can reproduce inequalities just as much as it has the capacity to make children and young people's lives better. In discussing what counts as a 'good' education, it is important to look for ways to recognise and celebrate the wide variety of ways in which children build their resources and are successful.

References

Abbott, I., Rathbone, M., and Whitehead, P. (2013) *Education Policy*. London: Sage.

Aries, P. (1996) *Centuries of Childhood*. London: Penguin Books.

Ball, S. (2021) *The Education Debate* (4th ed.). Bristol: Bristol University Press.

Biesta, G. (2019) 'What kind of society does the school need? Redefining the democratic work of education in impatient times', *Studies in Philosophy of Education*, 38(6), pp. 657–668.

Biesta, G. (2020) 'What constitutes the good of education? Reflections on the possibility of educational critique', *Educational Philosophy and Theory*, 52(10), pp. 1023–1027.

Boronski, T., and Hassan, N. (2015) *Sociology of Education*. London: Sage.

Bourdieu, P. (1986) 'The forms of capital', in J. G. Richardson (ed.) *Handbook of Theory and Research for the Sociology of Education*. New York: Greenwood, pp. 241–258.

Bradbury, A. (2021) *Ability, Inequality and Post-Pandemic Schools: Rethinking Contemporary Myths of Meritocracy*. Bristol: Policy Press.

Bruner, J. (1997) *The Process of Education*. Cambridge, MA: Harvard University Press.

Chitty, C. (2014) *Education Policy in Britain* (3rd ed.). London: Macmillian.

Deuchar, R., and Bhopal, K. (2017) *Young People, Social Control and Inequality: Problems and Prospects From the Margins*. London: Palgrave Macmillan.

Dewey, J. (2016) *Democracy and Education*. New York: Free Press.

Emirbayer, M. (1996) 'Durkheim's contribution to the sociological analysis of history', *Sociological Forum*, 11(2), pp. 263–284.

Fensham-Smith, A. J. (2021) 'The rise in elective home education: issues related to recognition, collaboration and successful partnerships', in J. Wearmouth and K. Lindley (eds.) *Bringing the Curriculum to Life: Engaging Learners in the English Education System*. London: McGrawHill, pp. 43–62.

Gillborn, D., and Youdell, D. (2001) 'The new IQism: Intelligence, 'ability' and the rationing of education', in J. Demaine (ed.) *Sociology of Education Today*. London: Palgrave Macmilan, pp. 65–99.

Kellet, M. (2010) 'Children's experiences of education', in Karen Littleton, Judith Kleine Staarman and Clare Wood (eds.) *International Handbook of Psychology in Education*. Bingley: Emerald Group Publishing Limited, pp. 465–498.

Martin-Denham, S. (2020) 'An investigation into the perceived enablers and barriers to mainstream schooling: the voices of children excluded from school, their caregivers and professionals', *Project Report*. University of Sunderland, Available at: http://sure.sunderland.ac.uk/eprint/11914 (Accessed 13th May 2021).

McGillicuddy, D., and Devine, D. (2020) 'You feel ashamed that you are not in the higher group' – children's psychosocial response to ability grouping in primary school', *British Educational Research Journal*, 46(3), pp. 553–573.

Rix, J., and Ingham, N. (2021) 'The impact of education selection according to notions of intelligence: a systematic literature review', *International Journal of Educational Research Open*, 2(2).

Siraj, I., and Mayo, A. (2014) *Social Class and Educational Inequality: The Impact of Parents and Schools*. Cambridge: Cambridge University Press.

Smith, E. (2018) *Key Issues in Education and Social Justice* (2nd ed.). London: Sage.

Thatcher, M. (1975) 'Let our children grow tall', speech to the institute of socio-economic studies, 15th of September, New York, *BBC Sound Archive Transcript*. Available at: www.margaretthatcher.org/document/102769 (Accessed 5th April 2021).

Thomas, G. (2021) *Education: A Very Short Introduction* (2nd ed.). Oxford: Oxford University Press.

UNESCO (2020) 'Inclusion and education: all means all', *Global Education Monitoring Report*, Available at: https://en.unesco.org/gem-report/report/2020/inclusion (Accessed 10th May 2021).

United Nations Convention on the Rights of the Child (1989) Geneva, United Nations.

Vygotsky, L. S. (1962) *Thought and Language*. Cambridge: Wiley.

Ware, H., and Singal, N. (2018) *Research for Change: Inclusive Quality Education for Children with Disabilities*, FERSA University of Cambridge Blog. Available at: https://fersacambridge.com/2018/02/06/research-for-change-inclusive-quality-education-for-children-with-disabilities/ (Accessed 1st April 2021).

Wood, D., Bruner, J., and Ross, G. (1976) 'The role of tutoring in problem solving', *The Journal of Child Psychology and Psychiatry*, 17(2), pp. 89–100.

Yosso, T. (2006) 'Whose culture has capital? A critical race theory discussion of community cultural wealth', *Race Ethnicity and Education*, 8(1), pp. 69–91.

8 Models of disability and their effects on children's lives

Kieron Sheehy, Budiyanto, Sri Widayati, and Khofidotur Rofiah

Introduction

This chapter presents a real-life issue concerning the life opportunities and educa-tion of disabled children. The chapter presents the historical background to this situation, highlighting some international agreements that aim to make children's lives better. This is followed by a discussion of different ways of thinking about disabled children's lives using 'models of disability' and how these affect our per-ceptions and, consequently, impact children's experiences. The chapter then introduces a teaching approach developed by the authors that draws on a model of disability to begin to address the exclusion of disabled children from kinder-garten education. Finally, there is a discussion of why different models might be needed and where an inspiration for a different way of thinking might come from.

A real-life issue

Indonesia has the world's most culturally diverse multi-ethnic population, with over 273 million people (Review, 2021) living across more than 17,524 islands (Direktorat Pembi-naan Sekolloah, 2008). The Indonesian government aims to give all children at least 12 years of education from the age of 7, with early years education being optional. This includes those who would have previously been excluded from education. This is in a context where over 75% of disabled children or those with additional learning needs have no access to any form of schooling (Faragher *et al.*, 2021). The goal is to create a situation where all children can be educated together: an inclusive education system where potentially excluded children join their peers in the same schools. As we'll see, this idea arose from an international movement which believes that disabled children and those with additional learning needs have the right to the same education as others.

Indonesian policy makers and educationalists have highlighted the importance of kindergartens in facilitating educational inclusion and creating better provision for the country's children (Ediyanto *et al.*, 2017). An ongoing collaborative project (Inclusive Indonesian Classrooms) between Universitas Negeri Surabaya (UNESA, the State Univer-sity of Surabaya, Indonesia) and The Open University (United Kingdom) aims to support schools in developing teaching strategies and approaches that enable positive educational and social outcomes for all learners (Budiyanto *et al.*, 2017). However, whilst gradual

DOI: 10.4324/9781003358855-9

change has occurred in other parts of the school system, change has been problematic at kindergarten level (Poernomo, 2016). If this situation is to be addressed, then it is helpful to understand why providing disabled children with access to education is important and why creating inclusive classrooms might be difficult. To do this, we will first consider how inclusive education became an aspiration and what it means.

Inclusive education

The Indonesian situation reflects an international trend in which countries and international organisations have attempted to implement positive visions of how disabled children should be treated. For example, the United Nations Convention on the Rights of the Child (UNCRC, 1989), which was discussed in Chapter 1, was the first human rights treaty that contained a specific reference to disability and highlighted that disabled children are at risk of social exclusion and marginalisation. The subsequent Salamanca statement (Reindal, 2015), signed by 92 government representatives and 25 international organisations, was an explicit agreement that children would 'receive the support required, *within the general education system*, [our emphasis] to facilitate their effective education' (Article 24). (You can read more about these agreements in Chapters 1, 7, and 10.)

For almost three decades, there has been widespread agreement across countries to address the exclusion of disabled children in society and aim for inclusive education, with all children being educated within their general education systems. This intention has been supported by large-scale international studies that examine the outcomes for inclusive classrooms, in which disabled children and those with additional needs learn

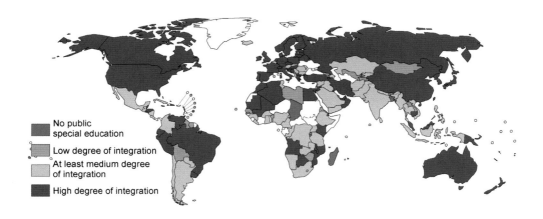

Is inclusive education available for children with disabilities?

- No public special education
- Low degree of integration
- At least medium degree of integration
- High degree of integration

Source: WORLD Policy Analysis Center, Education Database, 2014

Figure 8.1 Map showing countries offering inclusive education.

together with their peers. For example, a systematic review from 25 countries highlighted clear and consistent evidence that these settings 'confer substantial short and long-term benefits for students with and without disabilities' (Hehir *et al.*, 2016, p. 2). This is in contrast to a lack of evidence, from national and international research, that teaching children 'separately' in special schools produces better social or academic outcomes (Banks and Shevlin, 2021). However, a vital factor is quality of teaching, which similar studies highlight as being more important than setting (Cooper, Montgomery and Sheehy, 2018).

It might seem odd, therefore, that the education of disabled children needed to be repeatedly stated as a thing to be achieved. At first glance, it would appear to be working amazingly well. Take for example Figure 8.1, a map of inclusive education for disabled children around the world.

This map and the terms it uses illustrates a problem with the international agreement to strive for inclusive education: there is not an 'official' definition of what it means in practice (Mizunoya, Mitra and Yamasaki, 2018). Consequently, when different governments, parents, and educators speak of inclusive education, they may not be mean the same thing at all.

The United Nations Committee on the Rights of Persons with Disabilities proposed the following distinction between inclusive and other types of education. This is illustrated in Figure 8.2.

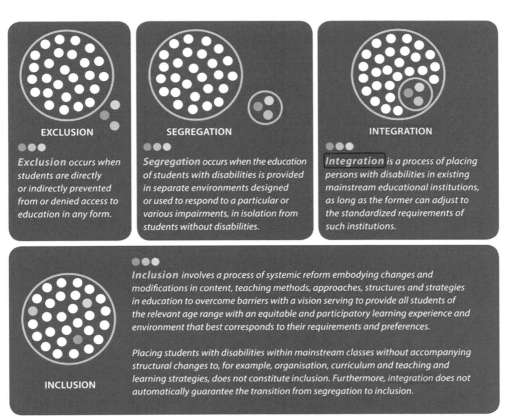

EXCLUSION

●●●

Exclusion occurs when students are directly or indirectly prevented from or denied access to education in any form.

SEGREGATION

●●●

Segregation occurs when the education of students with disabilities is provided in separate environments designed or used to respond to a particular or various impairments, in isolation from students without disabilities.

INTEGRATION

●●●

Integration is a process of placing persons with disabilities in existing mainstream educational institutions, as long as the former can adjust to the standardized requirements of such institutions.

INCLUSION

●●●

Inclusion involves a process of systemic reform embodying changes and modifications in content, teaching methods, approaches, structures and strategies in education to overcome barriers with a vision serving to provide all students of the relevant age range with an equitable and participatory learning experience and environment that best corresponds to their requirements and preferences.

Placing students with disabilities within mainstream classes without accompanying structural changes to, for example, organisation, curriculum and teaching and learning strategies, does not constitute inclusion. Furthermore, integration does not automatically guarantee the transition from segregation to inclusion.

Figure 8.2 Definitions of inclusive and other education.

If one considers Figure 8.1, and drawing on the UNCRPD definitions (shown in Figure 8.2), it is clear that the terms 'integration', 'special education', and 'inclusion' have been used interchangeably. In some countries (and for the authors of the Figure 8.1 map), the term 'inclusive education' is synonymous with integration or special education. One reason why these different terms and types of schooling are seen as being 'inclusive' is because the implementation of inclusive education is influenced by 'historical, cultural, social and financial reasons' (Mitchell, 2015, p. 121). For example, decisions about where and how children are taught must fit in with the existing range of provision or lack of it. The policy language might change to refer to inclusive education, but the provision remains similar, with children allocated to existing special or integrated provision. Another significant factor influencing how inclusive education is implemented are the different ways in which we think about disability (Wardhani, Fauzi and Andika, 2021). This contributes significantly to the exclusion of disabled children from education, which remains an international issue (UNICEF, 2019), and also why the education of disabled children with children not identified as disabled or having additional learning needs is an often controversial issue and varies widely in its implementation between and within nations (Qu, 2022).

These different ways of thinking about disability are known as *models of disability*, and they can be seen in government policies, people's discussions, and educational decisions.

Models of disability

A model (introduced in Chapter 6) is a framework for understanding an issue or experience by deeming particular aspects as important. In this way, a model defines what the issue is in relation to the emphasised features and shapes how to understand and respond to the issue. It creates a particular version of events (Burr, 1995). For example, at one time, a *religious* or *moral* model of disability was widely used to think about disabled children, reflecting different religious traditions (Retief and Letšosa, 2018), and still exists today. In this model, disability could be seen as a punishment from God for a moral transgression by the person themselves or their parents (Gammeltoft, 2008) or ancestors (Budiyanto *et al.*, 2020). Alternatively, the child's impairment might be perceived as a test of faith. Consequently, prayer would be seen as the appropriate way to help or support a disabled person. Damon Rose described his own experience of this:

> I get approached in the street by Christians who tell me they want to pray for me to get my sight back. Since I became blind as a teenager this has been a regular yet annoying by-product of being an independent disabled person who can walk about on the street.
>
> (Rose, 2019, www.bbc.co.uk/news/uk48054113)

Not only can a model of disability influence the way that people think about and act towards disabled young people, but it can also have a significant effect on how the young person sees themselves: 'The message I've taken from the Christians who've offered me healing is that I need to be "fixed"' (Rose, 2019). The life experiences and opportunities of disabled children and the way in which we (including disabled children themselves) talk about them reflect our beliefs about the nature of difference and disability.

> We develop these ways of talking, sometimes called discourses, through our personal experiences and by being part of a particular society at a particular time.
>
> (Montgomery and Sheehy, 2016, p. 183)

From the mid-1800s, an alternative way of thinking emerged, the medical model. This has profoundly shaped how modern society thinks about, labels, and responds to children's differences (Montgomery and Sheehy, 2016).

The medical model

The medical model (introduced in Chapter 6) is way of thinking about a person's health. It involves assessing and identifying the relevant signs and symptoms, linking these to a diagnostic category and then prescribing specific treatments for this diagnosed condition. This approach has had a profoundly positive impact on children's lives, for example, the identification and treatment of innumerable childhood physical problems, diseases, and challenges to children's health and wellbeing. For disability, the medical model can be seen when medical thinking is applied, equating disability to illness or disease. Some scholars and activists have argued that problems arise when this way of thinking is applied to complex or lifelong disabilities that cannot be 'mended' (Shakespeare and Watson, 2002).

This criticism is primarily because the medical model focuses on, and pathologises (see Chapter 6), a child's mental or physical limitations which are seen as largely unconnected to their social environment. This way of thinking has been applied to areas of life such as children's social development and can commonly be heard in educational discussions and decision making about disabled children. As a mother of a disabled child highlighted, it creates a perception that they are abnormal, 'different from *what is considered to be normal*' (Cologon, 2016). This changes how people 'see' and react to them. Parents of a disabled child explained how:

> At preschool, the children were told that if our son attempted to hug them that they should high five him. However, when the other children tried to hug each other that was allowed. Our son was portrayed by the teachers as 'different' therefore the children did too. (Mother and father, family #118)
>
> (Cologon, 2016)

This occurred even though there was no medical reason why the child should not be included in hugs by friends. This way of thinking explains the things children do through the lens of a diagnostic label. It can (potentially) take an everyday action or behaviour (such as hugs) and see it as an 'abnormal behaviour', perhaps linking it to a specific condition (Goodley, 2001).

A consequence of this model has been that 'The child or young person's education becomes centred around their impairment, and how to minimise this' (The Alliance for Inclusive Education, 2021), and the child's experiences are positioned as being outside or different from the mainstream. This might involve not only the designation of separate professional services but also a separation from their peers in order to access standard and support services (Drake Music, 2021). Historically within the United Kingdom, this way of thinking placed many disabled children or those with additional learning needs in various segregated settings, such as asylums or institutions or outside of education in 'mental handicap' hospitals (Sheehy and Kellett, 2003), and gave power over this situation to nondisabled professionals. The purposes of these settings has been argued as being to cure them, to shelter them, or to protect society from them (Rix, 2015).

Key points

- The medical model of disability locates the problem within an individual child.
- Disabled children risk being pathologised and seen as 'broken', wrong, or abnormal and in need of mending.
- The medical model is still used, *often implicitly*, as a way of understanding children's lives and experiences and influencing policy and practice.

The social model of disability

The United Nations Convention on the Rights of Persons with Disabilities (United Nations, 2007) states its position that disabled children have the right to education without discrimination due to disability. However, this convention also reflects a change in how disability could be conceptualised and illustrates a move away from medical model thinking. For example, Article 1 states that:

> Disability is an evolving concept and that disability results from the interaction between persons with impairments and attitudinal and environmental barriers that hinders their full and effective participation in society on an equal basis with others.
>
> (United Nations, 2007, p. 1.)

This is important because this convention sees disability as something that is created in the physical and societal interactions of children. This way of thinking is different from a view in which disability arises purely because of a child's 'abnormality'.

This change reflected a movement that had its origins largely within the United Kingdom. The Union of the Physically Impaired Against Segregation (UPAS) had argued that they were not disabled by their impairments but by barriers within society (UPAS, 1976). Disability Studies scholar Mike Oliver (2013) subsequently crystallised this view when he introduced the concept of the social model of disability, of which Shakespeare and Watson (2002, p. 1) say:

> Replacing a traditional, 'medical model' view of disability – in which the problems arose from deficits in the body – with a social model view – in which the problems arose from social oppression – was and remains very liberating for disabled individuals. Suddenly, people were able to understand that they weren't at fault: society was. They didn't need to change: society needed to change. They didn't have to be sorry for themselves: they could be angry.

Over time, the social model of disability began to be used beyond people with physical impairments and as a way to consider the issues and experiences of 'people with sensory impairments, intellectual and mental health conditions' (Berghs *et al.*, 2019, p. 6), which strengthened a perspective that it was society that had to be changed. This facilitated a global movement that aimed to remove disabling barriers in society, and it is this view that is seen in the UNCPRD (2007). In this model, a person is disabled by the impact of social and environmental barriers, and therefore, it is these barriers that need to be addressed. This idea is expressed in Figure 8.3, where the barrier is not just physical but also in the attitude of the person clearing the snow and where an inclusive solution has the potential to benefit a greater number of children.

A child might have a physical or sensory impairment, such as cerebral palsy or a visual impairment, but they are disabled by social and environmental factors. The social model has helped people to think differently about notions of disability, 'being' disabled, and how to develop an inclusive society.

Key points

- The social model of disability locates disability within society and rejects the idea that disability is located within the individual.
- The social model distinguishes between an impairment and society's reaction to it and argues that society needs to change, not individuals.
- The social model sees disability as a product of societies' attitudes and environments rather than biology and looks at how society provides opportunities to take part in everyday activities.
- The social model is also a political statement challenging society to be more inclusive.

The social model in different contexts

By focusing on factors external to the child, some disabled people have argued that the social model underplays 'internal' experiences of impairment, such as pain (Crow, 2010), and that all disabled people are oppressed by society and should have a 'disability identity' (Diamond, Nedergaard and Rosamond, 2020). The social model can

**CLEARING A PATH
FOR PEOPLE WITH SPECIAL NEEDS
CLEARS THE PATH FOR EVERYONE!**

Figure 8.3 The benefits of an inclusive approach.

been seen as presenting a simplistic view of the medical model and underplaying the complex interaction between the intrinsic and extrinsic factors that affect individuals (Shakespeare, 2006). Consequently, it has developed in different ways in different countries. Nordic countries have implemented models that focus on normalising the environment (Shakespeare, 2004; Wiseman, 2014 cited in Berghs *et al.*, 2019), whereas in North America, disability is more commonly constructed in relation to a minority group, whose culture, for example, deaf culture (Chapman, 2021) requires protection and political representation (Sabatello and Schulze, 2013 cited in Berghs *et al.*, 2019).

Despite these criticisms and developments, the 'British' social model remains widely used by professional services, disability activists, and organisations (Drake Music, 2021). Its simplicity is also its strength. It is easily explained to policy makers and has informed positive social changes. As illustrated in Table 8.1 below, educators often draw on the social model as a way of thinking about inclusive education, and contrast it with the medical model thinking which underpins special or segregated education.

Because the social model sees disability as arising largely from disabling environments, this leads to a view 'that through collaboration and cooperation at a societal level, disabled young people can be included in education' (Sheehy, 2014, p. 241). This contrasts with the stance that if the child's impairment cannot be 'fixed', then they 'may not be able to fit in the society' (Priyanti, 2018) or learn together with their peers.

Models of disability and how they apply in the classroom

Practitioners who work with children have beliefs that guide the decisions they make about how to best support or teach them, and these beliefs also affect if and how teachers work with the disabled children in their classes. For example, Anne Jordan (2013) assessed teachers' beliefs regarding the extent which they held medical or social perspectives which she described as 'pathognomic' or 'interventionist'. Pathognomic (P) beliefs reflect a traditional medical perspective on children's disabilities. In contrast, interventionist (I) beliefs see disabilities as arising from socially constructed barriers. These two categories map onto the two columns within Table 8.1, of medical and social models respectively. Jordan found that teachers in inclusive classes who attribute students' abilities to environmental factors (I beliefs) spent more time engaging

Table 8.1 Medical and social models of disability

Medical model	Social model
Child is faulty	Child is valued
Child is diagnosed	Strengths/needs defined by self and others
Child is labelled	Barriers are identified and solutions developed
Attention is focused on impairment	Outcomes-based programmes designed
Teaching resources follow diagnosis and are typically 'attached' to individuals	Teaching resources are assigned to remove barriers for all
Assessment, monitoring	Resources made available and reviewed
Segregation and alternative services	Training for parents and professionals
Ordinary needs put on hold	Relationships nurtured
Re-entry to school if meets standards to 'fit in' or permanent exclusion	Diversity welcomed; child is welcome
Separate (or add on) teaching practices for disabled pupils and those with special educational needs	Pedagogy designed to work as well as possible for diverse classrooms
School structures and practices remain unchanged	School structures and practices evolve

(Adapted and extended from Rieser, 2001, p. 139.)

with disabled students and felt it was their responsibility to do so. Teachers who saw abilities as fixed 'genetic' characteristics (P beliefs) felt, and took, less responsibility for disabled pupils and saw them as the responsibility of others (such as health care professionals and special education support teachers). Those with I beliefs worked at higher levels of engagement with disabled pupils but also engaged in this way with others in the class, producing better outcomes for all the class (Jordan, Glenn and McGhie-Richmond, 2010). These findings illustrate how teachers' implicit beliefs (reflecting a medical or a social model) can profoundly influence the inclusion, or not, of disabled children and, thereby, their education and life experiences.

The previous examples have used models of disability to understand why disabled children might be seen and treated differently in different countries or by different people. The next section looks at how awareness of models of disability can inform practical changes to support inclusion.

Inclusive Indonesian kindergartens: A case study

Creating inclusive Indonesian kindergartens is important because of the positive impact that kindergartens can have on the development of children previously excluded from education (Jenkins *et al.*, 2018) and also because kindergartens are able to act as sites for 'initiating an inclusive cultural shift' (Raičević, 2020). However, they remain rare (Ujianti, 2021), and the inclusive Indonesian classrooms project identified three factors that influenced this situation.

- Stigmatisation (introduced in Chapter 3 and Chapter 6) was explicitly linked to societal beliefs about disability, reflecting medical or religious ways of thinking (Priyanti, 2018), and this stigma also applied to teachers and parents of disabled children (Budiyanto *et al.*, 2020). The stigmatisation of children with additional learning needs was exacerbated by beliefs that they will 'hinder the development of other "normal" children' (Anggia and Harun, 2019, p. 181) and disagreement with the idea that 'All children have a right to education with their peers' (Budiyanto *et al.*, 2020). Consequently, even kindergartens deemed to be inclusive might not admit disabled children or make enrolment difficult (Sabila and Kurniawati, 2019).
- There was also a lack of practical, research-informed, inclusive educational approaches for teachers to use (Kristiana and Hendriani, 2018).
- Teachers felt they lacked the training and resources to teach inclusively (Diana *et al.*, 2020).

These three factors combined to create a situation where 'kindergartens do not train or buy resources because they have no pupils with special educational needs. They have no pupils with special educational needs because they do not have the resources or training' (Rofiah *et al.*, p. 3).

The project team had discussions with teachers and parents about this issue. We were seeking to create learning opportunities that would be sufficiently available for all children rather than using teaching and learning strategies that were suitable for most, alongside 'add-ons' for children experiencing difficulties (Florian and Black-Hawkins, 2011). We attempted to think about addressing this situation using a social model approach, which led to the idea of having the appropriate resources and teaching prac- tices in place *before* disabled children applied to enrol, as part of everyday classroom activities.

Based on our discussions, the everyday activity of storytelling was chosen, and we discussed how to make it inclusive and engaging. The outcome of this was Sign Sup- ported Big Books.

The team created Big Books for a whole class storytelling time. These featured a simple story, and on the reverse of each page, visible to the teacher, was a Signalong Indonesia sign. Signalong Indonesia is a type of key word signing, which takes manual signs from Indonesian sign languages and some British Sign Language signs (see Figure 8.4).

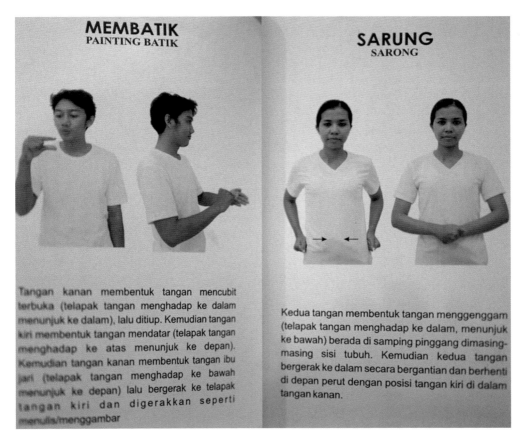

Figure 8.4 Signalong Indonesia signs for 'batik' and 'sarong'.

Signalong Indonesia is not a sign language and is much simpler than the signed languages of Deaf communities, which have their own grammatical structure and form. Signalong Indonesia (and all key word signing approaches) follows the order of spoken language, and signs accompany only the key word(s) in each sentence. Signalong Indonesia is sign-supported communication approach, and a range of studies have shown that this approach is beneficial for supporting the communication of children with learning and language difficulties (Grove and Launonen, 2019).

Initially, we chose to evaluate the use of these books in a small number of mainstream kindergartens (i.e., without any disabled children). The findings suggested the following:

- Children and teachers enjoyed using the books and signs. They were fun to use, and fun was seen as a central element of teaching.
- Compared to children who had the same books but without signs, children had significantly improved story comprehension and engagement.
- Teachers were keen to use Signalong Indonesia to support other books and story activities.

(Rofiah *et al.*, 2021)

The project sought to find something that would work well for all children and teachers, in keeping with the social model features (see Table 8.1). The research suggested that it was possible to put in place simple inclusive activities without this being necessitated by having a disabled child in the classroom that this approach facilitated, rather than hindered, children's learning and that when presented in this way, teachers were keen to adopt it. The simple resources were not 'attached' to the assessment of a particular child's disability (see Table 8.1) but instead addressed barriers to inclusion (language support, attitudes, resources, and training) within the school. When presented in this way, signing was not stigmatised. We felt that the approach had potential as a proactive means of beginning to address some of the barriers for inclusive kindergartens. Following refinements, the Big Book project materials and training were rolled out to approximately 3,500 children in kindergartens across Indonesia, which includes those with disabled children. Evaluations of this sample suggest that the majority of teachers enjoy using the approach and feel it supports all children, including those with additional learning needs.

Future possibilities

The models of disability used, when thinking about education, have a significant impact on children's lives. Consequently, other models have been developed to understand how to improve, or give alternative perspectives, on making decisions about important issues. Indeed, the term 'medical model' was first used by Ronald Laing, a psychiatrist interested in developing a better understanding of mental health issues (Sarto-Jackson, 2018). Elsewhere in this Reader, you will find references to other models, such as the biopsychosocial and biomedical models (Chapter 6). These have arisen within European and American societies in the global North, and the social model has been criticised because it was 'mainly advocated by white western men with physical impairments' (Berghs *et al.*, 2019, p. 7). Educators have argued that the dominant notion of inclusive education reflects Euro-American ways of thinking, which other countries are then exhorted to adopt by aid agencies (Armstrong, Armstrong and Spandagou, 2011). This might contribute to why inclusive practice appears to be 'often incompatible with the lived realities of people with disabilities in non-western contexts' (Kalyanpur, 2016, p. 16). If we wish to improve or consider alternative ways of thinking about disability and difference, then perhaps we should seek ideas that might lead to non–Euro-American models.

One possible source for informing a different way of thinking about inclusion and disability is *Ubuntu*. This commonly used term comes from a Zulu phrase 'Umuntu ngumuntu ngabantu' and the Setswana phrase 'Motho ke motho ka batho', which translates as 'a person is a person through other people' (Bennett, 1984, p. 73). This belief is held by many people in Southern Africa (Ramose, 2004). It emphasises community, cooperation, and sharing responsibility and available resources and is not premised on a resource-rich context. Many African educators have highlighted that the philosophy of Ubuntu seems to resonate with the principles of inclusive education (Chiwaya, Dreyer and Damons, 2021).

> Inclusive education is a connectedness between learners, educators and communities of learning, which provides a positive environment which in turn positively affects self-worth, self-belief and achievement. The ability to learn depends on these networks of support. This is the essence of ubuntu – that we live in a delicate web of interconnectedness and interdependence with each other. 'I am because we are'. If I diminish, insult or mistreat another person, I do so similarly to myself. So, inclusive education calls for mutual respect and support.
>
> (Majoko and Phasha, 2018, p. 10)

Ubuntu locates disability within a framework of democracy in which all citizens are equal and interdependent (Berghs, 2017). Teachers should affirm and respect difference by being sensitive to building on the experiences and ideas that learners bring with them and also to be aware of their own beliefs (Shockley, 2011). Whether Ubuntu might be able to inform a model of disability is not yet known, and its (mis)interpretation has be associated with the exclusion of disabled people (Ngubane-Mokiwa, 2018). However, in a world where disabled children remain the most excluded and vulnerable group (Sheehy, 2021), the development of new models should be explored.

Conclusions

Models of disability influence how society treats disabled children. These models are found in international and national policies aiming to improve children's lives, with a trend for legislation to reflect a social model of disability. However, the medical model remains a pervasive way of thinking about disability in local policies and individuals' beliefs, and the term inclusion has been used to represent ideas and practices that are underpinned by a medical model. Although subject to valid criticisms, the social model remains a useful way of thinking about how to improve the lives of disabled children and can inform innovative positive change. However, there is a need for new models, and the philosophy of Ubuntu offers a possible starting point – when we look to develop better ways of thinking about children's lives.

References

The Alliance for Inclusive Education (2021) *The Medical Model*. Available at: www.allfie.org.uk/def initions/models-of-disability/medical-model-disability/ (Accessed 4th January 2022).

Anggia, D., and Harun, H. (2019) 'Description of implementation inclusive education for children with special needs in inclusive kindergarten', *Advances in Social Science, Education and Humanities Research*, 26, pp. 181–187. https://doi.org/10.2991/icsie-18.2019.34.

Armstrong, D., Armstrong, A. C., and Spandagou, I. (2011) 'Inclusion: by choice or by chance?', *International Journal of Inclusive Education*, 15(1), pp. 29–39. doi:10.1080/13603116.2010.496 192.

Banks, J., and Shevlin, M. (2021) 'Inclusion at a crossroads special education in Ireland', *Research Outreach*, 127. doi:10.32907/ro-127-1990267982.

Bennett, J. (1984) 'Motho ke motho ka batho babang (a person is a person because of other people)', *Social Dynamics*, 10(1), pp. 90–93. doi:10.1080/02533958408458362.

Berghs, M. (2017) 'Practices and discourses of ubuntu: implications for an African model of disability?', *African Journal of Disability*, 6, pp. 1–8. doi:10.4102/ajod.v6.292.

Berghs, M., Chataika, T., El-Lahib, Y., and Dube, K. (2019) *The Routledge Handbook of Disability Activism*. London: Routledge.

Budiyanto *et al.* (2017) 'Developing Signalong Indonesia: issues of happiness and pedagogy, training and stigmatisation', *International Journal of Inclusive Education,* 22(5), 543–559. doi:10. 1080/13603116.2017.1390000.

Budiyanto *et al.* (2020) 'Indonesian educators' knowledge and beliefs about teaching children with autism', *Athens Journal of Education*, 7(1), pp. 77–98. doi:10.30958/aje.7-1-4.

Burr, V. (1995) *An Introduction to Social Constructionism*. London: Routledge. https://doi. org/10.4324/9780203133026 Pages 208 eBook ISBN9780203133026.

Chapman, M. (2021) 'Representation and resistance: a qualitative study of narratives of deaf cultural identity', *Culture and Psychology*, 27(3), pp. 374–391. doi:10.1177/1354067X21993794.

Chiwaya, S., Dreyer, L., and Damons, L. (2021) 'Ubuntu in inclusive education: A Malawian experience', in J. M. Ngwaru and L. M. Dreyer (eds.) *Inclusivity in Response to Diversity and Equal Human Rights*. Masvingo: Reformed Church University and the Centre for African Collaboration, Stellenbosch University, pp. 130–139.

Cologon, K. (2016) 'What is disability? It depends whose shoes you are wearing": Parent understandings of the concept of disability', *Disability Studies Quarterly*, 30(1). Available at: https:// dsq-sds.org/article/view/4448/4212.

Cooper, V., Montgomery, H., and Sheehy, K. (2018) *Parenting the First Twelve Years: What the Evidence Tells Us*. London: Pelican.

Crow, L. (2010) 'Including all of our lives: renewing the social model of disability', *Equality, Participation and Inclusion 1: Diverse Perspectives*, 1996, pp. 124–140.

Diana, Sunardi, Gunarhadi, Munawir Yusuf (2020) 'Preschool teachers' attitudes toward inclusive education in Central Java, Indonesia', *Advances in Social Science, Education and Humanities Research*, 397, pp. 1361–1368.

Direktorat Pembinaan Sekolloah (2008) 'Profil Pendidikan Inklusif di Indonesia', *Inclusive Education Profile in Indonesia*, 1.

Drake Music (2021) *Understanding Disability Part 3*. Available at: www.drakemusic.org/blog/nim-ralph/understanding-disability-part-3-the-medical-model/ (Accessed 4th January 2022).

Ediyanto, E. *et al.* (2017) 'Inclusive education in Indonesia from the perspective of Widyaiswara in centre for development and empowerment of teachers and education personnel of kindergartens and special education', *IJDS: Indonesian Journal of Disability Studies*, 4(2), pp. 104–116. doi:10. 21776/ub.ijds.2017.004.02.3.

Faragher, R. *et al.* (2021) 'Inclusive education in Asia: insights from some country case studies', *Journal of Policy and Practice in Intellectual Disabilities*, 18(1), pp. 23–35. doi:10.1111/jppi.12369.

Florian, L., and Black-Hawkins, K. (2011) 'Exploring inclusive pedagogy', *British Educational Research Journal*, 37(5), pp. 813–828. https://doi.org/10.1080/01411926.2010.501096.

Gammeltoft, T. M. (2008) 'Childhood disability and parental moral responsibility in northern Vietnam: towards ethnographies of intercorporeality', *Journal of the Royal Anthropological Institute*, 14(4), pp. 825–842. doi:10.1111/j.1467-9655.2008.00533.x.

Goodley, D. (2001) '"Learning difficulties", the social model of disability and impairment: challenging epistemologies', *Disability & Society*, 16(2), pp. 207–231. doi:10.1080/0968759012 0035816.

Grove, N., and Launonen, K. (2019) *Manual Sign Aquisition in Children with Developmental Disabilties*. New York: Nova Science Publishers. Available at: Nova Science.

Hehir, T. *et al.* (2016) 'A summary of the evidence on inclusive education', *Instituto Alana*, pp. 1–34. Available at: http://alana.org.br/wp-content/uploads/2016/12/A_Summary_of_ the_evidence_on_inclusive_education.pdf.

Jenkins, J. M. *et al.* (2018) 'Do high-quality kindergarten and first-grade classrooms mitigate preschool fadeout?', *Journal of Research on Educational Effectiveness*, 11(3), pp. 339–374. doi:10.1 080/19345747.2018.1441347.

Jordan, A. (2013) 'Fostering the transition to effective teaching practices in inclusive classrooms', in S. E. Elliott-Johns and D. H. Jarvis (eds.) *Perspectives on Transitions in Schooling and Instructional Practice*. Toronto, ON: University of Toronto Press, pp. 1689–1699. doi:10.1017/ CBO9781107415324.004.

Jordan, A., Glenn, C., and McGhie-Richmond, D. (2010) 'The supporting effective teaching (SET) project: the relationship of inclusive teaching practices to teachers' beliefs about disability and ability, and about their roles as teachers', *Teaching and Teacher Education: Elsevier Ltd*, 26(2), pp. 259–266. doi:10.1016/j.tate.2009.03.005.

Kalyanpur, M. (2016) 'Inclusive education policies and practices in the context of international development. Lessons from Cambodia', *ZEP: Zeitschrift für internationale Bildungsforschung und Entwicklungspädagogik*, 39(3), pp. 16–21.

Kristiana, I. F., and Hendriani, W. (2018) 'Teaching efficacy in inclusive education (IE) in Indonesia and other Asian developing countries: a systematic review', *Journal of Education and Learning (EduLearn)*, 12(2), p. 166. https://doi.org/10.11591/edulearn.v12i2.7150.

Majoko, T., and Phasha, N. (2018) *The State of Inclusive Education in South Africa and the Implications for Teacher Training Programmes*. Johannesburg: British Council.

Mitchell, D. (2015) 'Inclusive education is a multi-faceted concept', *CEPS Journal*. Available at: http://nbn-resolving.de/urn:nbn:de:0111-pedocs-106113.

Mizunoya, S., Mitra, S., and Yamasaki, I. (2018) 'Disability and school attendance in 15 low- and middle-income countries', *World Development*, 104, pp. 388–403. doi:10.1016/j.worlddev.2017. 12.001.

Montgomery, H., and Sheehy, K. (2016) 'Understanding disabled children's experiences', in L. Farrington-Flint and H. Montgomery (eds.) *An Introduction to Childhood Studies and Child Psychology*. Milton Keynes: Open University, pp. 181–202.

Nations, U. (2007) *Convention on the Rights of Persons with Disabilities*. Available at: https:// treaties.un.org/doc/Publication/CTC/Ch_IV_15.pdf.

Ngubane-Mokiwa, S. A. (2018) 'Ubuntu considered in light of exclusion of people with disabilities', *African Journal of Disability*: AOSIS, 7. doi:10.4102/AJOD.V7I0.460.

Oliver, M. (2013) 'The social model of disability: thirty years on', *Disability and Society*, 28(7), pp. 1024–1026. doi:10.1080/09687599.2013.818773.

Poernomo, B. (2016) 'The implementation of inclusive education in Indonesia: current problems and challenges', *American International Journal of Social Science*, 5(3), pp. 144–150.

Priyanti, N. (2018) 'Representations of people with disabilities in an Indonesian newspaper: a critical discourse analysis', *Disability Studies Quarterly*, 38(4).

Qu, X. (2022) 'A critical realist model of inclusive education for children with special educational needs and/or disabilities', *International Journal of Inclusive Education*, 26(10), pp. 1008–1022. doi:10.1080/13603116.2020.1760366.

Raičević, T. D. (2020) 'Kindergarten is important for every child regardless of where they grow up', *UNICEF*. Available at: www.unicef.org/montenegro/en/stories/kindergarten-important-every-child-regardless-where-they-grow (Accessed 1st February 2020).

Ramose, M. (2004) 'Transforming education in South Africa: paradigm shift or change?', *South African Journal of Higher Education*, 17(3), pp. 137–143. doi:10.4314/sajhe.v17i3.25413.

Reindal, S. M. (2015) 'Discussing inclusive education: an inquiry into different interpretations and a search for ethical aspects of inclusion using the capabilities approach', *European Journal of Special Needs Education*, Routledge, 31(1), pp. 1–12. doi:10.1080/08856257.2015.1087123.

Retief, M., and Letšosa, R. (2018) 'Models of disability: a brief overview', *HTS Teologiese Studies/ Theological Studies*, 74(1), pp. 1–8. doi:10.4102/hts.v74i1.4738.

Review, W. P. (2021) *Indonesia Population 2021*. Available at: https://worldpopulationreview.com/countries/indonesia-population.

Rieser, R. (2001) 'The struggle for inclusion: the growth of a movement', in L. Barton (ed.) *Disability, Politics and Struggle for Chang*. London: David Fulton Publishers.

Rix, J. (2015) *Must Inclusion Be Special?: Rethinking Educational Support Within a Community of Provision*. Taylor & Francis. Available at: https://books.google.co.uk/books/about/Must_Inclusion_Be_Special.html?id=d92-oAEACAAJ&pgis=1 (Accessed 16th April 2016).

Rofiah, K. *et al.* (2021) 'Fun and the benefits of sign supported big books in mainstream Indonesian kindergartens', *International Journal of Early Years Education*, pp. 1–5. doi:10.1080/09669760.2021.1956440.

Rose, D. (2019) 'Stop trying to "heal" me', *BBC News*. Available at: www.bbc.co.uk/news/uk-48054113 (Accessed 22nd December 2021).

Sabila, H., and Kurniawati, F. (2019) 'Parental attitudes of preschool children toward students with special needs in inclusive and non-inclusive kindergartens: a comparative study', *Advances in Social Science, Education and Humanities Research*, 229(Iciap 2018), pp. 602–609. https://doi.org/10.2991/iciap-18.2019.51.

Sarto-Jackson, I. (2018) 'Time for a change: topical amendments to the medical model of disease', *Biological Theory*, Springer Netherlands, 13(1), pp. 29–38. doi:10.1007/s13752-017-0289-z.

Shakespeare, T. (2006) *Disability Rights and Wrongs*. London: Routledge.

Shakespeare, T., and Watson, N. (2002) 'The social model of disability: an outdated ideology?', *Research in Social Science and Disability*, 2, pp. 9–28.

Sheehy, K. (2014) 'Educational psychology and the development of inclusive education', in A. Holliman (ed.) *Routledge International Companion to Educational Psychology*, pp. 235–245. London: Routledge. doi:10.1017/CBO9781107415324.004.

Sheehy, K. (2021) 'Eugenics and the lives of disabled children', in V. Cooper and N. Holford (eds.) *Exploring Childhood and Youth*. London: Routledge, pp. 163–175.

Sheehy, K., and Kellett, M. (2003) 'The creation of difference', in *Inclusive Education: Learning for All: Thinking it Through*. Milton Keynes: Open University, pp. 9–54.

Shockley, K. (2011) 'Reaching African American students: profile of an Afrocentric teacher', *Journal of Black Studies*, 42(7), pp. 1027–1046. doi:10.1177/0021934711403739.

Ujianti, P. R. (2021) *The Implementation of Inclusive Education Program for Early Childhood*. Proceedings of the 2nd international conference on technology and educational science (ICTES 2020), 540(Ictes 2020), pp. 175–178. doi:10.2991/assehr.k.210407.233.

UNCPRD (2007) *United Nations Convention on the Rights of Persons with Disabilities*. Available at: https://www.un.org/disabilities/documents/convention/convoptprot-e.pdf.

UNCRC (1989) *United Nations Convention on the Rights of the Child*. Available at: https://www.unicef.org.uk/wp-content/uploads/2016/08/unicef-convention-rights-child-uncrc.pdf.

UNICEF (2019) *Introduction, Disabilities*. Available at: www.unicef.org/disabilities (Accessed 1st September 2019).

The Union of the Physically Impaired Against Segregation and The Disability Alliance (UPAS) (1976) Fundamental Principles of Disability.

Wardhani, N. W., Fauzi, M., and Andika, F. (2021) 'Inclusive education and social justice for all Indonesians', in *2nd International Conference on Innovation in Education and Pedagogy (ICIEP 2020)*. Dordrecht: Atlantis Press, pp. 135–139.

9 Race(ism) and ethnicity

Anthony Gunter

Introduction

Childhood can often be understood and characterised as a protected time of inno-cence and purity. From this common-sense Euro-American perspective, young chil-dren are thought to be 'colour blind' and not to make distinctions or hold prejudices on the basis of skin colour or appearance. However, psychological research indicates that even very young children are aware of perceived racial and ethnic differences, shaped through their observational learning and their early social interactions with parents, adults, and their peers. Not only might children understand themselves as belonging to a particular ethnic group, but they might also adopt racist attitudes and themselves experience racist bullying in early childhood.

This chapter will explore how psychology and the social sciences more broadly have contributed to our understanding of race/racism and ethnicity, including how children and young people's social and cultural interactions shape their develop-ment and behaviours throughout childhood and into early adulthood and how their lived experiences are shaped by the impact of structural and institutional racism, whether it be via education or the criminal justice system. The notions of race and ethnicity are quite complex and have often been the focus of negative attitudes, prejudice, and discrimination. The chapter will also consider how views of race and ethnicity have changed over the years and how children and young people learn about these concepts. Moreover, the chapter will detail ways in which children and young people directly experience racism.

Race(ism) and ethnicity: Key concepts

'Identity' – as introduced in Chapter 4 – is an 'interpretation of the self that estab-lishes what and where the person is in both social and psychological terms' (Guiber-nau and Rex, 1997, p. 4). This means that through identity, individuals construct meaning beyond their individual selves, placing themselves within one or more group or collective identities. Race and ethnicity are collective identities that have been historically and culturally constructed.

- *Race* is applied to groups defined by 'perceived common physical characteristics that are held to be inherent' (Cornell and Hartman, 1998, p. 24). This definition

DOI: 10.4324/9781003358855-10

and the term 'race' itself are highly contentious, because they pre-suppose that biologically different races of people do actually exist. However, as we shall see in this chapter, despite superficial physical differences between some groups of people, scientific evidence does not support this argument.

- *Ethnicity*, as a concept, broadly refers to distinct cultural practices and beliefs of a group of people who share a collective identity and common heritage. Ethnicity can best be viewed as a matter of contrast, for example, 'to draw a boundary between "us" and "them" on the basis of the claims we make about ourselves and them, that "we" share something that "they do not"' (Cornell and Hartman, 1998, p. 20). Whereas 'race' (as a concept) is ascribed to perceived interracial physical differences, such as skin colour, for example, between Black and White people, *ethnicity* can also include intra- (or within) 'racial' differences related to nationality, language, and/or culture, for example, between Irish Americans and Polish Americans.

- *Racism*, broadly, 'may be taken as any practice which, intentionally or not, excludes a "racial" or "ethnic" minority from enjoying the full rights, opportunities, and responsibilities available to the majority (or dominant minority) population' (Richards, 1997, p. x). There are different kinds of '*racisms*': (i) individual-level or interpersonal racism; (ii) group-level or institutional racism, for example, in schools or the workplace; and (iii) structural racism, the totality of ways in which racial discrimination is enacted via the policies and practices of multiple institutions across society, for example, in housing, education, health care, and criminal justice.

Race 'science'

From the 17th century, 'Age of Reason' philosophers in Europe developed a new worldview, challenging the absolute and divine power of monarchs and religious leaders and presenting new 'truths' to be proven scientifically. The Swedish natural scientist Carl Linnaeus aimed to classify and name the whole natural world of plants, animals, and people, including those recently 'discovered' (to European eyes) in his *Systema Naturae* (*Systems of Nature*), first published in 1735. Initially, Linnaeus described four types of humans, corresponding to Europe, Asia, Africa, and the Americas. Building on these ideas, during this period, other European scientists set about further organising and classifying people, postulating the existence of distinct races, including 'White', 'Yellow', 'Black', 'Malay', and 'American' [indigenous], thought to be more or less fixed, physically distinct, and morally and psychologically different – e.g., the European was described by Linnaeus as 'White, sanguine, and muscular'; the Asian, 'sallow, melancholic, and stiff; the African, 'Black, phlegmatic, and lazy'; and the American 'is Red, choleric, and straight-backed'.

Significantly, these European scientists argued that reason and civilisation were attributes possessed solely by White Europeans. Those who were not of European descent, manifested by different facial and physical characteristics, were thought to be uncivilised (savages), lacking in reason.

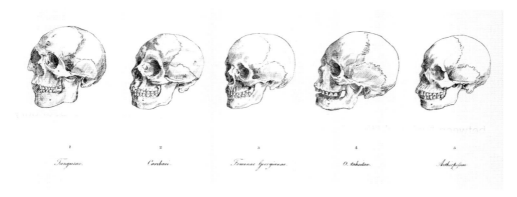

Figure 9.1 Scientists have used skull measurements to seek to classify brain size and intelligence across human types according to geographical origin.

Source: Bhopal (2007)

This was the starting point for 'race science', a new discipline proclaiming the exist-ence of a human 'racial' hierarchy: the 'White race' regarded as superior and the 'Yellow race' inferior to the 'White' race but superior to 'Black' and 'Indigenous' races. This think-ing, often termed 'scientific racism', also discouraged racial mixing, which was thought to result in contamination of the superior 'White race' and the dilution of 'White blood'.

European colonialism and the enslavement of Africans, driven by greed and profit, was in full swing well in advance of the development of 'race science'. However, the new thinking about the existence of different, inferior 'races' provided a ready-made moral justification for Europeans' continued domination, exploitation, and subjugation of non-White people and their lands. The convergence of colonialism and race science underpinned the political ideologies of European colonialism and slavery in the 18th and 19th centuries and led to the annihilation of indigenous peoples and their cul-tures, as well as the physical and psychological violence of the transatlantic slave trade and chattel slavery (Fryer, 1984).

The idea of different races as 'scientific fact' was gradually questioned by some social and natural scientists in the 20th century. In particular, biological anthropolo-gists and human geneticists were discovering that there was huge biological and genetic *variation within* population groups, as well as great *similarities between* them. Despite differences in appearance – for example, between White Europeans and Black Africans in relation to skin pigmentation ('colour') and hair type/texture – modern science indicates that humans are, by and large, genetically almost identical:

> Research has repeatedly shown that race is not a scientifically valid concept. Across the world, humans share 99.9% of their DNA. The characteristics that have come to define our popular understanding of race – hair texture, skin colour, facial features – represent only a few of the thousands of traits that define us as a species.

> (Nelson, 2019, pp. 440–441)

Furthermore, humans certainly share the same ancestral roots, as science writer Angela Saini (2019) explains (see text box). The history of human migration from one setting to different environments explains the variations found in a few average characteristics between population groups in different locations, and also the fact that the most genetic diversity is found *within* Africa, not *between* population groups around the world.

Human migration and genetic diversity

The greatest genetic diversity within Homo sapiens is found in Africa, because this continent contains the oldest human communities. When some of our ancestors began to migrate into the rest of the world sometime between 50,000 and 100,000 years ago, the groups that moved were genetically less diverse than the ones left behind for the simple reason that they were made up of fewer people.

The human variation we see across different regions today is partly the result of this 'founder effect'. Of course, groups of people have average physical differences, as a result of their biological and environmental histories. It has been estimated that ten thousand generations separate every single one of us from the original little band of people in what is now Africa, but we look different because of the characteristics we happened to take with us when we migrated. As these small migrant populations spread, bred, and adapted to their local environments, they began to look ever more different from the relatives they left behind generations earlier and more like each other. And as small members of these groups, again, left for new territory, they would become slightly genetically different again because of a serial founder effect.

Saini (2019, p. 70)

Similarly, anthropological research found that human differences lay in language and culture, not biology, and many academics had to concede that race was not an accurate or reliable way to think about human variation. The world's most noted scientists, in the fields of biology, genetics, psychology, sociology, and anthropology, with international diplomats and lawmakers, attended the 1949 United Nations Educational, Scientific and Cultural Organization (UNESCO) meeting in Paris to redefine race based on the scientific evidence. UNESCO released its first statement on race in 1950, drafted by eight experts from New Zealand, Mexico, Brazil, India, France, the USA, and the UK, and incorporated comments from a further 12 global experts, underlining that fundamental differences between so-called races did not exist:

Scientists have reached general agreement in recognizing that mankind is one: that all men belong to the same species, Homo sapiens . . . [the] genes responsible for the hereditary differences between men are always few when compared to the whole genetic constitution of man and to the vast number of genes common to all human beings regardless of the population to which they belong. This means that the likenesses among men are far greater than their differences.

(Beaglehole *et al.*, 1950, p. 8)

Stripped of genetic validity, race can be understood as a set of socially constructed categories which specifies how individuals should be grouped and identified, categories that change over time and place. In the USA, for example, the 'one-drop' rule was a social and legal principle that classified individuals with any African ancestry as 'Black' or 'Negro'. By way of contrast, in Brazil, there is an additional racial category of 'Brown' or '*Mestizo*' that sits between White and Black, the equivalent of what in the UK is often referred to as 'mixed race'.

It is important not get too bogged down by the sometimes complex, but often emotive, discussions about race with regards to human differences based on biology or genetics.

A key take-away from this chapter is that the concept of race is based upon European race-science thinking of the 17th–19th centuries, which purports that non-White people are inferior to White Europeans. Although these theories have since been discredited by scientists in the 20th century, commonly held stereotyped assumptions rooted in race-science thinking about indigenous, Black, and Asian people continue to exist up to the present day and are the reason why non-White groups experience racism.

Racism, ethnicity, and intersectionality

'Race', if defined as genetic difference between people (of which there are few differences), then, holds little use for credible scientists. Yet the idea of grouping people in this way has come to appear quite obvious or 'natural' because it is based on superficial physical characteristics, as a result of which society treats individuals as belonging to a particular racial group and individuals regularly identify and understand themselves this way. The hundreds of years of White Euro-American political and economic domination over the global majority is a fundamental reason why false ideas about race difference still exert such a powerful influence in the world today. The general population in many countries continue to believe that particular psychological and moral characteristics are associated with physiological ones, which can lead to acts of racial prejudice and racial discrimination – or what is commonly referred to as racism. For example, longstanding and common negative stereotypes held by White Australians about Indigenous Australians include that they are 'primitive', 'drunks', 'violent', and 'lazy'. To this end, researchers at the Australian University (ANU) ana-lysed the implicit (or unconscious) bias of more than 11,000 Australian participants over a ten-year period and found that 75% of them held a negative implicit bias against Indigenous Australians. According to the ANU researchers, this implicit neg-ative bias against Indigenous Australians is more than likely the cause of the racism they experience (Shirodkar, 2019).

While *prejudice* refers to *negative attitudes and ideas* held about an individual or group of people based solely on their membership of that group, *discrimination* refers to *negative actions or behaviour* towards an individual or group of people. We can place racism within individual and institutional contexts: an example of individual racism might be a child making racist/offensive comments to another child in the school playground, whilst institutional racism be seen where schools (via teachers' actions) are disproportionately excluding large numbers of Black pupils. Additionally, structural racism allows us to see how the combined interaction of multiple institu-tions – via their ideologies, cultural practices, and discriminatory processes – results in racial inequities across health, education, housing, criminal justice, and employment.

In light of the controversy surrounding the concept of race, ethnicity has become a more acceptable way of describing difference. Importantly, it understands human difference as being socially constructed through culture and tradition. While different physical characteristics, including skin colour, may distinguish ethnic groups, the soci-ologist Anthony Giddens says that 'the most usual ones are language, history or ancestry (real or imagined), religion and styles of dress or adornment' (Giddens, 2009, p. 633). Ethnicity might also encompass such things as diet, religious beliefs, tradi-tions, rituals, and ceremonies, providing a sense of belonging and history across generations.

The significance of ethnicity may vary for different people, however, and become more or less salient at different times. The sociologist and cultural theorist Stuart Hall (1992) refers to 'New Ethnicities' to explain that people do not possess a singular or fixed identity rooted in either a cultural or biological essence. The self can identify with multiple groupings depending on the occasion. For example, an individual 'racialised' as Black can occupy a range of further identities that incorporate class, gender, sexu-ality, and ethnicity. Today, Black feminist critical scholars drawing on the work of US critical race theorist Kimberlé Crenshaw (1989) talk about 'intersectionality' (see the introductory chapter, 'Understanding children and young people's lives'). This important analytical framework highlights that because individual and group identities 'intersect', a person or group can experience multiple oppressions and disadvantages. For example, a working-class Black woman may be subject to discrimination(s) based on the overlapping identities of her 'race', gender, and social class.

Like race, ethnicity can be the focus of negative attitudes, prejudice, and discrimi-nation, and the International Convention on the Elimination of All Forms of Racial Dis-crimination (United Nations, 1965) recognises that racism exists on the basis of both race and ethnicity. Moreover, sociologists have charted the rise of a 'new racism' in Britain. Since speaking about racial difference has become less acceptable, this focuses on cultural differences as a threat to the 'British way of life', whatever we might understand that to be.

A key concern for many psychologists and sociologists has been the formation of negative racial attitudes among children and the effect on their interactions with peers, a topic discussed in the following section.

Key points

- '*Race*' refers to the claim that biological/genetic distinctions can be made between groups of people who differ in physical appearance.
- As humans share 99.9% of DNA, there is no scientific evidence to support the idea of biologically distinct races, and to this end, 'scientific racism' has been widely discredited.
- Many individuals, groups, and organisations still hold on to false beliefs that inherent moral and psychological characteristics are linked to physical appearance, such as skin colour. These beliefs can result in prejudicial and/or discriminatory actions, or '*racism*', that manifest in an individual, institutional, and/or structural context.
- *Ethnicity* has come to be a more acceptable way of describing human difference; it includes both physical and cultural distinctions between individuals. Like race, ethnicity can be the source of individual and group prejudice and discrimination.
- People do not possess a singular or fixed identity rooted in biology or any given culture; rather, the self can identify with various groupings. This is what Stuart Hall refers to as the concept 'New Ethnicities'.
- 'Intersectionality' draws on the work of Black feminist scholars like Kimberlé Crenshaw to explain how people can experience multiple oppressions and disadvantages that directly relate to their multiple intersecting identities.

Race(ism), ethnicity, and childhood

Given that childhood has been portrayed as a state of innocence, adults have often assumed that children are 'colour blind' and do not distinguish between people on the basis of race or develop racist attitudes until later in life. There is now, however, quite an established body of research to suggest that young children are far from naïve and show an awareness of issues relating to 'race' and ethnicity even from a very young age (Quintana, 2010). This research evidence comes from psychological, sociological, and criminological accounts of childhood and the youth life stage.

Psychological studies

Within psychology, there has been a long history of research into the development of children's racial attitudes. The consistent message from these studies is that young children have the capacity to recognise physical differences in such things as skin colour from about the age of 2 years and can begin to ascribe attitudes to people with these differences from about the age of 3 years (Quintana, 2010). Psychologists have shown that as children start to learn about the world, even from early childhood, they learn about race and ethnicity (and racial bias) from their parents, community, books, television, peers, social media, and wider culture (Rizzo *et al.*, 2020). They become keenly aware that race, as opposed to shoe size or height, is a category of some significance in our society and begin to attach social meaning to race as they absorb the conscious and unconscious racial prejudices that are prevalent in our society.

Psychological studies of racial bias have often involved presenting children with racial stimuli, like images or dolls with different 'racial' characteristics, and then asking questions about their preferences and evaluations of each image/doll. They might, for example, be asked which is good/bad, clean/dirty, good-looking/ugly, as well as which they look more like. Early work in this field was carried out in the USA by psychologists Kenneth Clark and Mamie Phipps Clark in the 1940s, both of whom were African American researchers. Their studies involved presenting Black children with two dolls that were identical in everything but skin and hair colour. One doll was pale with yellow hair; the other was brown with black hair. The Clarks then asked their sample of children, who were aged between 3 and 7 years and from different schools, a series of questions about the dolls. The children were asked which doll they would rather play with, which one was the nice doll, which one looked bad, which one had the nicer colour, and so on. The majority of Black children selected the White doll as the one they would rather play with and the one that was nice. The Clarks argued that their experiment provided clear evidence of 'pro-White bias' (as it is known) in their sample of children (Winkler, 2009; Jarrett, 2016).

Of particular significance for these researchers, though, was the observation that when Black children were asked to choose the doll that looked most like them, one third of them picked the White doll. From the findings of this pioneering study, there was evidence that Black children potentially suffered from low self-esteem because they were aware of and internalised negative views of their race. Psychologists have repeated this kind of study many times with children of different ethnicities in both the UK and the USA. While this 'out-group preference' (as it is known by psychologists) among Black children appears to have diminished somewhat over time, the consistent finding is that 'pro-White bias' in both White and Black children remains pronounced. Both Black and White children display a preference for White as opposed to Black skin colour, and when asked to describe the differences in skin colour of dolls, they often assign more positive characteristics to White- than Black-skinned ones (Winkler, 2009; Jarrett, 2016).

Interestingly, while psychologists have noted that this pro-White, anti-Black racial bias is evident even among young children, this tends to decline in middle childhood, particularly around the age of 7. It is thought that the immature cognitive structures of pre-schoolers make them likely to develop racial bias, as they are only able to identify physical differences before later acquiring cultural associations.

As children develop the capacity for more sophisticated reasoning about the world, they evaluate people in a more balanced way, and it is suggested that their racial atti-

Figure 9.2 Kenneth Clark conducting one of the famous doll studies in the 1940s.

tudes may lessen as they become older (Winkler, 2009). Studies that use racial stimuli to examine children's racial bias, however, have been criticised. One of the key concerns is that these methods require children to make definitive choices, which they perhaps might not ordinarily make, and there is little room to explore variations in attitude or the basis upon which decisions are made. Choosing one stimulus over another, for example, may not symbolise outright rejection of the other. Moreover, as these experiments are conducted in an artificial environment, they give us little understanding of how this bias plays out in children's everyday lives. If a child demonstrates 'White bias' in an experiment, for example, does that necessarily mean that he/she will discriminate in practice?

Sociological and criminological studies

Moving beyond psychological accounts of racial attitudes in childhood, sociological and criminological studies have examined how children and young people's racial attitudes can manifest into harmful behaviours and actions. In contrast to most psychological studies, however, this research provides a close-up examination of children and young people's cultural and social worlds by utilising ethnographic research methods, including observation, in-depth interviews, and case studies. Drawing directly on children and young people's experiences, these studies have sought to provide a deeper and more holistic understanding of the place, and impact, of racism in their everyday lives (Troyna and Hatcher, 1992; Connolly, 1998; Westwood, 1990; Webster, 1996). All of these studies were carried out in the 1990s, and it is unfortunate – due to the continuing scarcity of research on children and young people's experiences of race and racism in the UK – that I am not able to include more recent studies alongside these older texts.

There is research evidence which highlights that in addition to racist name-calling, some children and young people also engage in acts of racist violence (racist hate crime). An investigation by the National Society for the Prevention of Cruelty to Children (NSPCC, 2019) found that race hate crimes against children in the UK had reached a three-year high; in the period 2017–18, there were 10,571 recorded offences compared to 8,683 in 2015–16. Of course, the issue of racist violence amongst children and young people is part of a much wider and longstanding societal problem. Indeed, none of the various racial and ethnic groups that have settled in Britain during the last 200 years have managed to escape widespread animosity; they have been the victims of verbal abuse, physical attacks, mob violence, and murder (Panyani, 1993). The racist murder of the teenager Stephen Lawrence at a bus stop in 1993 – alongside the failed police investigation and his family's dogged fight for justice – would become one of the key watershed moments in modern British history. Of course, there have been many other young victims of racist violence whose names and personal stories have never managed to capture the British public's attention.

This section on race, ethnicity, and childhood has focused primarily on the development of racial bias among children. But it is important to note that ideas of race and ethnicity can and do have a positive impact on children and young people's lives. Ideas of race and ethnicity can provide a positive sense of belonging and pride for children as they learn to think of themselves as belonging to a particular group with a specific history and/or customs. Moreover, despite evidence of racism in children's peer relationships, some children and young people do create very positive, long-lasting inter-ethnic friendships.

In my ethnographic study *Growing Up Bad* (Gunter, 2010), I examined the role and significance of 'Road culture' on Black and White young people's post-16 transitions in an East London neighbourhood. Road culture is a Black-influenced youth subculture – which informed the young people's dress styles, speech patterns, leisure interests/activities, and musical preferences – that is largely played out in public settings: 'on Road' (streets). However, it would be incorrect to define or portray Road culture in exclusively racial/ethnic terms, as this 'Black' reading fails to recognise the participation of large numbers of White and other minority ethnic urban youth. Road culture was central to the lives of all the young people growing up in the local neighbourhood and cuts across ethnicity and gender. All of the young people would invariably spend large amounts of time 'hanging about' together within their local neighbourhood. As such Road culture, alongside a strong attachment to their 'endz' (local neighbourhood), resulted in the creation of genuine interracial friendship groups.

Key points

- Although children are often thought to be 'colour blind', there is a strong body of evidence to suggest that children as young as 3 years begin to absorb the conscious and unconscious racial prejudices that are prevalent in our society.
- Psychological studies have focused on exploring children's responses to racial stimuli, but these experiments tell us little about the place of racism in children's everyday lives.
- In-depth sociological and criminological studies focus more on children and young people's cultural worlds and reveal how racism is mobilised in their everyday encounters.
- Whilst children and young people can absorb negative attitudes about race and ethnicity, it is important to recognise that ideas about race and ethnicity can and do provide a positive sense of belonging and pride for children and young people.
- Despite evidence of racism in children and young people's peer relationships, some children and young people do create very positive, long-lasting inter-ethnic friendships.

Racism, schooling, and criminal (in)justice

To examine whether Black boys are given the same protections of childhood as their White peers, Philip Goff *et al.* (2014) undertook four experimental studies utilising laboratory and field work. This group of social psychologists found evidence that Black boys are seen as older and less innocent and that they prompt a less essential conception of childhood than do their same-age White peers. These four studies built on previous research which also shows that the strong historical link between Black people and animals (and apes specifically) may still influence the distinctive ways in which individuals dehumanise Black people. In the USA, Black children are found to be 18 times more likely than White children to receive a prison sentence and due to the near-universal protection ordinarily reserved for children in the West, Goff *et al.* maintain that it is this process of dehumanization which explains why Black children are particularly susceptible in being treated as adults. Similarly, in a survey study, Rebecca Epstein, Jamilia Blake, and Thalia González (2017) provide evidence demonstrating that adults are more likely to view Black girls, between the ages of 5 and 14 years, as more adult-like and less innocent than their White peers. Viewed within the broader context of disparities and negative outcomes in US public education and juvenile justice systems, the study findings suggest that the perception of Black girls as less innocent is a potential contributing factor to receiving harsher punishment in schools and juvenile justice settings.

There has also been a longstanding discussion about the disproportionate punitive treatment of Black children and young people in the UK education and criminal justice systems. As early as 1971, Grenadian politician Bernard Coard published a scathing attack on the British educational system, highlighting a trend of placing Black children in schools for the 'educationally subnormal' (as they were called at the time). Coard (1971, p. 28) described how Black children were made to feel 'inferior in every way' in school and how prejudice and patronising attitudes were widespread among teachers. While Black children were told at school that their language was second rate, the teaching resources depicted all the greats of history as being White. Teachers' expectations of Black children were also found to be low, which also impacted on their sense of their own ability to achieve. Coard's ground-breaking research was very influential in the UK, and it kick-started many of the educational multicultural and anti-racist educational policies of the 1970s and 1980s. Findings from observational studies have also supported Coard's arguments, with many researchers arguing that Black and White pupils are treated differently in schools (Gillborn, 2008). All of the Black young people in my study (Gunter, 2010) talked about the ongoing conflict between themselves and their White teachers, resulting in many of them being excluded from school and/or underperforming academically. These studies suggest that Black students typically experience greater amounts of criticism and conflict in their relationships with teachers than their White peers.

Even outside the school environment, Black British youth have had to contend with the effects of structural racism. In particular, during the past five decades, they have found their activities and behaviours on the streets scrutinised and violently targeted by the police, resulting in longstanding racial disparities in the use of stop and search by police.

Stop and search and Black youth

I carried out a five-year ethnographic study examining youth crime prevention practice and policing in one East London borough (Gunter, 2017, pp. 157–158). In addition to direct observations, the study comprised in-depth biographical interviews with 66 young adults aged 14–24, as well as interviews with 34 practitioners and key stakeholders – including police officers, youth workers, housing officers, local residents, and parents.

In the study, I recount how there were a number of incidents and occasions where I observed police offices harassing countless numbers of Black young men – even threatening myself and other concerned adults who attempted to intervene. Often, they would publicly humiliate their young victims by making them take off their socks, footwear, and any outer clothes garments; throw them forcibly up against walls; make racist comments; and insult their mothers. Unfortunately, it was such an everyday occurrence that many Black young people in the two neighbourhoods viewed it to be 'normal', as two interviewees, Jamal and T-jay, describe:

JAMAL: To be honest like, I get stopped on a regular when it first happened I was like angry and that because they can get rude and a bit hyper. They try to intimidate you and get a reaction and all the good cop bad cop s**t, and when you are younger it like kinda works. But now, after a while I just got used to it, like I thought it was normal . . . You know to be true like, I been stopped too many times, I can't really remember how many but definitely too many (Black male, 16).

T-JAY: [laughs] yeah. . . . one day I think I was stopped about seven times (Black male, 17).

INT: Why, did they give you a justifiable reason?

T-JAY: Apparently, I fit the description of someone that robbed a gang. Well, I'm not robbing a gang. And, what was the other one? The other one was because I was riding a bike, er, I was doing a wheelie round the park, they said it was reckless riding, but really, I'm not on the road so I'm allowed to do that, they just kept stopping me as well.

INT: This was all in one day?

T-JAY: One, yeah.

INT: And other than that, have you been stopped and searched as well?

T-JAY: Oh yeah, there's been like a month where I have, like every day I go out, I get stopped and searched.

INT: So it's a regular occasion for you.

T-JAY: Yeah.

Whilst the use of stop and search fell by 75% between 2010–11 and 2016–17, Black people were still found to have been stopped and searched nearly nine times more often than White people, whereas Asian people were three times more likely to be stop-searched than Whites (Shiner *et al.*, 2018). The ethnic penalties arising through stop and search and other police actions continue on through to prosecution, conviction, and sentencing. Between 2006 and 2016, the proportion of young people aged 18 and under in prison who were Black, Asian, and minority ethnic rose from 25% to just over 40% (Lammy, 2017). As of May 2020, 51.9% of the youth custodial population were from a Black, Asian, and minority ethnic background: 29% Black, 11.7% mixed, and 11.2% Asian and other (HM Government, 2020). The general 10–17-year-old population is 4% Black, 4% mixed, 10% Asian and other, and 82% White.

Key points

- Research by social psychologists in the US has found evidence that Black boys and girls are viewed as more adult-like and less innocent than their same-age White peers.

- The adultification of Black children is a potential contributing factor as to why they receive harsher punishment in schools and juvenile justice settings.
- In the UK, there has been a longstanding concern about the disproportionate punitive treatment of Black children and young people in the education and criminal justice systems.
- Studies examining racism in schools suggest that Black British students typically experience greater amounts of criticism and conflict in their relationships with teachers than their White peers.
- During the past five decades, Black British youth have found their activities and behaviours on the streets scrutinised and violently targeted by the police, resulting in longstanding racial disparities in the use of stop and search by police.

Conclusion

This chapter began by exploring the concepts of race, ethnicity, and racism and their place in contemporary society. While the idea of biologically distinct races has been discredited, race still remains a pervasive concept in society and can lead to acts of racism. In the light of the controversy surrounding race, it is suggested that the concept of ethnicity has become a more acceptable way of describing human difference. Psychological and sociological studies of children and young people's racial attitudes have revealed that they are susceptible to the racist attitudes prevalent in society and use these as powerful tools in their peer-to-peer relationships. While we may often think that matters of race and racism are far removed from the lives of children, this chapter illustrates that children have a sophisticated understanding of race and racism. These issues are central to, and have a real impact on, the lives of both children and young people. Lastly, we discussed the adultification of Black children and it being a potential contributing factor as to why they receive harsher punishments in schools and criminal justice settings in comparison to their same-age White peers.

References

Beaglehole, E., Comas, J., Costa-Pinto, L. A., Frazier, F., Ginsberg, M., Kabir, H., Levi-Strauss, C., and Montagu, A. (1950) 'The scientific basis for human unity', *UNESCO Courier*. Available at: https://unesdoc.unesco.org/ark:/48223/pf0000081475.nameddest=81490 (Accessed 26th October 2022).
Bhopal, R. (2007) 'The beautiful skull and Blumenbach's errors: the birth of the scientific concept of race', *BMJ*, 335(1308).
Coard, B. (1971) *How the West Indian Child is Made to Feel Educationally Subnormal in the British School System*. London: New Beacon Books.
Connolly, P. (1998) *Racism, Gender Identities and Young Children*. London: Routledge.
Cornell, S., and Hartmann, D. (1998) *Ethnicity and Race: Making Identities in a Changing World*. London: Pine Forge Press.
Crenshaw, K. (1989) *Demarginalizing the Intersection of Race and Sex: A Black Feminist Critique of Antidiscrimination Doctrine, Feminist Theory and Antiracist Politics*. University of Chicago Legal Forum (Vol. 1989), article 8. Available at: http://chicagounbound.uchicago.edu/uclf/vol1989/iss1/8.
Epstein, R., Blake, J., and González, T. (2017) *Girlhood Interrupted: The Erasure of Black Girls' Childhood (June 27, 2017)*. Available at SSRN: https://ssrn.com/abstract=3000695 or [online] doi:10.2139/ssrn.3000695.

Fryer, P. (1984) *Staying Power: The History of Black People in Britain*. London: Pluto Press.

Giddens, A. (2009) *Sociology*. London: Polity Press.

Gillborn, D. (2008) *Racism and Education: Coincidence or Conspiracy?* Abingdon: Routledge.

Goff, P., Culotta, C., DiTomasso, N., Jackson, M., and Di Leone, B. (2014) 'The essence of inno-cence: consequences of dehumanizing Black children', *Journal of Personality and Social Psychology*, 106(4), pp. 526–545.

Guibernau, M., and Rex, J. (1997) *The Ethnicity Reader: Nationalism, Multiculturalism and Migration*. Cambridge: Polity Press.

Gunter, A. (2010) *Growing up Bad: Black Youth, Road Culture and Badness in an East London Neigh-bourhood*. London: The Tufnell Press.

Gunter, A. (2017) *Race, Gangs and Youth Violence: Policy, Prevention and Policing*. Bristol: Policy Press.

Hall, S. (1992) 'New ethnicities', in J. Donald and A. Rattansi (eds.) *Race, Culture and Difference*. London: Sage Publications and Open University.

HM Government, UK Parliament. (2020) *Children and Young People in Custody* (Part 1). Available at: https://publications.parliament.uk/pa/cm5801/cmselect/cmjust/306/30609.htm (Accessed 21st October 2022).

Jarrett, O. (2016) 'Doll studies as racial assessments: A historical look at racial attitudes and school desegregation', in M. M. Patte and J. A. Sutterby (eds.) *Celebrating 40 Years of Play Research: Connecting Our Past, Present, and Future*. New York: Hamilton Books, pp. 19–37.

Lammy, D. (2017) *The Lammy Review: An Independent Review into the Treatment of, and Outcomes for, Black, Asian and Minority Ethnic Individuals in the Criminal Justice System.* London: Lammy Review. Available at: https://assets.publishing.service.gov.uk/government/uploads/system/uploads/attachment_data/file/643001/ (Accessed 21st October 2022).

Nelson, R. (2019) 'Racism in science: the taint that lingers', *Nature*, 570, pp. 440–441.

NSPCC (2019) *Talking to Children about Racism*. Available at: www.nspcc.org.uk/keeping-children-safe/support-for-parents/children-race-racism-racial-bullying/ (Accessed 21st October 2022).

Panyani, P. (1993) *Racial Violence in Britain, 1840–1950*. Leicester: University of Leicester Press.

Quintana, S. M. (2010) 'Ethnicity, race and children's social development', in P. K. Smith and C. H. Hart (eds.) *The Wiley-Blackwell Handbook of Childhood Social Development* (2nd ed.). Oxford: Wiley Blackwell, pp. 231–239.

Richards, G. (1997) *Race, Racism and Psychology: Towards a Reflexive History*. London: Routledge.

Rizzo, M., Green, E., Dunham, Y., Bruneau, E., and Rhodes, M. (2020) 'Beliefs about social norms and racial inequalities predict variation in the early development of racial bias', *Developmental Science*, 25(2), e13170.

Saini, A. (2019) *Superior: The Return of Race Science*. London: HarperCollins.

Shiner, M., CaRre, Z., Delsol, R. *et al.* (2018) *The Colour of Injustice: 'Race', Drugs and Law Enforce-ment in England and Wales Stop Watch*. London, Stop Watch. Available at: www.stop-watch.org/what-we-do/research/the-colour-of-injustice-race-drugs-and-law-enforcement-in-england-and-wales/ (Accessed 26th October 2022).

Shirodkar, S. (2019) 'Bias against indigenous Australians: implicit association test results for Australia', *Journal of Australian Indigenous Issues*, 22(3–4), pp. 3–34. https://search.informit.org/doi/10.3316/informit.150032703197478.

Troyna, B., and Hatcher, R. (1992) *Racism in Children's Lives: A Study of Mainly-white Primary Schools*. London: Routledge.

United Nations (1965) *International Convention on the Elimination of All Forms of Racial Discrimina-tion*, UN General Assembly resolution 2106 (XX). Available at: www.ohchr.org/en/instruments-mechanisms/instruments/international-convention-elimination-all-forms-racial (Accessed 21st October 2022).

Webster, C. (1996) 'Local heroes: violent racism, localism and spacism among Asian and white young people', *Youth and Policy*, 53, pp. 15–27.

Westwood, S. (1990) 'Racism, Black masculinity and the politics of space', in J. Hearn and D. Morgan (eds.) *Men, Masculinities and Social Theory*. London: Unwin Hyman.

Winkler, E. N. (2009) 'Children are not colorblind: how young children learn race', *PACE: Practical Approaches for Continuing Education*, 3(3), pp. 1–8.

10 Global childhoods

Afua Twum-Danso Imoh and Heather Montgomery

The origins of a global childhood

In the 21st century, a particular conception of childhood has become almost universal across diverse societies around the world. This conception – which has become seen as the gold standard of childhood – places an emphasis on childhood as a phase of life characterised by innocence, protection, dependency, inexperience, and immaturity (both physical and mental), in which children require shielding from the vices of the adult world, including being protected from exposure to issues relating to sex, gambling, drugs, alcohol, and also from work. The world of children has become characterised by activities relating to learning, especially that which takes place in schools (as you learned in Chapter 7), and work and responsibility (of any kind) have been substituted with play. Crucially, childhood has become separated from the adult world as a time of precious, if precarious, difference. It has also become defined by age so that, for most people, childhood refers to all those below the age of 18.

> **The global North and the global South**
>
> Throughout the chapter, the term 'global North' is used as a shorthand for the industrialised countries of Europe, North America, and Australia/New Zealand, and the 'global South' is used to describe newly industrialising countries elsewhere, especially the poorer ones in Africa and Asia. This is a crude distinction, and there are large variations and inequalities within and between these societies; however, it is used here for convenience and clarity.

Yet as Chapter 1 and other chapters in this Reader have shown, ideas of childhood are social constructions which have changed considerably over time as well as place. This chapter will examine how this modern concept of childhood came into being. It will trace its roots in the political and economic developments that took place in Europe from the 17th century onwards and will look at how it has since been exported, and even sometimes imposed, on countries outside the West (Cunningham, 2020).

The origins of these contemporary ideas around childhood are disputed by historians, but almost all acknowledge the importance of the ideas promoted and discussed by the philosophers of the European Enlightenment (Heywood, 2017). The Enlightenment refers to the intellectual and philosophical movement that swept across Europe in the 17th and 18th centuries which formulated new ideas about the nature of humans and society and promoted ideals such as liberty, toleration, rights, and happiness. The work of French philosopher Jean-Jacques Rousseau (1712–1778) has been especially influential, and it was Rousseau who arguably pioneered the ideology of

DOI: 10.4324/9781003358855-11

childhood as a protected, separate, and innocent time of life, on which the modern Western conception of childhood is based (Cunningham, 2020).

Rousseau's *Emile*

In 1762, Rousseau published his landmark novel, *Emile, or On Education*, in which he argued that children were born innocent but were corrupted by adults. In the arresting opening sentence, he wrote: 'God makes all things good; man meddles with them and they become evil' (1966/1762, p. 5). In *Emile*, Rousseau argued that childhood and adulthood were fundamentally different and that they should be kept separate. Childhood, in his belief, was a special, innocent, and, in many ways, better time of life than adulthood which adults should cherish and protect:

> Love childhood, indulge its sports, its pleasures, its delightful instincts. Who has not sometimes regretted that age when laughter was ever on our lips, and when the heart was ever at peace? Why rob these innocents of the joys which pass so quickly, of that precious gift which they cannot abuse?
>
> (Rousseau, 1966/1762, p. 43)

Children (and unusually, he discussed girls as well as boys), he argued, should be allowed to develop at their own rate in natural surroundings, where their goodness could be isolated from the artificiality and misery of the adult world. They should not be forced into school or formal learning and, until the age of 12, should exist in a state of idyllic innocence when they should be free and happy with 'nothing [to do except] to run and jump all day' (1966/1762, p. 71). 'Leave childhood to ripen in your children' (1966/1762, p. 58), he exhorted.

Emile had a great impact on societal attitudes towards children across Western Europe, and Rousseau is often seen as one of the first to call attention to the needs of children and to argue that childhood was a worthy subject of study, interesting in themselves, not just for what they would become in the future.

The separation of the worlds of children and adults became increasingly evident in schools in Europe and North America in the 18th and 19th centuries where middle- and upper-class boys (girls were rarely educated outside the domestic realm) were grouped together by age and moved from class to class according to their age. Life in schools centred on discipline and conformity and turning children into the right sort of adults, the focus being on the end product, not on the child himself. Yet childhood was still seen as something separate and in need of protection, and increasingly, children began to wear different clothes from adults, literature was censored to ensure that 'innocent' children were not exposed to inappropriate content, and gambling and alcohol were banned in schools as unsuitable pastimes for children (Plumb, 1972). In Medieval Europe, games such as hide-and-seek would be played by anyone, regardless of age,

Figure 10.1 An 18th-century classroom where only the wealthier boys were educated.

but by the 19th century, the child's world of irresponsible play was firmly set against the adult's world of responsibility and work (Cunningham, 2020; Heywood, 2017).

Due to the exclusion of girls and working-class boys from schools, those most affected by these new constructions of childhood in Europe were upper-class boys who were in education (Fletcher, 2008). Once this conception of childhood had been established for elite boys, middle-class reformers began to turn their attention to girls and working-class boys and, by the middle of the 19th century, a 'good' childhood was widely seen as one where children were separated from adults, where their correct place was in the home or school, where their innocence was protected, and where they were sheltered from the harsh realities of adult life. The 1870 Education Act, which represented the beginning of compulsory mass schooling in England (also discussed in Chapter 7), was based on a particular vision of childhood which was to be imposed on all children regardless of their social background. They were expected to learn, through school-based education, their place in society and to strive to grow up to be citizens who accepted, unquestioningly, their social roles. The ideal childhood was seen as a universal one: children were to be protected by adults but also controlled by them (Hendrick, 1997).

Key points

•   The modern concept of childhood emerged as a result of the political and economic developments in Western Europe from the 17th century.

- Childhood became characterised as a time of innocence, immaturity (physical and mental), dependency, and inexperience, when children must be kept separate from the adult world.

How contemporary childhoods became globalised

Today, the conception of childhood as a separate, protected, and precious space can be found in many societies which historically had different understandings of what childhood means and how it is defined. This is the result of several factors, both historical and contemporary, which this section will explore.

Historically, the most notable to highlight is the role of Christian evangelisation through the activities of missionary groups from the 15th century onwards. While each missionary group adopted different approaches based on their denomination, all left Europe with the explicit goal of transmitting 'proper', or 'civilised', ideas about family life, marriage, and child-rearing to what they considered to be primitive peoples who were some shade of black or brown. One key strategy adopted by many missionary groups was schooling, due to their belief that focusing their conversion strategies on the young in the community was an effective way of having an impact in the long term on a society. Thus, the institution of the school was used to impart, systematically, 'proper' values to children and to construct a certain kind of childhood in 'far-flung' places (Twum-Danso Imoh, 2020).

In the process of 'civilising' the indigenous people they encountered in various locales, missionaries also sought to counter what they viewed as the negative influence of the families and cultures of children they were converting. In some contexts, boarding schools were adopted as the most effective method of delivering formal education as well as 'proper' values to children, as they provided an environment which ensured the transmission and consolidation of the missionaries' ideas and values. They also ensured that children were cut off from the daily cultural life of their families and were influenced by the missionaries rather than the community elders. Children attending these schools were taught to perceive their culture and families as inferior, ultimately leading, in some contexts, to tensions and conflicts between generations (see, for example, Ncube, 1998; Balagopalan, 2014; Twum-Danso Imoh, 2020; Wells, 2021).

These missionary endeavours often preceded the formal colonisation of many countries in Asia and Africa by a small group of European countries, including Britain, during the 18th and 19th centuries. This colonisation not only constituted a political and economic conquest of the lands of subjugated peoples but also formalised many of the missionaries' ideals through the imposition of laws which aimed to eliminate undesirable 'primitive' practices and also to ensure that 'native' children grew up to know their place in the social hierarchy, enforcing their inferiority and backwardness in comparison to their colonisers and supposed 'civilisers'.

What is globalisation?

While today, direct colonial rule may have disappeared, its legacies in terms of laws, ideologies, unequal trading relationships, and inter-ethnic conflicts live on and

Figure 10.2 A British missionary, Mrs. Stannard, with a group of boys in the Congo, taken some-time between 1900 and 1915. Note that once the children become older, they are expected to be Christians and wear 'civilised' clothes.

What is globalisation?

The term globalisation suggests a move towards the worldwide integration of eco-nomic, financial, trade, and communica-tion systems. It also implies the increasing similarity of politics and social values, particularly those based on a democratic model dominant within the global North. In some respects, globalisation has brought benefits to children's lives, particularly through the many international initiatives and attempts to invest in children's devel-opment and alleviate poverty, although there have also been unintended and neg-ative consequences.

continue to inform children's daily lives and experiences. Unequal power rela-tions between countries and the eco-nomic and political dominance of the global North continue to impact chil-dren's lives, and while contemporary forms of globalisation may bring bene-fits to some, they are experienced by others as a new form of colonialism (Naftali, 2014; Balagopalan, 2014; Twum-Danso Imoh, 2019). Although glo-balisation is not a new concept or process, the late 20th century witnessed a significant intensification of global processes largely driven by the develop-ment of new technologies that facilitated closer interactions and connections between different parts of the world. This not only related to the flows of goods and capital but also of people, ideas, international legislation, and social policy. All of these have implications for understandings of childhood in diverse parts of the world (Stephens, 1995).

The United Nations Convention on the Rights of the Child

International children's welfare legislation is often presented as a positive feature of globalisation, with talk of an 'international community' caring for the world's children. This is most evident in discussions of children's rights which, while first discussed in the 19th century, gathered momentum during the 20th century through a series of international declarations and other initiatives and culminated in the adoption of the Convention on the Rights of the Child (UNCRC) by the UN General Assembly on 30th November 1989. This child-focused international treaty, which took ten years to draft, covers a wide range of civil, political, economic, social, and cultural rights and is based on the underlying principles of non-discrimination, participation, survival, and development and the best interests of the child (this was explored in Chapter 1). Upon the adoption of the UNCRC, the governments of many countries were quick to ratify it, with Ghana the very first to do so in February 1990. In under a year, the required 20 states had ratified the UNCRC, thus bringing it into force by September 1990 (de Waal, 2002). Significantly, however, the USA has signed but refused to ratify, arguing that it interferes with the rights of individual states to set their own laws and that parents are the best guardians of children's rights. While many commentators have taken such rapid and widespread ratification as a sign of a universalisation in understandings between governments about what childhood is and how children should be treated, the politics underpinning this process need to be considered. De Waal (2002) has suggested that some governments of countries in sub-Saharan Africa ratified the UNCRC in expectation of reward in terms of more aid from Western governments. Thus, while the UNCRC represents an achievement, the number of countries that have ratified it and its rapid rate of ratification should not be automatically seen as representing a consensus in attitudes towards children by the world's governments. Indeed, there is much reservation around the UNCRC among many countries in the global South, who feel it is insensitive to their needs and traditional values and local childhood experiences, as will be discussed later.

In the years since its adoption, the UNCRC's impact has been wide reaching in numerous respects – certainly at the level of law and policy. As Stahl (2007, p. 805) argues, 'the UNCRC has influenced the world, both in how societies regard children and in how they react to children as people'. International organisations, particularly the UN children's agency, UNICEF, have played a significant role in promoting the UNCRC and encouraging others to adhere to its standards and have drawn on its provisions to inform their strategies and programmes. This support cannot only be seen at the level of the international community but also in national contexts. For instance, as ratification requires governments to ensure that their national laws are in line with the UNCRC's standards, many governments have reviewed their child-focused laws and amended them accordingly. Furthermore, local actors – either as individuals or as collectives, including children and young people themselves – have called for action that would facilitate the UNCRC's standards within their contexts (Twum-Danso Imoh, 2019).

It is important to note, however, that the UNCRC's understandings of childhood are not neutral or value-free but are an outcome of the evolution of the modern conception of childhood that emerged in Western Europe from the 17th century onwards, as discussed earlier. This is apparent in numerous places throughout, especially in the preamble (the opening section) which includes the following statements in paragraphs 7 and 8:

> Considering that the child should be fully prepared to live an individual life in society, and brought up in the spirit of the ideals proclaimed in the Charter of the United Nations, and in particular in the spirit of peace, dignity, tolerance, freedom, equality and solidarity.
>
> (UN, 1989, para 7)

> Bearing in mind that, as indicated in the Declaration of the Rights of the Child, 'the child, by reason of his physical and mental immaturity, needs special safeguards and care, including appropriate legal protection, before as well as after birth'.
>
> (UN, 1989, para 8)

The image of childhood in parts of the preamble clearly indicate the extent to which the individual – as opposed to the family or wider community – is seen as the key unit of the society. This emphasis on the individual child is very much linked to developments that took place in Europe during the Enlightenment and, as the next section will argue, does not always hold true in other places where the key unit of society is seen as the family or a wider collective.

Key points

- The conception of childhood that emerged in Western Europe from the 17th century can now be identified in diverse contexts, including in the global South.
- This concept 'travelled' to other contexts due to historical and contemporary factors, including the activities of missionary groups, colonial rule of much of the South by a small group of Western European countries, and the intensification of globalisation processes.
- A key component of global processes that had an impact on exporting this conception of childhood was international social policy, especially the United Nations Convention on the Rights of the Child (UNCRC).

Different contexts, different childhoods

It is important to note that although the conception of childhood that emerged in Western Europe and North America can now be identified in other parts of the world, including in the global South, its spread has not been evenly felt across regions or

Figure 10.3 Children in Ghana collecting water as part of their daily chores.

even countries. Numerous laws are now in line with the UNCRC and often have strong support from social elites, but not everyone within a continent, country, city, town, or village supports this notion of childhood, including the idea of a fixed chronological age to define the end of childhood.

In sub-Saharan Africa, for example, much of the evidence shows that becoming an adult in many societies is based on factors other than chronological age. Historically, boys determined their transition to adulthood through economic independence, the ability to look after oneself and others, and having their own house or land, while for girls, it was marriage and/or becoming a mother that signified their transition to adulthood. The key attribute for both boys and girls was the acquisition of a dependant (for boys, through marriage; for girls, through motherhood). Such transitions exist not just historically but also remain very evident in numerous contexts in the region. Mozambican anthropologist Alcinda Honwana (2012), for example, has developed the concept of 'waithood' to describe the situation of young people who are recognised as adults by law yet have not attained the markers required in the contexts in which they live their everyday lives to become fully recognised by their communities as adults (transitions to adulthood will be discussed further in Chapter 14). This persistence of cultural notions about when childhood ends is also seen in some communities in Ethiopia where motherhood remains a key indicator for the attainment of womanhood and, hence, full adult status (Tafare and

Chuta, 2020). Even today, a boy of 14 can be recognised as an adult, as he has achieved the social markers set for the attainment of adulthood, while a man of 40 may be denied this very recognition because he has not (de Waal, 2002; Honwana, 2012).

While marriage (and motherhood for girls) is the principal requirement for the recognition of an individual's full adult status, it is also important to consider that even before these life events occur, child-rearing and socialisation are geared towards preparing children for the role they will eventually play once they achieve adult status. In fact, children's undertaking of responsibilities, both within and outside the home, is a form of learning, based on consideration of their competence and their gender, that is seen to provide them with important life skills vital for their everyday lives as adults. Generally, therefore, while many children in the global North are often separated from adults through schools where their education is future oriented, in other societies, significant numbers of children learn alongside parents and are gradually included in adult endeavours until they become competent to take on full roles in adult society.

Children's learning in the Niger Delta of Nigeria

In partnership with an NGO called Safe Child Africa, I undertook research in the Niger Delta of Nigeria in 2012 on the continuing importance placed on children's work as part of training and as part of reciprocal arrangements in families. I found that children were expected to support adults' endeavours, and a crucial part of this is to undertake what are considered to be light domestic tasks. This norm and expectation was evident in the accounts of both adult and child research participants in the study. In the adult focus group discussions, it was stressed that such contributions by children are highly valued and partly inform attitudes to children. One adult told me:

> It is very much valued in our community, it is in practice, and they help us to do the farm work. I have seen children clean village streets where parents do not have a chance to do so. Those who do not do it are classified as bad or lazy children and nobody likes them.

The children, who had themselves come to recognise these chores as part of their duties, also suggested that they were quite happy to perform them as long as these tasks were not overly taxing. Mary, aged 10, told me: 'the roadside is for the older ones; that is why I like it when they ask me to go and fetch the water'.

Indeed, when they were asked to take pictures to show the things that make them happy in their society, many of the children, such as 10-year-old Nse, came back with images which featured them sweeping, cooking, cleaning, and performing other household chores. When I asked Nse about which pictures made him happy, he pointed to a picture of himself sweeping and said: 'This one makes me happy . . . this is how I'm sweeping and this one makes me happy because this is the job, they give to me. I like this job . . . this job is not too hard for me'.

The research showed that the children cook for their families, do the laundry, take care of their siblings, and clean the church, school compound, and over-grown communal pathways and that such activities are integral to what it means to be a child in this context (Twum-Danso Imoh, Okyere and Secker, 2012; Twum-Danso Imoh and Okyere, 2020).

The 'chore curriculum'

The work that children are expected to undertake as part of the socialisation process in diverse African contexts is carefully thought out. Both Nse and Mary talked about their satisfaction with the chores allocated to them because they were in line with what they were capable of undertaking effectively. Chores are constantly monitored by family members who gradually increase their responsibility as children prove their competence in a particular skill or task until it is clear they are able to engage in tasks normally reserved for adults. From the perspective of development psychology (see the next section), Bame Nsamenang (2004) claims that there are ways parents or caregivers in the broader West African context are able to judge a child's ability to undertake certain chores at different developmental stages. Serpell (1993), writing specifically of Zambia, supports this by arguing that adults keep a mental tally of the proportion of errands that a given child performs adequately, and this serves as an index of how mature the child is. These skills form the basis of what anthropologist David Lancy (2012) calls 'the chore curriculum', a term he uses to demonstrate that children's work within families involves careful thinking and close monitoring to ensure that the responsibilities allocated to children are always commensurate with their abilities, enabling them to become self-sufficient and effective contributors to the domestic economy.

This linkage between children undertaking tasks and the gradual maturation process is key to understanding the importance of children having duties or responsibilities in contexts across the continent. These duties, which primarily centre around work, either within or outside of the house as part of a broader family enterprise, are seen as an important part of preparing children for their roles as adult men or women and providing adults the opportunity to monitor their progress and make judgements about their maturity. Thus, the way families use children's household work to assess maturity and competence further illustrates approaches other than chronological age which determine transitions through different phases of childhood.

Despite all this, however, Article 1 of the UNCRC states categorically the following:

For the purposes of the present Convention, a child means every human being below the age of eighteen years unless under the law applicable to the child, majority is attained earlier.

(UN, 1989)

Although this definition provides space for governments to set the age of majority at a younger age, the age of 18 has, in effect, become the fixed age to define the boundary between childhood and adulthood in laws and policies not only in countries in North America and Western Europe but also more globally. For example, in trying to bring their child-focused laws in line with the UNCRC's standards in the years following their ratification of the treaty, most countries included the definition of childhood as ending at 18 as opposed to other markers mentioned previously.

The African Charter on the Rights and the Welfare of the Child

This alignment in definitions of the age of majority can be further seen in the regional laws relating to childhood that exist. The most notable of these, perhaps, is the African Charter on the Rights and Welfare of the Child which was drafted with the specific aim of foregrounding 'African civilisation' and:

> the virtues of their cultural heritage, historical background and the values of the African civilization which should inspire and characterize their reflection on the concept of the rights and welfare of the child.
>
> (preamble, OAU, 1990, para 6)

Despite this plea for context and cultural relevance, however, the definition of childhood used by the Charter is similar, and arguably more rigid, than the Convention, as it leaves no room for manoeuvre by governments. Article 2 stipulates that 'a child means every human being below the age of 18 years' (OAU, 1990). The question that arises from this is: why would a treaty that seeks to consider 'African civilisation' define the ending of childhood with an arbitrary chronological age as the cutoff point, when this is at odds with historical understandings of childhood in many African societies? The answer may be that while the Charter referred to Africa as a single entity sharing a single civilisation (a rather simplistic notion), it also recognised prevailing conditions across the continent at the time of the drafting and adoption of the Charter and their impact on many African children. Specifically, beyond a desire to foreground the culture and historical traditions in the regional instrument, it also sought to address the specific contexts and challenges faced by contemporary African states. The third paragraph of the preamble sets forth some of these issues:

> Noting with concern that the situation of most African children, remains critical due to the unique factors of their socio-economic, cultural, traditional, and developmental circumstances, natural disasters, armed conflicts, exploitation, and hunger, and on account of the child's physical and mental immaturity he/ she needs special safeguards and care.
>
> (OAU, 1990, para 3)

Hence, the circumstances facing many African countries at the time were critical to informing the drafting of the Charter. During the 1980s, many African countries witnessed severe economic decline, which, in turn, led to food insecurity. There was also political instability which, in some contexts, resulted in civil wars in which children bore the brunt as victims as well as perpetrators. By the end of the 1980s, the impacts of the global epidemic of HIV/AIDS had specific and severe implications for children not only through infections but also in terms of loss of care due to the death of parents or caregivers. Thus, given the context facing young people in Africa at the time, the Organisation of African Unity (OAU, now known as the African Union), an organisation founded on principles of African Unity and Pan-Africanism, adopted a Charter which defined childhood in more rigid terms than that stipulated in the UNCRC, even though the UNCRC is widely accepted as a document that is firmly embedded in Western cultural and political traditions (Twum-Danso-Imoh, 2020).

This flow globally of a fixed age of majority centred around the age of 18 is an indication of how ideas about childhood have 'travelled' around the world and become globalised. As a result, these ideas are now frequently used in everyday discussions about what it means to become an adult in different parts of the world. Furthermore, as a result of the UNCRC, those under the age of 18 are now categorised in a range of countries as being in a special and precarious phase of life which needs protection and care if complete and responsible adulthood is to be achieved.

Key points

- Global conceptions of childhood co-exist with other conceptions, in contexts which historically had their own understandings of childhood.
- Marriage and parenthood continue to be key markers of the distinctions between adulthood and childhood in sub-Saharan Africa and elsewhere.
- The responsibilities children are assigned as part of the socialisation process show how communities use ways other than chronological age to assess maturity and determine when an individual is ready to progress to a different phase of childhood or has achieved adulthood.
- Despite these local understandings, international legislation has standardised the definition a child as anyone under the age of 18.

Different childhoods, different psychologies

These understandings of childhood are underpinned by different notions of children's roles and responsibilities and point to very different ideas about how children should be socialised and how best to understand children's psychological and social development. In Chapter 2, it was noted that there has been some more recent unease about developmental psychology's setting of universal standards and its tendency to use concepts and observations derived from studies of middle-class White children from privileged cultures within the global North as the developmental norms by which all children are measured. Indeed, psychological concepts like 'attachment' or 'self-esteem' do not readily translate into all other languages, or if they do, they may have different characteristics; and as discussed previously, other cultures may have radically different ideas about what is normal or typical for children at particular ages or, indeed, what is desirable and beneficial to a child.

One of the key thinkers and innovators in the field of local or indigenous psychologies was Cameroonian psychologist Bame Nsamenang (1951–2018), whose ideas around children's responsibilities have already been referred to in this chapter. Beginning with research in the Nso region of Cameroon, where he was born, he studied children's development in his own community as a way of exploring human development from perspectives other than Western ones. Central to his arguments was the belief that, in general, and as you learned in Chapter 4, societies in the global North were more focused on separate individuals than the family or community as African ones were (while acknowledging the large differences between and among both African and Western societies). Therefore, the development of the individual self was less relevant to understanding Nso children, and others in West Africa, than it would be to studies of child development in North America or Europe (Nsamenang, 2006).

Nso children, Nsamenang argued, attained their sense of self by being recognised and valued by the broader community, and he emphasised the importance of children's social and cultural – rather than individual – development. Socialisation, Nsamenang believed, was acquired not through academic pursuits but through local cultural traditions and learning, which emphasised the importance of obedience and social responsibility, rather than self-expression or independence. Socialisation, he argued, should 'teach social competence and shared responsibility within the family system and the ethnic community' (Nsamenang and Lamb, 1994, p. 137).

Using his work with the Nso to generalise more widely, he argued that parents in many African communities value responsibility and obedience over independence and autonomy and are more concerned with children becoming integrated into everyday social life and becoming part of the collective. Children's responsibilities, Nsamenang (2004, p. 111) argues, are 'an indigenous instrument used to integrate them into the social fabric and economic life with little deliberate effort'. In most Western cultures, adults see children as needing to develop independence but not having many capabilities when young. In contrast, adults in Africa make very different assumptions about children, seeing them as capable, socially responsible, and obedient from an early age. Children are raised to be responsible for others, to do what adults tell them, and to take on particular roles when they are considered mature enough, as discussed in the previous section on the chore curriculum. Life stages depend on 'social rather than biological signposts' (Nsamenang and Lamb, 1994, p. 137) which are linked to children's observed levels of competence rather than their biological maturation. Children learn through observing and imitating the adults around them, through folktales and metaphorical stories, and perhaps most importantly, through peer socialisation. Adults usually take a 'hands-off' approach to child-rearing, and children are rarely directly taught by their parents but gradually take on more and more responsibility in certain roles (such as childcare or farming tasks) until they are able to do them competently. They then move onto roles which require more responsibility until finally, they are able to assume adult roles.

Nsamenang always emphasised the practicality of his work and the need for it to make an impact on the lives of children and young people. This was particularly evident during the AIDS epidemic of the 1980s and 1990s, when there was a rush to call in foreign experts who were often unaware of the cultural and psychological contexts they were dealing with and did not grasp the capabilities of African communities to look after chil-dren who had lost parents. Lacking understanding of key values such as social responsib-ility and obedience, and the localised psychologies of the communities they were 'helping', these experts overlooked the possibility of sibling caretakers and wider com-munity care for children who had lost their parents. Instead they favoured orphanages and centralised care, these were sometimes hundreds of miles away, thereby adding to the psychological vulnerabilities of already fragile groups of children and families.

Bame Nsamenang was a pioneer, and his call for more localised psychology has led to many other scholars examining culturally appropriate psychologies for their own communities, including discussions of localised conceptions of intelligence and advo-cacy for contextually relevant developmental services. His work is also an exemplar for the way Childhood and Youth Studies and Psychology can work together to inform studies of how children develop psychologically, socially, and culturally. He wrote of Nso children:

> knowledge is not separated into discrete disciplines, but all strands of it are interwoven into a common tapestry, which is learned by children at different developmental stages, who participate in the cultural and economic life of the family and society.
>
> (Nsamenang, 2006, p. 293)

Key points

- One of the criticisms of developmental psychology is that it is based on concepts and ideas from the global North that do not always readily translate into other societies.
- Bame Nsamenang, a psychologist from Cameroon, dedicated his life to developing studies of African child development; local, or 'indigenous', psychologies; and their practical application.
- He argued that children's development should not be understood through a developmental lens dominated by ideas from the global North but should be seen in terms of children learning social competence and shared responsibility within the family system and their ethnic communities.

Conclusion

This chapter has looked at how and why the idea of a global childhood has become such an important part of contemporary Childhood and Youth Studies. It has exam-ined the origins of the European Enlightenment's idea of childhood as a separate and protected space and stage of life and how these ideas have developed and become universalised. Through a brief discussion of missionary work, colonialisation, and globalisation, the chapter has looked at how contemporary notions of childhood from the global North have travelled across the world and how they have been incorporated into the idea of a universal global child, looked after by the 'international community'. Finally, the chapter discussed how these ideas have been resisted by parents and communities in other places who have very different understandings of their children's capabilities and different expectations of their children's roles. This had led to the emergence of a new field of local psychology, pioneered by those such as Bame Nsamenang, applying local ideas and cultural values to studies of human development.

References

Balagopalan, S. (2014) *Inhabiting 'Childhood': Children, Labour and Schooling in Postcolonial India*. London: Palgrave Macmillan.

Cunningham, H. (2020) *Children and Childhood in Western Society Since 1500* (3rd ed.). Abingdon: Routledge.

de Waal, A. (2002) 'Realising child rights in Africa: children, young people and leadership', in A. de Waal and N. Argenti (eds.) *Young Africa: Realising the Rights of Children and Youth*. Trenton, NJ and Asmara: Africa World Press.

Fletcher, A. (2008) *Growing up in England. The Experience of Childhood 1600–1914*. New Haven: Yale University Press.

Hendrick, H. (1997) 'The constructing and reconstructing of British childhood: An interpretative survey 1800 to the present', in A. James and A. Prout (eds.) *Constructing and Reconstructing Childhood: Contemporary Issues in the Sociological Study of Childhood* (2nd ed.). Basingstoke: The Falmer Press.

Heywood, C. (2017) *A History of Childhood*. Cambridge: Polity.

Honwana, A. (2012) *A Time of Youth. Work, Social Change and Politics in Africa*. Sterling, VA: Kumarian Press.

Lancy, D. (2012) 'The chore curriculum', in G. Spittler and M. Bourdillon (eds.) *African Children at Work: Working and Learning in Growing Up*. Berlin: Lit Verla.

Naftali, O. (2014) *Children, Rights, and Modernity in China: Raising Self-Governing Citizens*. London: Palgrave Macmillan.

Ncube, W. (1998) 'The African cultural fingerprint? The changing concept of childhood', in W Ncube (ed.) *Law Culture, Tradition and Children's Rights in Eastern and Southern Africa*. Aldershot: Ashgate/Dartmouth.

Nsamenang, A. B. (2004) *Cultures of Human Development and Education: Challenge to Growing up African*. New York: Nova Science Publishers Inc.

Nsamenang, A. B. (2006) 'Human ontogenesis: an indigenous African view on development and intelligence', *International Journal of Psychology*, 41(4), pp. 293–297.

Nsamenang, A. B., and Lamb, M. (1994) 'Socialization of NSO children in the Bamenda Grassfields of northwest Cameroon', in P. M. Greenfield and R. R. Cocking (eds.) *Cross Cultural Roots of Minority Child Development*. Hillsdale, NJ: Lawrence Erlbaum, pp. 133–146.

Organization of African Unity (OAU) African Charter on the Rights and Welfare of the Child, African Charter on the Rights and Welfare of the Child, OAU Doc. CAB/LEG/24.9/49 (1990). (umn.edu).

Plumb, J. H. (1972) *In the Light of History*. London: Allen Lane.

Rousseau, J. J. (1966 [1762]) *Emile, or on Education*. London: J. M. Dent and Sons.

Serpell, R. (1993) *The Significance of Schooling: Life-Journeys in an African Society*. Cambridge: Cambridge University Press.

Stahl, R. (2007) 'Don't forget about me: implementing article 12 of the United Nations convention on the rights of the child', *Arizona Journal of International and Contemporary Law*, 24(3), pp. 803–842.

Stephens, S. (1995) 'Children and the politics of culture in late capitalism', in S. Stephens (ed.) *Children and the Politics of Culture*. Princeton: Princeton University Press, pp. 3–48.

Tafere, Y., and Chuta, N. (2020) *Transitions to Adulthood in Ethiopia Preliminary Findings: Summary and Policy Issues*. Oxford: Young Lives.

Twum-Danso Imoh, A. (2019) 'Terminating childhood: dissonance and synergy between global children's rights norms and local discourses about the transition from childhood to adulthood in Ghana', *Human Rights Quarterly*, 41(1), pp. 160–182.

Twum-Danso Imoh, A. (2020) 'Situating the rights vs. culture binary within the context of colonial history in sub – Saharan Africa', in J. Todres and S. King (eds.) *Oxford Handbook on Children's Rights Law*. Oxford: Oxford University Press.

Twum-Danso Imoh, A., and Okyere, S. (2020) 'Towards a more holistic understanding of child participation: foregrounding the experiences of children in Ghana and Nigeria', *Child and Youth Services Review*, 112(2020), pp. 1–7.

Twum-Danso Imoh, A., Okyere, S., and Secker, E. (2012) *Facilitating Children's Participation in the Niger Delta of Nigeria*, unpublished Project Report Funded by the University of Sheffield R&D Collaborative Scheme.

United Nations (1989) *United Nations Convention on the Rights of the Child*. Convention on the Rights of the Child | OHCHR.

Wells, K. (2021) *Childhood in a Global Perspective*. Bristol: Policy Press.

11 Gender in childhood and youth

Naomi Holford

Introduction: Defining categories

Imagine a newly born pair of twins in the hospital, wrapped in blankets. You have been told that one is a boy and one is a girl – but it might be difficult to tell which is which. Five years later, you can probably answer the question very easily – even though the twins are probably still very similar in height, weight, and bone structure. There are now many clues in their hairstyle, clothing, appearance, and behaviour that help you determine the boy and the girl. Indeed, if you are uncertain, you might feel uncomfortable asking. But why is this?

This chapter will explore how gender comes to be so important in shaping how adults think about and treat children and how children and young people think about themselves and experience the world. It introduces the concept that gender is a social construction, rather than solely defined by biology. This means that the way gender is thought about and experienced can vary between different societies and across history. For example, in the UK and other global North societies today, high-heeled shoes are seen as women's clothing. However, in 17th-century Britain, high-heeled shoes were considered men's clothing. While this may be fairly trivial, it is an illustration that aspects of gender we take for granted are socially constructed.

Language and terminology

Language around gender is changing and contested as people seek compelling and comfortable ways to describe themselves. This chapter aims to use accurate and respectful language, seeking to use words that respect the terms individuals and communities use for themselves. However, different terminology may be current by the time you read this chapter, and different groups or individuals may find different terms preferable or members of a group may disagree on the terms they prefer.

Like all children, the twins in the first paragraph have been assigned a sex at birth – designated as a boy or girl, based on the biological factors discussed in the box later. *Sex* usually refers to the biological features associated with being a man or woman. Many of these do not emerge until puberty, when hormonal signals initiate changes to

DOI: 10.4324/9781003358855-12

Figure 11.1 Babies marked out as boy and girl through their clothing and accessories.

the body (e.g., in muscle and fat distribution and body hair growth). These are known as secondary sexual characteristics. Primary sexual characteristics are those directly related to reproduction and present from birth – the genitals and gonads (ovaries or testes).

Gender can be defined as the social, cultural, and psychological characteristics and meanings associated with being a man or a woman or someone with another gender identity. Gender is flexible, expressed in different ways in different places. For example, in many countries, most childcare is carried out by women; bearing, nurturing, and caring for children is often considered part of being a woman. However, in some societies, men do as much infant and childcare as women, and it is central to their role as men; for example, fathers in the Aka society of central Africa hold their children almost 50% of the time and women are as likely, or more likely, to hunt.

Although gender is constructed socially, it is also psychological and individual. *Gender identity* is a person's internal sense of the gender they feel they are. Most children develop a gender identity consistent with the sex they are assigned at birth – for example, a child assigned as a boy will think of themselves as a boy. However, some grow up to be transgender, meaning they identify with a gender other than that assigned at birth. That can mean that a child assigned as a boy thinks of themselves as a girl, or it can mean that they identify neither as a boy nor as a girl but as non-binary (or another gender), meaning their gender is neither male nor female. In recent decades, transgender experience and the idea of gender identities beyond male and female have become more visible – although they have always existed in some form (see, for example, Peletz, 2009; Surtees, 2020).

Despite this, the dominant conception of gender in many contemporary societies is binary – it has two categories, classifying all people into two genders, seeing masculinity and femininity as distinct and opposite. Boys are seen as different from girls, with different social and cultural norms for how each gender is expected to behave. These norms differ across and within societies, but gender norms and expectations exist everywhere.

The gender binary is not equal. Men generally have more social, political, and economic power. However, men and boys can also be disadvantaged by the gender binary. For example, masculinity may be associated with an expectation that men should be self-reliant and suppress fear or sadness, which can contribute to men not seeking help for mental or physical health problems. In addition, gender is not experienced separately from other aspects of identity. Gendered experiences and inequalities are affected by factors such as race and ethnicity, age, and social class. ('Gendered' means something is affected by gender or divided along gender lines. A 'gendered school uniform', for example, has different requirements for boys and girls.)

In the rest of this chapter, you will explore the role of gender in children and young people's lives. The chapter looks at how gender norms are produced within different environments, how children navigate binary gendered expectations, and how they understand and express their own gender in different ways, influenced by other aspects of identity. It covers experiences of boys and girls whose gender identity corresponds with their sex assigned at birth, and of transgender children, who face particular challenges in societies structured by binary gender.

Key points

- Gender is an important category in shaping how adults think about children and how children and young people think about themselves and experience the world.
- Gender is socially constructed: its meanings can vary between different societies and across history.
- Gender identity is a person's internal sense of gender – what gender they feel they are.
- Many contemporary societies view gender as binary.

Establishing categories: Infancy and adult expectations of gender

Gender is central to children's experiences of themselves and of the world. One of the first questions asked of many expecting parents is, 'Will it be a boy or a girl?' Or, 'Do you know what you're having?' The second question is usually automatically understood, even though the words are not specific, because of a shared assumption that gender is fundamental to what a baby will be. While the question technically refers to a baby's sex, it is considered so important because of the role of gender in shaping expectations about a child.

You have already learned about the interplay between nature and nurture: whether particular characteristics result from biological or social causes, or a combination. Popular media and everyday discussions often talk about gendered characteristics as natural and inevitable. Boys may be described as more boisterous than girls in the nursery. But since children are defined as boy or girl before, or at, birth, it is almost impossible to separate biological influences from social and cultural expectations and ideas about gender. Before birth, those who know the sex of their foetus describe boys' movements as 'vigorous' or 'strong' while talking about girls' movements as more gentle. But for those who don't know, there is no difference in the way boys' and girls' movements are described (Rothman, 1994).

At birth, there are minimal differences between boys' and girls' physical, emotional, cognitive, and social abilities. However, adults treat infants differently, shown by psychological research that looks at how adults behave. The 'Baby X' experiment was first carried out in the 1970s in Chicago, USA (Seavey, Katz and Zalk, 1975). A 3-month-old baby, dressed in a yellow sleepsuit, was introduced to volunteers as either 'Mary' or 'Johnny'. Volunteers were asked to play with the baby, using a choice of three toys left in the room – a rag doll, a football, and a teething ring. None of the male volunteers presented a football to what they supposed was a girl, but 89% presented her with a doll; meanwhile, 80% of the women gave 'the boy' a football, and 75% presented 'the girl' with a doll. More recent studies have similarly found that adults behave differently towards children based on their gender in multiple aspects of life.

One study looked at US mothers' judgements of their children's physical development, asking them to estimate their 11-month-old infants' crawling abilities before they tried a new task: crawling down a steep slope (Mondschein, Adolph and Tamis-LeMonda, 2000). Mothers of girls underestimated, and mothers of boys overestimated, their performance, although boys and girls did not differ in actual crawling ability.

Psychologists Melissa Clearfield and Naree Nelson (2006) looked at mothers' language and play with their 6-, 9-, and 14-month infants. Again, there were no differences in infant behaviour, but mothers talked differently, asking more questions of girls, expecting them to be more verbally expressive while being more instructive to boys (saying 'come here' or calling their name). They also played more with girls, leaving boys to play independently. Psychologist Ashley Leavell *et al.* (2012) studied low-income African American, Latino, and White fathers of 2–4-year-olds across the USA over three years, surveying them about how often they carried out caregiving (e.g., feeding), physical play (e.g., chasing games), literacy (e.g., reading books), and social activities (visiting friends or family) with their children. Fathers carried out more physical play with boys and more literacy-related activities with girls; interestingly, African American fathers engaged in play, caregiving, and visiting more with sons than with daughters.

Many psychological studies, therefore, suggest that parents, caregivers, and even strangers consciously and unconsciously treat children differently based on their (assumed) gender and have different expectations of many abilities – even when differences don't exist. Some of these studies were experiments in controlled environments, isolating and changing specific factors to see how these affect behaviours. Of course, children do not grow up in controlled environments. There are many influences on their gendered development and experience, and children themselves play an active role interacting with adults, peers, and the environment. After the box below, the next section will consider the ways in which children start to learn about, and explore, their own gender.

Variations in gender – and even sex

Most babies are assigned a sex – male or female – at birth, if not before. This is usually straightforward – the doctor looks at the baby's genitals. If it has testes and a penis, it is called a boy; if it has a vagina and a clitoris, it is called a girl. But it is not always that simple.

Biologically, there are five factors that go towards determining a baby's sex. These are the following:

1   Chromosomes, which carry the genetic information in body cells. Usually, girls have two X chromosomes, and boys have one X and one Y chromosome.
2   Whether the baby has testes (which will make sperm) or ovaries (which will make eggs).
3   The sex hormones (hormones are chemicals that produce particular effects, and men and women tend to have different levels of sex hormones).
4   The internal reproductive organs (like the uterus).
5   The external genitals (like the penis or clitoris).

Most people have a combination of these factors allowing easy assignation of sex, but for some, the combination is not clear cut. People whose five factors aren't all typically male or typically female are described as having 'differences in sex development' (DSD), sometimes referred to as 'intersex' conditions. In every 2,000 babies, 1–2 (1.7%) are born with ambiguous genitals: they can't be easily placed into the category of male or female. This is about the same number as children born with cystic fibrosis, Down syndrome, or red hair. These ambiguities can take a number of physical forms. For instance, a person might be born with a large clitoris or without a vaginal opening or a particularly small penis. Not everyone with DSD is aware of this. Some forms may not become evident until puberty, and some never do so.

The treatment of intersex people provides insight into social ideas about sex and gender. Doctors often perform genital surgery for a more typical appearance. From the 1950s until recently, this was carried out without informing the child (who would never be told) and sometimes without even informing the parents (who would be aware that their child was undergoing surgery but not why). It was thought important for children's healthy development that they feel 'normal'. For instance, people who were considered male in most of the five respects but had very small penises had these surgically removed and were raised as girls. Hormone therapy was also sometimes used when children reached the age of puberty.

There is often no clear physiological reason to carry out genital surgery on babies with ambiguous genitals, and surgery can cause a diminishing or loss of sexual sensation in later life. In general, the approach taken with children thought to be girls was to focus on later fertility, with sexual sensation seen as unimportant. In contrast, for children thought to be boys, the eventual size and function of the penis was considered most important. This indicates the medical construction of sex based on gendered norms: the ideal of femininity prioritises motherhood and the ability to bear children, while the ideal of masculinity focuses more on later sexual prowess than the ability to bear children. Depending on the specific type of intersex condition, some children may start to develop unexpected body characteristics when they reach puberty, which can be confusing or distressing. As adults, some intersex people identify as the sex they were assigned at birth, while others do not.

In the past few years, an intersex activist movement (e.g., Organisation Intersex International Europe) has campaigned for a changed approach. They argue children ought to be left to decide later if they want to change their genitals. They ought not to be given surgical or hormonal treatment until they can give informed consent. This is contested and can lead to different problems. It is not easy for parents or medical professionals to know the best approach. It is very difficult to raise a child without gender, so a gender is usually 'picked'. But children who appear different – for instance, because their genitals are significantly different to the norm – may feel confused about their own identities and may be teased or excluded by others. The intersex movement seeks to provide support and community for intersex people. It is one example of how new identities and communities can be formed around aspects of the human experience that have always existed (see later 'Changing categories: Shifting norms and gender diversity').

As noted previously, around 1.7% of people have biological sex characteristics that do not fit typical male or female categories. These variations indicate that even based on biological sex, children cannot be categorised into two distinct, different groups. For gender, variations are much greater. This chapter gives examples of how gender affects behaviour and how boys' and girls' experiences differ (whether the reasons are biological, social, or both). However, it is important to note that they also share many similarities. Where differences exist, these are differences between *averages*, rather than between every girl and every boy.

One way to visualise this is through overlapping normal distribution curves. Many measurable traits – for example, height or running ability – are 'normally distributed' within a population. This means that if you take 100 people at random and plot their traits on a graph, most will be somewhere in the middle, while fewer will be at the extremes (e.g., very tall or very short). This results in a 'normal distribution curve'. Normal distribution curves can be plotted for different groups, for example, men and women. The example later shows the distribution of male and female heights in adult humans. It shows that on average, men are taller than women, but there is a significant overlap: some women are taller than some men.

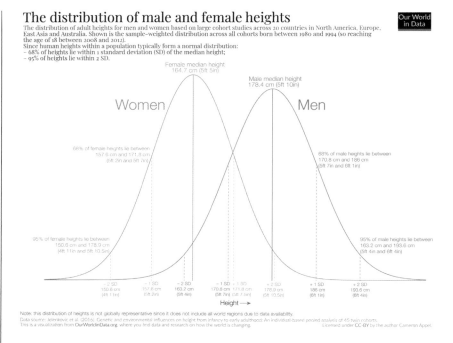

Figure 11.2 Men and women's heights across the world. On average, men are taller than women, but there is substantial crossover between men and women.

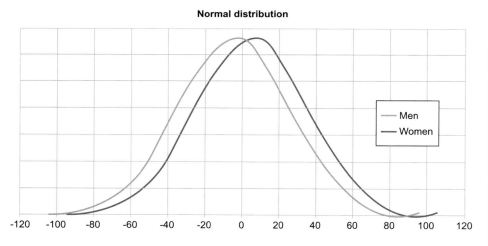

Figure 11.3 An example of overlapping normal distributions for male and female groups, showing that most individuals fall somewhere in the middle.

Height is substantially sexually dimorphic in humans – meaning that sexes tend to exhibit different characteristics. However, most behaviours and traits studied in social sciences do not exhibit clear sexual dimorphism. Distributions are more likely to fit a pattern like Figure 11.3.

The overlapping area represents most people – showing that even where average differences do exist, most people of all genders fall within the same overall range. In most ways, boys and girls are more similar than they are different. Remember, for example, in Chapter 4 that although boys and girls differed in some favourite activities, the meanings they attached to these were the same, and their social selves were very similar.

Importantly, the vast majority of psychological and sociological research on gender differences and similarities has been carried out based on binary sex assigned at birth, without accounting for multiple or fluid gender identities and rarely accounting for transgender experience or asking children about their own gender identity. So the research discussed in this chapter does not fully account for the range of children's experience and their own understandings of themselves. As understandings of gender change, research will change too.

Key points

- Adults treat children differently based on their gender from before birth and have different expectations of boys and girls.
- Children are assigned a sex at birth based on biological characteristics, but not everyone fits easily into the male or female category.
- For any behaviour or trait, even if there is a difference in average performance or development, there are wide variations within genders. In most areas, boys and girls are more similar than they are different.

Learning categories: Gender in early childhood

Developmental psychology indicates that children first acquire a gender identity around the age of 2 1/2 or 3 – when they can identify their own gender and that of others (although, as discussed in the previous section, they are affected before this age by ideas about gender) (Martin and Ruble, 2010). But they do not yet think of gender as permanent and unchangeable. It is not until about 5 years that they acquire what is known as 'gender stability' – believing that boys will grow up to be men and that girls will grow up to be women. But they may still define gender by concrete external factors, such as clothing, hair, or physical appearance – rather than a more general idea of a person's gender.

Research on gender identity development has assumed that gender *is* stable – rather than fluid or flexible. Research on transgender children's identity development is still limited. It has become more common for children to socially transition in early childhood – that is, for a child assigned as one sex to identify as a different gender in everyday life. The available research suggests that transgender children who transition early in life go through similar stages of gender identity development to other children, although they may be more likely to believe that gender might not stay the same between childhood and adulthood (Fast and Olson, 2018; Gülgöz *et al.*, 2021).

With developing gender identity, children begin to apply gendered ideas about what is appropriate, and inappropriate, to their own lives and choices – such as what they play with. From very early, these choices are influenced not only by their own desires but also by their perceptions of what others may think. Parents have substantial influence. Even when parents said they would be happy for their children to play with a toy not associated with their gender (such as a boy playing with a doll or a girl with a truck), many children said their parents wouldn't like it if they played with the 'inappropriate' toy (Morawska, 2020).

Children are also influenced by peers and keen to fit with social norms. Ethnographic research in sociology, where children are observed in their natural environments, indicates that children modify gendered behaviours among peers. Researcher Jennifer Lyttleton-Smith (2019) spent a year observing 3–4-year-old children at preschool. Children showed nuanced and changing understandings of their own and others' gendered behaviours. At first, there were no strong gender differences, but over the year, particular spaces became associated with girls' or boys' play. Boys began to avoid the 'home corner', which was cluttered, enclosed, and private, and associated with homemaking, caring, and dress-up play. Girls began to avoid the 'small world', a more open space with storage for mathematics materials and trains, cars, and bricks. By the end of the year, these different spaces were mostly divided along gendered lines.

From early childhood, boys' toy preferences tend to become more rigid, while girls' become more flexible. They are more willing to play with toys considered 'masculine' (Eliot, 2010). This reflects social and cultural trends, as masculinity is generally more

Figure 11.4 Toys are often marketed and used in gendered ways. These LEGO Minifigures representing different jobs (photographer, painter, magician, beautician) represent some different options.

highly valued than femininity. Boys, or children assigned male at birth, are more likely to be socially punished or excluded for behaviours or traits considered feminine than girls are for behaviours considered masculine. Early gendered perceptions shape children and young people's interests and understandings of themselves and others. For example, gendered perceptions of intellectual ability emerge early. In an American study, by age 6, girls were more likely to identify boys as 'really, really smart' and avoid activities aimed at 'really, really smart' children (Bian, Leslie and Cimpian, 2017).

As children learn about gender, it becomes part of their identity. There are gendered associations with play, friendship, physical activity, clothing, reading and viewing, and school subjects. These do not have to be explicit for them to become part of children's understanding of themselves and the world. Nor do they have to be conscious. Like many aspects of children's life, gender becomes embodied. Anne Fausto-Sterling, a biologist specialising in gender identity development, describes embodiment as being 'automatic, unintentional, and found in all aspects of our nervous system' and gender 'a biosocial sediment built up over a lifetime' (Fausto-Sterling, 2019). Social experience influences the body and brain, which simultaneously influence people's social experiences. She gives the example of a young girl choosing not to climb trees: perhaps because her dress makes climbing difficult and she has been warned not to get it dirty; or because her parents worry more about her hurting herself than her brother; or other girls around are not climbing trees. In any case, she does not climb trees, and so she does not develop her physical climbing abilities.

As children learn about gender, they also learn about many other aspects of the world, including other identities. Children's experiences and understandings of gender are intersectional: they are influenced by other aspects of identity, including race/ethnicity and social class. Social and cultural inequalities affect how children think about gender. One psychological study (Lei, Leshin and Rhodes, 2020) found that children aged 7–11 were slower and less accurate in categorising Black women's gender than categorising Asian or White women or Black men, suggesting that children saw Black women as less representative of their gender. Another study with younger children found that both Black and White children in the US responded less positively to Black boys than they did to Black girls, White boys, and White girls. By age four, children perceive Black men as exhibiting more negative masculine stereotypes (such as aggression) than White and Asian men. As you learned in Chapter 9, early stereotypes can be connected to wider inequalities and social attitudes, such as the disproportionate criminalisation of Black men.

Key points

- Children develop a gender identity at about 3 years, when they can identify their own gender and that of others.
- Young children learn about 'appropriate' gendered behaviours, modify their behaviour to fit, and monitor other children's behaviour based on gender.
- Ideas about 'appropriate' gendered behaviours are also influenced by other aspects of identity, like race.

Maintaining categories: Gender in young children's peer groups

As you saw in Chapter 7, most societies require children to attend school for at least some time. School becomes important beyond children's educational and cognitive development, for their social and emotional development. This includes their gender identities, influenced by their interactions with adults and other children. Research on gender (often ethnographic) involves observing their everyday school environments and talking to children about what they are doing.

Although gender is often considered to be natural and instinctive, a consistent research finding is the effort it takes for children to work out and fit into gender norms. Theories of gender performance (or performativity) focus on the child's active role in making their gender identity. Theorists argue that gender is a continual process – something we do, or perform (an idea influenced by the work of feminist philosopher Judith Butler, 1990). A boy is always making himself into a boy, through the way he talks, walks, and dresses. With constant repetition, he makes the category of 'boy' seem natural and unchangeable. But at the same time, the category is funda-mentally precarious and unstable, so he can never stop performing. The careful and intricate work that people put into achieving seemingly natural performances of gender in social interaction have been studied by sociologists since the 1960s (Garfinkel, 1967). This is not necessarily conscious but embodied and deeply rooted.

Different environments have different gender 'rules'. Within settings, like school, there are usually various types of masculinity and femininity. These are often hierarchical – where one type is seen as better than another. Sociologist Diane Reay's (2005) study of Year 3 children in England (aged 7–8) found different types of femi-ninity: the girls called themselves 'nice girls', 'spice girls', 'girlies', and 'tomboys'. 'Nice girls' were very focused on schoolwork and seen as well-behaved, but also boring, by peers. 'Girlies' were interested in relationships with boys, writing love letters and flirting, but often called 'dumb' by boys, although they were achieving quite highly educationally. 'Spice girls' were also interested in relationships with boys but retaliated against boys when teased and were seen as intimidating and quite often in trouble with school. Finally, 'tomboys' rejected traditional ideas of femininity, were hostile to girls, and enjoyed playing with boys. Some children moved between groups – although more remained within the same friendship groups through the study.

Different forms of gender expression are shaped by the children's lived contexts. Deevia Bhana and Emmanuel Mayeza's (2019) work on gender in South Africa used focus group discussions to explore how girls aged 10–12 in a KwaZulu-Natal town-ship used different forms of femininity to manage gendered and sexual violence from boys at school. Some responded with violence, emphasising their strength and resistance and a need to fight back for their safety. Others used the concept of Ubuntu (care, collective responsibility, and empathy; see Chapters 4 and 8) to argue for cooperation in ending violence. The researchers concluded, 'femininity is fluid and . . . the same context and conditions can give rise to highly divergent forms' (p. 106).

Key points

- Children take an active role in performing their gender, requiring substantial conscious and unconscious effort in peer groups.
- Different environments have different gendered expectations, with varying types of masculinity or femininity within one environment.

Changing categories: Shifting norms and gender diversity

Focusing on how children fit certain norms is an important part of gender research, but it can overlook ways that children don't fit those norms.

Sociologist Barrie Thorne (1993), in an influential ethnography of gender in US schools, developed the term 'borderwork' to refer to how children and adults build and reinforce boy-girl divisions – for example, a group of boys might refuse to let a girl join a football game (seen as a 'boys' game' in her research, as often elsewhere). Borderwork can occur when boys and girls play together within gendered groups – for example, when teams of girls chase boys. It can be reinforced by adults, for example, when they split the class into groups based on gender. The school institutional setting tended to emphasise gender divisions, and sometimes gender did not matter much. Most children Thorne studied played together across gender outside school.

As well as 'borderwork' (maintaining gendered boundaries), Thorne describes 'border crossing', entering spaces normally identified for the other gender. This might mean playing with them, like the 'tomboys' in Reay's study, or dressing differently, for instance, a boy wearing nail varnish or a dress. As discussed previously, it is often easier for girls to border cross. There is usually greater anxiety from others if a boy wears 'feminine' clothes than if a girl wears 'masculine' clothes. Context affects border crossing: a girl might be happy to play with boys in her street but not at school. Children who border cross (deliberately or involuntarily) are often punished by peers, through teasing, exclusion, or bullying.

It is important to realise that almost all children struggle with gender norms at times. Childhood Studies scholar EJ Renold *et al.* (2017) conducted research with 10–11-year-olds in England, which showed they feel pressure trying to get gender 'right'. Even if very 'girly' or 'boyish', there were constantly new situations to work out rules for, and maintaining a gendered identity may mean giving up some friends or activities.

More recently, there is increasing understanding that not all people identify with the sex they were assigned at birth, and transgender experience has become more visible in the media and politics. In some contexts, children and young people who experience a strong discomfort with their assigned gender (known as 'gender dysphoria') have options to describe and understand their identity, and for some, this may involve gender transition. Social transition is where a child begins to live according to the gender they identify as. A child assigned female at birth may adopt a new name, be referred to as a boy, and called 'he' or 'him' by his family and school or may be referred to as a non-binary person and called 'they' or 'them'. Children who strongly and persistently identify with a gender other than that assigned at birth may select medical transition, undergoing medical treatments to align their sex characteristics with their gender identity. For those under 18, this usually involves puberty blockers, delaying the physical effects of puberty so they do not develop sex characteristics which conflict with their gender, although as discussed in Chapter 1, this is highly controversial and children's right (or otherwise) to access this medical treatment has been contested. They can later choose to undergo hormone therapy so their sex characteristics better match their gender identity. Medical transition is rare and difficult to access in most countries, including the UK, requiring the approval of doctors after extensive psychological assessment.

There is limited research on transgender identities, but they are thought to develop similarly to other children's gender identities (Tate, Youssef and Bettergarcia, 2014). Trans young people may experience different trajectories of gender development, with some feeling clear discomfort with their assigned gender from a very early age while others developing gender dysphoria around puberty as Annie Pullen Sansfaçon found (Sansfaçon *et al.*, 2020). Others may come to an understanding of their trans identity in older young adulthood or indeed in adulthood. These trajectories might be influenced by social and family support or information availability. For example, some young people in Sansfaçon's study remembered feeling discomfort in their assigned gender at an early age but experienced resistance from parents, so they suppressed these feelings until they became difficult to ignore during puberty.

For trans children, experiences of gendered childhood institutions can be particularly difficult. Aoife Neary's research in Irish primary schools, interviewing educators and parents of trans children aged between 5 and 13 years (Neary, 2021), found celebratory occasions, like birthdays and religious rituals, were especially challenging. Gender came very obviously into view. A pre-school had pink or blue bunting for a child's birthday, or children had to wear gendered clothing for their First Communion – 'mechanisms that marked out the boundaries of belonging, often with exclusionary and deeply isolating effects for their children' (p. 9). Birthday parties, usually single gender (inviting all the boys or girls in the class), also caused significant distress. One child, assigned female at birth, wanted a boys-only party, but no boys attended and the child was not invited to any birthday parties that year.

The pressure of gendered institutions was also a focus of Tori Howell and Louisa Allen's (2021) research with fa'afāfine and fakaleiti young people in an all-boys' faith-based secondary school in Aoteoroa, New Zealand. The Samoan term 'fa'afāfine' translates as 'in the manner of a woman', referring to people assigned male at birth whose gendered behaviours are, to varying degrees, feminine. Fakaleiti is the equivalent term for Tongans. They highlighted verbal insults and physical violence at school and being blamed for assaults against them. Curriculum, especially religious studies and physical education (PE), was especially marginalising, as were experiences of using the boys' toilets, with participants often avoiding them altogether. Uniforms and dress codes punished students if they attempted to grow their hair long or wear make-up. School prefects petitioned the board of trustees, trying to get fa'afāfine and fakaleiti students expelled for 'bringing shame on the school due to their feminine appearance' (p. 425).

Such research emphasises how central the gender binary is to children's lives and the harms it can do to those who do not fit within it. Most children discussed in Neary's research identified strongly as a boy or a girl, in contrast to their sex assigned at birth, and experienced difficulties when they were put in the 'wrong box'. However, some experienced a more fluid gender identity. An increasing number of children and young people (and adults) identify as non-binary, or gender diverse: they do not see themselves as either a boy or a girl but as neither or a combination of both. This kind of identity may be more likely to emerge later in childhood, as children develop the ability to understand flexibility and complexity in categories. Sara Bragg *et al's* (2018) research with young people aged 13–19 in England indicated that young people felt their generation was more accepting of gender diversity and equality. Participants expressed support for gender fluidity, rejecting rigid gender binaries. However, they also described continuing gendered expectations, including sexual harassment and bullying for not fitting into gendered roles.

The qualitative research discussed in this chapter suggests that children and young people often find rigidly enforced binary gender norms potentially harmful to their wellbeing. This is supported by quantitative research: surveys of the rates of mental health difficulties indicate that transgender and non-binary children and young people are more likely to experience self-harm, suicidality, and eating disorders compared to their peers across different countries (Connolly *et al.*, 2016; Kingsbury *et al.*, 2022). But if children are supported in their gender identity by adults and peers – for example, using their chosen name and pronouns and allowing them to use facilities associated with their gender – they can thrive. Trans children who are supported to socially transition do not show greater mental health difficulties than children overall (Olson *et al.*, 2016). Studies on mental health across populations indicate that transgender young people who go through medical transition do not differ in mental health difficulties to the overall population and have better outcomes than those who wanted but could not access this (Turban *et al.*, 2022).

Key points

- Most children struggle to some extent with binary gendered expectations of societies and institutions.
- Some children are transgender, developing a gender identity that does not correspond with the sex they were assigned at birth.
- Transgender children often experience discrimination and mental health difficulties, but supporting gender identity leads to greater wellbeing.

Conclusion

Gender is a key social division in how adults think about children and how children grow to think about themselves. Gender is often assumed to be binary – consisting of two separate and opposite categories, based on the sex a child is assigned at birth – and adults consciously and unconsciously treat boys and girls differently. However, evidence shows there are more similarities than differences between girls and boys.

Children develop a gender identity at a young age, influenced by social context but also deeply internally felt. Gender identity is embedded in unconscious, embodied habits and developed and maintained through interaction with others – adults and children – and through constructions of gender in the media and commercial worlds. Although we think of gender as 'natural', children actively make their gender identities and constantly aim to get their gender performance 'right'. Exactly what counts as 'right' is socially constructed: it differs across settings and times and is influenced by factors like race and social class. Almost all children cross some gender boundaries at certain times. Yet they frequently punish each other socially for doing gender 'wrong'.

Gendered perceptions and understandings have an impact throughout life: many occupations are highly gendered and unequal – occupations dominated by women tend to be lower paid than occupations dominated by men.

Most children develop a gender identity that is consistent with the sex they are assigned at birth. However, some develop a transgender identity outside the traditional binary of male and female, and although these have always existed, it is becoming more common for children and young people to express them. For trans and non-binary children and youth, navigating childhood's binary gendered landscape can be particularly challenging. However, adults listening to and respecting children and young people's identities and wishes and creating supportive environments encouraging children and young people to express their identity without being constricted by gender expectations can be beneficial to all – whatever their gender.

References

Bhana, D., and Mayeza, E. (2019) 'Primary schoolgirls addressing bullying and negotiating femininity', *Girlhood Studies*, 12(2), pp. 98–114.

Bian, L., Leslie, S.-J., and Cimpian, A. (2017) 'Gender stereotypes about intellectual ability emerge early and influence children's interests', *Science*, 355(6323), pp. 389–391.

Bragg, S. *et al.* (2018) '"More than boy, girl, male, female": exploring young people's views on gender diversity within and beyond school contexts', *Sex Education*, 18(4), pp. 420–434.

Butler, J. (1990) *Gender Trouble, Feminism and the Subversion of Gender*. London: Routledge.

Clearfield, M. W., and Nelson, N. M. (2006) 'Sex differences in mothers' speech and play behavior with 6-, 9-, and 14-month-old infants', *Sex Roles*, 54(1), pp. 127–137.

Connolly, M. D. *et al.* (2016) 'The mental health of transgender youth: advances in understanding', *Journal of Adolescent Health*, 59(5), pp. 489–495.

Eliot, L. (2010) *Pink Brain, Blue Brain: How Small Differences Grow into Troublesome Gaps – and What We Can Do About It*. London: Oneworld Publications.

Fast, A. A., and Olson, K. R. (2018) 'Gender development in transgender preschool children', *Child Development*, 89(2), pp. 620–637.

Fausto-Sterling, A. (2019) 'Gender/sex, sexual orientation, and identity are in the body: how did they get there?', *The Journal of Sex Research*, 56(4–5), pp. 529–555.

Garfinkel, H. (1967) *Studies in Ethnomethodology*. Englewood Cliffs, NJ: Prentice-Hall.

Gülgöz, S. *et al.* (2021) 'Transgender and cisgender children's essentialist beliefs about sex and gender identity', *Developmental Science*, 24(6).

Howell, T., and Allen, L. (2021) '"Good morning boys": Fa'afāfine and Fakaleiti experiences of cisgenderism at an all-boys secondary school', *Sex Education*, 21(4), pp. 417–431.

Kingsbury, M. *et al.* (2022) 'Suicidality among sexual minority and transgender adolescents: a nationally representative population-based study of youth in Canada', *CMAJ*, 194(22), pp. E767–E774.

Leavell, A. S., Tamis-LeMonda, C. S., Ruble, D. N. *et al.* (2012) 'African American, White and Latino fathers' activities with their sons and daughters in early childhood', *Sex Roles*, 66(1–2), pp. 53–65.

Lei, R. F., Leshin, R. A., and Rhodes, M. (2020) 'The development of intersectional social prototypes', *Psychological Science*, 31(8), pp. 911–926.

Lyttleton-Smith, J. (2019) 'Objects of conflict: (re) configuring early childhood experiences of gender in the preschool classroom: gender and education', *Gender and Education*, 31(6).

Martin, C. L., and Ruble, D. N. (2010) 'Patterns of gender development', *Annual Review of Psychology*, 61, pp. 353–381.

Mondschein, E. R., Adolph, K. E., and Tamis-LeMonda, C. S. (2000) 'Gender bias in mothers' expectations about infant crawling', *Journal of Experimental Child Psychology*, 77(4), pp. 304–316.

Morawska, A. (2020) 'The effects of gendered parenting on child development outcomes: a systematic review', *Clinical Child and Family Psychology Review*, 23(4), pp. 553–576.

Neary, A. (2021) 'Trans children and the necessity to complicate gender in primary schools', *Gender and Education*, pp. 1–17.

Olson, K. R. *et al.* (2016) 'Mental health of transgender children who are supported in their identities', *Pediatrics*, 137(3), p. e20153223.

Organisation Intersex International Europe. Available at: https://www.oiieurope.org/ (Accessed 27th February 2023).

Peletz, M. G. (2009) *Gender Pluralism: Southeast Asia Since Early Modern Times*. Abingdon: Routledge.

Reay, D. (2005) '"Spice girls", "nice girls", "girlies" and "tomboys". Gender discourses, girls' cultures and femininities in the primary classroom', in C. Skelton and B. Francis (eds.) *A Feminist Critique of Education*. London: Routledge.

Renold, E. Bragg, S. Jackson, C., and Ringrose, J. (2017) *How Gender Matters to Children and Young People Living in England*. Cardiff University, University of Brighton, University of Lancaster, and University College London, Institute of Education. ISBN 978-1-908469-13-7

Rothman, B. K. (1994) *The Tentative Pregnancy: Amniocentesis and the Sexual Politics of Motherhood* (2nd ed.). London: Pandora.

Sansfaçon, A. P. *et al.* (2020) '"I knew that I wasn't cis, I knew that, but I didn't know exactly": gender identity development, expression and affirmation in youth who access gender affirming medical care', *International Journal of Transgender Health*, 21(3), pp. 307–320.

Seavey, C. A., Katz, P. A., and Zalk, S. R. (1975) 'Baby X: the effect of gender labels on adult responses to infants', *Sex Roles*, 1(2), pp. 103–109.

Surtees, A. (2020) *Exploring Gender Diversity in the Ancient World*. Edinburgh: Edinburgh University Press.

Tate, C. C., Youssef, C. P., and Bettergarcia, J. N. (2014) 'Integrating the study of transgender spectrum and cisgender experiences of self-categorization from a personality perspective', *Review of General Psychology*, 18(4), pp. 302–312.

Thorne, B. (1993) *Gender Play: Girls and Boys in School*. Rutgers, NJ: Rutgers University Press.

Turban, J. L. *et al.* (2022) 'Access to gender-affirming hormones during adolescence and mental health outcomes among transgender adults', *PLoS ONE*, 17(1), p. e0261039.

12 Digital childhood and youth

Life with screens

Lucy Caton and Mel Green

Introduction

Children and young people's lives have become enmeshed in technological developments that offer engaging, interactive, and thrilling online opportunities, and there is considerable discussion about children and young people's engagement with them. Smartphones, tablets, and gaming consoles are advancing at a rapid pace, shaping children and young people's experiences and relationships. Artificial intelligence (AI), virtual reality (VR), and augmented reality (AR) are further constructing how children and families interact with virtual and physical worlds. While many parents and media commentators are concerned that 'screen time' in general may damage children's sleep, health, and friendships, research findings indicate that it is more meaningful to think about the diverse forms and functions of digital screen use. Indeed, Isabela Granic, Hiromitsu Morita, and Hanneke Scholten (2020, p. 195) assert that the term screen time is 'meaningless in the current landscape of digital applications, platforms, and mobile ubiquity'. It may be more useful to think about the context in which screens are used, the content of the activity, and the potential connections that open up (Blum-Ross and Livingstone, 2016). The challenge, therefore, is how best to understand and manage both risks and opportunities that digital media present.

Context: Childhood in a digital age

Surveys from the global North report that younger children are using digital technologies ever more frequently and even more so during and since the global Covid-19 pandemic. For some time, research has suggested that pre-schoolers become familiar with digital devices before they are exposed to books (Hopkins, Brookes and Green, 2013), and the UK market research company YouGov found that, by age 6, 10% of children owned their own smartphone, with another 49% permitted use of a family device, while 40% of 6-year-olds had their own tablet, and 85% had access to one (Ibbetson, 2020). Many no longer type for digital searching, commands, and messages, instead favouring verbal and auditory communications via technologies such as Apple's Siri, Amazon's Alexa, and dictated voice notes. It is important to note that a longstanding 'global digital divide' (Lythreatis, Singh and El-Kassar, 2021) continues to persist – a significant inequality between and within the world's richest and poorest countries in

DOI: 10.4324/9781003358855-13

internet access that drives children and young people's experiences. In many countries in the global South, digital exclusion is widespread. This chapter addresses children's lives in the global North, where the internet is seen as a basic necessity for economic and human development. Here, too, however, digital exclusion affects the life chances of many children and young people in less resourced communities.

Children and young people's experiences in physical and virtual worlds can flow into one another to offer unique experiences and a new hybrid reality of childhood and youth (Granic, Morita and Scholten, 2020). For example, the *Pokémon Go* phenomenon, played by millions of people around the world, popularised AR. *Pokémon Go* uses location tracking via Global Positioning System (GPS) mapping services and the camera on smartphones to overlay popular Nintendo *Pokémon* cartoon characters into location images so they 'appear' on the screen as if in the physical world (Drake, 2016). In this way, players explore the physical world while chasing and training virtual *Pokémon*. This is an example of social gaming where offline and online experiences and activities are meshed together. However, darker sides to applications have been documented, such as the immersive '*Horizon Worlds*' VR in the Metaverse (from Meta, formerly Facebook), accessed through VR headsets that can track bodily information like eye movements, facial expressions, and body temperature. A report by the global, non-governmental community advocacy organisation SumOfUs (2022) detailed many harms quickly encountered in *Horizon Worlds*, including virtual grooming; sexual, homophobic, and racist activities; and failure to act against users who violate guidelines. These issues (among others) highlight the need to regulate digital media for children and young people's wellbeing, report violations, and create measures that protect children online while facilitating their rights to information and participation in digital media.

Children and young people's screen use through a global pandemic

In 2020, nearly 3 billion people worldwide were forced to shelter at home, as many countries enacted restrictions to limit the spread of Covid-19. Nearly 90% of children and young people in the global North were physically cut off from their schools and communities (Schwartz *et al.*, 2021), and technology quickly became central in their access to learning, peers, and virtual play. Social media and networking platforms replaced schools and playgrounds as places where many children connected with friends and family. This accelerated a focus on children and young people's use of technology. Some academics, such as psychologist Jean Twenge (2020), raised concerns that digital screen use is harming young people's social and emotional wellbeing, with claims that increased social media use is contributing to rising mental health problems, such as depression, anxiety, and suicidal behaviours. In contrast, other psychologists, such as Amy Orben (2020), conclude that social media use does not (from the data available to date) appear to be strongly associated with adolescents' wellbeing, including depressive symptoms. Other studies have found limited negative effects or even benefits with greater screen time (Przybylski and Weinstein, 2019) and, therefore, some social media use. To understand these contrasts, Orben (2020) suggests it might be useful to differentiate the emotional and social outcomes of social media use. For example, social media might have a negative effect on emotional outcomes (e.g., mood or depression) but a positive effect on social outcomes (e.g., social connectedness). However, there is still no clear answer because effects of social media vary across users and time frames. Twenge (2020) indicates that more research is needed before screen time limits are justified. Psychologists Candice Odgers and Michaeline Jensen (2020) note that current research is unable to deliver the clear guidance that policy makers, educators, parents, and adolescents themselves require. They argue for future investments in online research and interventions to better support adolescents who now spend much of their time in digital spaces.

In a qualitative study of children and their parents on technology use during the lockdown in Denmark in the spring of 2020, Thomas Lundtofte (2021) interviewed 20 children aged 2–12 years (and their parents) about their everyday lives, digital habits, social relations, and general wellbeing. Interviews were carried out using online video conference software (e.g., Zoom), and the children filled out so-called 'time capsules', where they could draw and write about their experiences beforehand. Although all children had used digital technologies more than usual for communication and entertainment, the research team highlighted significant differences between younger children (7 years and under) and older ones (8 years and above). Young children had little contact via social media with other children and were dependent on parents helping them with technologies for remote learning. Older children had more well-established digital practices, and they were able to maintain social relations with other children and independently use their digital devices for online learning. Children and parents experienced new ways of using digital technologies and while their encounters were not without conflict or frustration, some parents in the study expressed some level of surprise after realising how their (primarily younger) children had had positive experiences with digital technologies.

Much advice about screen time for children was first formulated prior to the Covid-19 pandemic. For example, the American Academy of Pediatrics (AAP, 2021), which had previously endorsed strict limits on screen time for young children, recommended rethinking this in light of the pandemic, instead focusing on the *activities* children are engaged in rather than the *time* children spend on screen. The AAP suggested that adults use screens along with younger children; that they set boundaries on where, when, and how adolescents use their devices; and that screen use should not replace physical activity or interfere with sleeping patterns and quality of sleep.

Lundtofte (2021) indicates that children and young peoples' use of screens to interact with people in their lives was beneficial in many ways during the strict periods of lockdown. However, what also emerged was the need for children and young people's equitable access to technology. As noted previously, even in high income countries, there are differences between households in the availability of reliable broadband internet connections and devices to support online education and communication.

Key points

- Children's physical everyday life and their virtual experiences (digital life) have become meshed together in a new hybrid reality.

- Much of the advice available about 'screen time' was written prior to the Covid-19 pandemic. Research involving children is required to clarify the impact of different kinds of screen use.
- Current research recommends considering the *activities* children are engaged in rather than the *time* children spend on screen.
- Greater safeguards are needed for immersive digital environments.
- There are significant inequalities between and within countries, and internet access and exclusion continue to affect children and young people's access and experiences.

Children and young people's screen use at home

Researchers face particular challenges when seeking to understand children's technology experiences in their homes. Parents and carers often maintain control over the digital devices and software that children and young people access, through direct parental surveillance or restrictive tools. Additionally, due to negative attitudes towards children and young people's technology use often presented in the media, some parents can be reluctant to share with researchers their child's home practices, play, and learning with technology due to fears of being judged negatively (Laidlaw, O'Mara and Wong, 2019). Laidlaw and colleagues noted that parents became less panicked as popular articles began to shift their focus to more 'balanced examinations' of the challenges and benefits of technology.

As children and young people are expert in their lives, it is good practice to involve them as active research participants. For example, when seeking to understand children's experiences of digital media in the home, 'show and tell' tours invite a child to lead the researcher around their home using a digital recording app, enabling a focus on their activities and passions. Jackie Marsh and her colleagues (2016) used a mixed-methods approach to collect data, when working with children aged up to 5 years, during six visits to each household. The researchers interviewed parents and children; videoed and photographed children whilst they used the apps (and asked parents to do so); and invited children to wear GoPro cameras attached to a chest harness and to lead researchers on play and creativity tours at home, identifying the spaces and places where they played, both on- and offline.

These play tours yielded rich information about how the digital and non-digital converge and diverge in children's play across virtual and physical worlds. Marsh *et al.* (2016) concluded that contemporary play draws on digital and non-digital properties and moves fluidly across boundaries of space and time. For example, LEGO continues to be a passion for many children and young people; they can move fluidly across virtual and physical spaces using LEGO apps on a tablet and smartphone as well as original LEGO bricks. LEGO fans participate in online communities by uploading videos of their physical LEGO play or producing digital films made in LEGO computer games using screen-capture software (Marsh *et al.*, 2017). This illustrates how physical toys can be used in virtual spaces and how the two modalities can flow into one another.

Engaging with, and listening to, the views and experiences of children and young people can enhance understanding of contemporary play and new ways of using and learning with technologies. It also provides opportunities to explore safety measures and reporting mechanisms that safeguard children and young people.

Key points

- Research exploring children and young people's own views and experiences can enhance our understandings of how they engage with, play, and learn from digital technology.
- Fruitful inquiry for contemporary hybrid realities could include what it means for children and young people to move fluidly across virtual and physical spaces, developing a deeper engagement with activities and their learning.

Digital play and learning

Psychologists have noted that play is essential for children's development. It not only supplements learning but is also necessary for it, as play-based learning (PBL) research shows (Taylor and Boyer, 2020). Digital play offers children opportunities to experience enjoyment and live out playful intentions in online spaces.

Types of digital play

As in the offline world, virtual games can offer children opportunities to explore and create. To enable playworkers to identify children's (offline) play, playworker Bob Hughes (2002) described 16 types of play. Marsh and her colleagues (2016) studied digital play in children under five years playing on tablets and observed most of these 16 types of play. A common feature of digital play with apps witnessed by Marsh *et al.* was *imaginative play*: for example, children treated digital pets as 'real' animals and pretended to care for them. Marsh *et al.* also observed *deep play* in a digital environment, such as when 3-year-old April played the app '*Temple Run*': though she described the game as 'scary', she also wanted to play it again. Marsh *et al.* (2016) highlighted that in deep digital play, children experience similar feelings of tension and fear as in risky offline play. It may be easier to switch some digital games off if they are causing too much emotional stress than it would be to leave deep play in a physical environment, suggesting children could have more control over digital play. However, game design often strategically deploys suggestion and reward to encourage players to continue, and a player's psychological drive to continue will often be strong, as demonstrated here by April.

In Marsh *et al.*'s (2016) study, they found one type of digital play that was not reflected in Hughes's framework of 16 play types. *Transgressive play* occurred when children played in a way that differed, or 'transgressed', from the app designers' intentions. In 3-year-old Arjun's activities when playing '*Alphablocks*' on the CBeebies Playtime app, rather than placing alphabet blocks on the line underneath a word he was supposed to spell, he swiped the block to the top of the screen to make it disappear, then released it to bounce back on the screen while saying, 'Peekaboo!'

Marsh *et al.* (2016, p. 250) propose adding 'transgressive play' to Hughes's frame-work with the following definition: 'Play in which children contest, resist and/or trans-gress expected norms, rules and perceived restrictions in both digital and non-digital contexts'. While Marsh *et al.* note this omission in Hughes's framework, ideas of transgression exist in other conceptualisations of play, games, and childhood (Duncum, 2009; Møller, 2015).

Furthermore, one of Hughes's 16 play types was missing from Marsh *et al.*'s ana-lysis of children's digital play: *rough-and-tumble* play. This relates to physical contact, such as a child climbing onto a parent's back who is on all fours, pretending the parent is a 'horsey'. Active or exergames (exercise games), like *WiiFit*, *Just Dance*, or VR games, offer physical activity and interactivity but cannot replicate the physical touch of offline rough-and-tumble play. Finally, one of Hughes's 16 types of play was difficult to identify in virtual environments. *Recapitulative play* can occur in all play types, where children might explore history, rituals, and myths and play in ways that resonate with the activities of our human ancestors (lighting fires, building shelters). It is seen offline when children build dens and shelters or light fires, usually in natural environments. However, Marsh *et al.* (2016) did observe it in children's play of a game called *Minecraft* (more on this later).

Marsh *et al.*'s (2016) study enables us to see that digital play can offer children similar experiences to offline play, and should not necessarily be viewed as harming children's cognitive development. Instead, Marsh *et al.* demonstrate that digital con-texts change what play looks like and the tools used to engage in it. In offline play, the physical features and social aspects come from seeing and being able to touch those who are playing. In online play, social aspects may come from playing online while in the same room as other players or in online communities where communica-tion takes place through text or voice chat. Despite looking and being different from play in the physical world, digital play can provide some of the same benefits. Granic, Lobel and Engels (2014) note that playing video games can foster social, emotional, and technical skills that can help children and young people to develop into rounded individuals.

Further studies show an overlap between young people's online and offline worlds. Young people were found to interact online with the same peers they socialised with at school, and online contexts strengthened offline relationships (Reich, Subrahmanyam and Espinoza, 2012). Indeed, researchers have long suggested that separating chil-dren and young people's engagement in physical and virtual environments is futile. Instead, we can note the fluidity of movement between these spaces, where experi-ences unfold, intersect, and merge along a continuum. One game that has become a global phenomenon and is world renowned for merging online with offline communities is *Minecraft*.

Minecraft replicates many positive aspects of play, so it challenges some of the blanket concerns expressed about virtual worlds or virtual gaming. However, as noted earlier, a key aspect of offline play not replicated by digital play includes tactile experi-ences. Exploratory tactile experiences, such as messy play, 'feely' bags, or cooking, are necessary for helping children to develop and understand sensory experiences and accept certain smells, tastes, and textures. Furthermore, as most digital games rely on sight and sound, they are inaccessible to children and young people with visual and/or hearing impairments. To evaluate the success of digital play opportunities for learning and play participation for all, it is important to consider how all children and young people have equal access to similar learning experiences.

Digital apps and children's physical development

Many educational smartphone and tablet applications have been developed to increase language, literacy, and STEM (science, technology, engineering, and mathematics) skills for pre-school children (Callaghan and Reich, 2018). Examples of organisations creating educational experiences or revision opportunities include BBC Bitesize (BBC, 2022). However, being on screen rather than in the physical world might cause under-development of physical skills, such as in the finger muscles. In a report in a UK news-paper, the Head Paediatric Occupational Therapist at the Heart of England Foundation NHS Trust, Sally Payne, highlighted that:

> Children are not coming into school with the hand strength and dexterity they had 10 years ago. Children coming into school are being given a pencil but are increas-ingly not able to hold it because they don't have the fundamental movement skills.
>
> (Hill, 2018)

Over-reliance on touchscreen and thumb use of game controllers reduces children's fine-motor abilities to grip pencils, which are necessary for handwriting. Children must be exposed to handwriting and drawing activities from an early age to establish the appropriate brain patterns that are beneficial for learning. However, this could occur either with a stylus and tablet or traditional paper and pencil (Askvik, van der Weel and van der Meer, 2020; Vinci-Booher, James and James, 2016). Some apps for young children provide opportunities to 'trace' over letters, replicating 'sand' or 'foam' writing activities.

Minecraft: An early 21st-century phenomenon

In August 2021, 13 years after its initial release, *Minecraft* had over 141 million players monthly (Mojang Studios, 2022), and players often include very young children (Marsh *et al.*, 2016). The enormous popularity has surprised many.

Minecraft is described by its developers, Mojang Studios, as a 'sandbox video game', akin to a creative sandpit in which children play, creating a new game each time. There are high levels of freedom and creativity in games like *Minecraft* and *The Sims* (another 21st-century game popular amongst young people), which often lack set objectives or predetermined goals, allowing for 'emergent game-play', where the player chooses how they interact with the game and create narratives. Although *Minecraft* provides tutorials for users, players can play in ways developers never anticipated. The 'open-world' virtual environment *Minecraft* provides is a perfect example of open-ended digital play. It incorporates all of Marsh *et al.'s* (2016) redefined 16 types of digital play apart from rough-and-tumble play. Many (e.g., Dezuanni, 2017) have described *Minecraft* as having similarities with Lego not least due to the block-like appearance of the characters and the environment but also the opportunity to develop spatial awareness skills and children's agency through choice.

Minecraft can be played alone, with friends and family over local area networks, or with other players over the internet, highlighting the social opportunities this game offers. It can also be played in two modes: Creative, where all resources are freely available, creative construction is allowed, and avatars can fly; and Survival, where players are more restricted. As their avatars are not able to fly, they can be injured by falls and hostile creatures, and they must manually collect resources to build structures. Survival mode creates competition and a lack of freedom that is not present in Creative mode. These gameplay features allow players to choose the level of skill required from the gaming experience, providing the player with a sense of control.

A final important feature is the opportunity for collaboration. Mavoa, Carter and Gibbs (2018) studied how children play *Minecraft*: nearly half of the parents reported their child most often played *Minecraft* with others. This suggests that claims about digital play being predominantly solitary (e.g., Mundy *et al.*, 2017) appear overstated, at least in the case of *Minecraft*. *Minecraft* might be the perfect example of how digital play can replicate offline play due to its open-ended nature, varying skill levels, creative engagement, and opportunities for collaboration.

Furthermore, many apps like Endless Reader ™ and Endless Numbers ™ (Originator Kids, 2013a, 2013b) can teach children to read with online tools to capture sound, write by tracing with their fingers, and conduct early maths calculations by playing independently. Children with developmental delays, non-verbal autistic children, and other neurodiverse children, who require language and communication support, can communicate using augmentative and alternative communication (AAC) on tablet devices, pressing pictures or symbols to have the assistive technology speak.

Other muscle-building gross- and fine-motor activities, such as cutting and sticking, climbing, running, and pulling ropes, are not represented in most digital play.

However, virtual reality (VR) and video game consoles with motion-sensitive features like Nintendo Switch™ offer in-game actions, such as running in place, squatting, jumping, and so on. Digital play and learning offer developmental opportunities that differ from those offline but that can also be beneficial.

Key points

- Physical and digital play and learning experiences can merge along a continuum.
- Although digital play occurs in a different context, it can replicate many experiences of playing physically with traditional toys and games.
- Digital devices cannot replicate all physical skill opportunities for all children and young people but offer developmental opportunities that may also be beneficial.
- Playing computer games can develop a range of developmental social, emotional, and technical skills.

Exploitation of children in virtual spaces

As we have seen, screen use at home, digital play, and digital learning opportunities offer ways for children and young people to merge and intersect their experiences between physical and virtual spaces with much success and offer excellent opportunities to learn, socialise, and play. However, risks should also be considered when exploring young people's virtual worlds, including how children and young people are treated and how spaces are regulated.

As Simone van der Hof *et al.* (2020) highlight, the virtual worlds in which children grow up are increasingly commercialised. Referring to rights articulated in the United Nations Convention on the Rights of the Child (UNCRC; see Chapter 1), van der Hof *et al.* note that in the virtual environment, children and young people need protection against a myriad of economically exploitative practices. An in-depth study for the European Commission (Lupiáñez-Villanueva *et al.*, 2016) of 25 of the most popular online games revealed that in all advergames (in which products are advertised), children and young people were not only subjected to embedded advertisements but also to multiple prompts to make in-app purchases. Advertisements and prompts to purchase had significant effects on behaviour, with children more likely to eat sweets after viewing adverts with high-energy snacks and more likely to spend money if prompted. Not all games contain embedded advertisements, and in-app purchases are usually locked for under 13s (assuming that their correct age has been entered), but it is important for families to understand the safeguarding and process for reporting violations that underpin games they are using.

Games that allow children to design digitally and to make and set the rules are becoming more visible in education, even in school lessons, indicating they may be a positive experience. Roblox, a game site launched in 2006, allows users to create games that they and others can play in a large virtual world. As of 2019, Roblox had a library of over 50 million user-generated games and more than 100 million active monthly players (Dredge, 2019). It is described by its developers as a 'global platform where millions of people gather together every day to imagine, create, and share experiences in immersive, user-generated 3D worlds' (Roblox Corporation, 2021). In August 2021, investigative video journalists (PMG, 2021) alleged that the platform encourages child game developers to make games for other users but makes it next to impossible to profit from the games they create, stating that 'it is very challenging to make money on Roblox, and Roblox profits from people trying'. They argue that encouraging children to create games for the platform but not renumerating them is a form of child labour. Conversely, Roblox state that instead of exploiting children, they feel they are providing them with the opportunities to build experiences by teaching them 'the fundamentals of coding, digital civility, and entrepreneurship' and that they have helped many begin their careers in science, technology, engineering, and mathematics (STEM) (D'Anastasio, 2021). Yet boundaries between work and play appear ambiguous, and further transparency around children's creative contributions is required. This may infringe Articles 31 and 32 of the UNCRC, that assert the child's right to relax and play, and to be protected from economic exploitation. This further indicates a need to understand the fluidity between physical and virtual worlds and the principle that the rights children hold offline also apply online.

Children can be further exploited online when data about them are used in the commercial world. In the current era, 'data can be used to learn, deduce or infer much more about individuals than ever before' (Children's Commissioner for England, 2018, p. 4). Children's online behaviour is continuously recorded, often sold, analysed, and acted upon (van der Hof *et al.*, 2020). Advergames, such as *Big Bumpin'*, an Xbox game paid for by Burger King, collect personal information from the player to make the game visually more attractive to them, thereby making them more susceptible to the product (Verdoodt, Clifford and Lievens, 2016). Internet-connected physical toys can record children's conversations, analysing and remembering them, and may integrate targeted references to products in those conversations (Milkaite and Lievens, 2019). These data can be used to build a profile that is sold on the internet to advertisers and others, contributing to a child's digital footprint, which games and other apps use to make automated marketing decisions, such as targeting them with ads with features they will respond to, offering or withholding certain rights or options, and establishing learning analytics about them. The UNCRC right to privacy (Article 16) encompasses the right to data protection; the collection and processing of personal data – for instance, to profile a child – should comply with legal requirements.

In sum, and as noted earlier in the chapter, online platforms currently facilitate many unsafe practices, through which children and young people can be exposed to harmful content and contact. Children can learn to understand regulations provided to protect them, consider how safe versus how vulnerable they feel in situations, and explore how the data they share with others will be used, yet the ways current system designs do not generally give them the option to act with agency – for example, choosing to play a game but opting out of having their data collected. Similarly, while parents and carers expect to monitor and protect children, expecting them to be able to do so within digital systems that are designed for exploitation and not suitably regulated for children and young people is unreasonable. Improving these systems is important not just to protect children and young people but also because over-protection can lead to them being treated as 'passive objects of concern, rather than moral agents in their own right' (Alderson and Morrow, 2020, p. 43).

There is also an opportunity to invite children to adopt a central role in technology research and innovation. Involving children in designing and making games through a participatory design agenda can be empowering and enjoyable. Games like Roblox can be seen as a tool for empowerment, and when integrated into children's education, they could help combat the digital divide (Iivari and Kinnula, 2018). However, this would require addressing power differences between adults and children and involving children as 'decision makers' (Iivari and Kinnula, 2018, p. 3). Children and young people enjoy and can benefit from being online; therefore, it is up to adult creators and policy makers to actively explore ways that successfully invite children and young people to contribute to the design of these online spaces to minimise risks and maximise opportunities.

Key points

- Children can be exploited online, and it is vital to consider the regulations and safeguards in place.
- Children and young people can be targeted through gameplay by corporations for marketing or game development, often as an infringement of their rights.
- Children have a right to separate play from economic gain, and game developers should be required to be transparent about intentions of game design.
- Children and young people are influential in the design of gaming experiences, and offering a sense of agency and voice in design can create positive experiences.

Conclusion

This chapter's discussion about children and young people's lives on and off screen has developed far beyond current mainstream media concerns about 'screen time', arguing that this oversimplifies children's current hybrid worlds of games, applications, and mobile activities. You may have been challenged by the view that children and young people may experience benefits and more opportunities when engaging and participating in virtual worlds. During the global Covid-19 pandemic, the virtual world facilitated communication and collaboration when the physical world was locked down. However, there were also barriers to engaging in these virtual worlds, particularly for those from more disadvantaged backgrounds.

This chapter has explored how children can move fluidly between physical and virtual spaces in their new hybrid reality. This can lead to online exploitation through exposure to harms, commercialisation, and infringements of privacy and other rights, but those virtual worlds can also provide opportunities to play in different contexts and acquire different skills. Virtual worlds can offer children opportunities to learn many skills and develop in a fast-changing world. Offering children and young people a voice and agency in the research and design of their online practices can create more positive experiences.

References

Alderson, P., and Morrow, V. (2020) *The Ethics of Research with Children and Young People: A Practical Handbook* (2nd ed.). London: Sage.

American Academy of Pediatrics (2021) 'Beyond screen time: a parent's guide to media use', *Pediatric Patient Education*. Available at: https://doi.org/10.1542/peo_document099 (Accessed 14th March 2023).

Askvik, E. O., van der Weel, F. R., and van der Meer, A. L. H. (2020) 'The importance of cursive handwriting over typewriting for learning in the classroom: a high-density EEG study of 12-year-old children and young adults', *Frontiers in Psychology*, 11(1810). doi:10.3389/fpsyg.2020.01810.

BBC (2022) *BBC Bitesize*. Available at: www.bbc.co.uk/bitesize (Accessed 9th September 2022).

Blum-Ross, A., and Livingstone, S. (2016) *Families and Screen Time: Current Advice and Emerging Research. Media Policy Brief 17*. London: Media Policy Project, London School of Economics and Political Science.

Callaghan, M. N. and Reich, S. M. (2018) 'Are educational preschool apps designed to teach? An analysis of the app market', *Learning, Media, and Technology*, 43, pp. 280–293. doi:10.1080/17439884.2018.1498355.

Children's Commissioner for England (2018) *Who Knows What about Me?* Available at: www.childrenscommissioner.gov.uk/publication/who-knows-what-about-me/ (Accessed 16th February 2022).

D'Anastasio, C. (2021) 'On Roblox, kids learn it's hard to earn money making games', *WIRED*, 19 August, Available at: www.wired.com/story/on-roblox-kids-learn-its-hard-to-earn-money-making-games/ (Accessed 24th October 2022).

Dezuanni, M. (2017) 'Material and discursive learning with Minecraft and Lego', in C. Beavis, M. Dezuanni and J. O'Mara (eds.) *Serious Play*. New York: Routledge, pp. 133–148.

Drake, D. (2016) *Reality Check: The Technology Behind 'Pokemon Go'*, Wharton University of Pennsylvania, 1 August. Available at: Reality Check: The Technology Behind "Pokemon Go" – Wharton Global Youth Program (upenn.edu) (Accessed 18th August 2022).

Dredge, S. (2019) 'All you need to know about Roblox', *The Guardian* (Digital), 28 September. Available at: www.theguardian.com/games/2019/sep/28/roblox-guide-children-gaming-platform-developer-minecraft-fortnite (Accessed 12th September 2022).

Duncum, P. (2009) 'Towards a playful pedagogy: popular culture and the pleasures of transgression', *Studies in Art Education*, 50(3), pp. 232–244.

Granic, I., Lobel, A., and Engels, R. C. (2014) 'The benefits of playing video games', *American Psychologist*, 69(1), pp. 66–78. doi:10.1037/a0034857.

Granic, I., Morita, H., and Scholten, H. (2020) 'Beyond screen time: identity development in the digital age', *Psychological Inquiry*, 31(3), pp. 195–223. doi:10.1080/1047840X.2020.1820214.

Hill, A. (2018) 'Children struggle to hold pencils due to too much tech, doctors say', *The Guardian*, 25 May. Available at: www.theguardian.com/society/2018/feb/25/children-struggle-to-hold-pencils-due-to-too-much-tech-doctors-say (Accessed 12th September 2022).

Hopkins, L., Brookes, F., and Green, J. (2013) 'Books, bytes and brains: the implications of new knowledge for children's early literacy learning', *Australasian Journal of Early Childhood*, 38(1), pp. 23–28.

Hughes, B. (2002) *A Playworker's Taxonomy of Play Types* (2nd ed.). London: PlayLink.

Ibbetson, C. (2020) 'How many children have their own tech?', *YouGov*. Available at: https://

yougov.co.uk/topics/education/articles-reports/2020/03/13/what-age-do-kids-get-phones-tablet-laptops- (Accessed 5th January 2022).

Iivari, N., and Kinnula, M. (2018) *Empowering Children Through Design and Making: Towards Protagonist Role Adoption*, PDC '18: Proceedings of the 15th participatory design conference, 1, 20–24 August 2018, Hasselt and Genk, Belgium.

Laidlaw, L., O'Mara, J., and Wong, S. S. H. (2019) 'Researching in the iWorld: From home to beyond', in Natalia Kucirkova, Jennifer Rowsell and Garry Falloon (eds.) *The Routledge International Handbook of Learning with Technology in Early Childhood*. Abingdon: Routledge, pp. 182–195.

Lundtofte, T. E. (2021) *The School Year 2020–2021 in Denmark During the Pandemic. Country Report*. Luxembourg: Publications Office of the European Union. doi:10.2760/41171JRC125452. Available at: https://ketlib.lib.unipi.gr/xmlui/bitstream/handle/ket/3779/jrc125452_edu_covid_denmark_report_2021.pdf?sequence=1&isAllowed=y (Accessed 18th October 2022).

Lupiáñez-Villanueva, F., Gaskell, G., Veltri, G., Theben, A., Folkford, F., Bonatti, F., Bogliacino, F., Fernández, L., and Codagnone, C. (2016) *Study on the Impact of Marketing Through Social Media, Online Games and Mobile Applications on Children's Behaviour*. Report for the European Commission's Consumers, Health, Agriculture and Food Executive Agency, Luxembourg: European Union. Available at: https://ec.europa.eu/info/sites/default/files/online_marketing_children_final_report_en.pdf (Accessed 18th October 2022).

Lythreatis, S., Singh, S. K., and El-Kassar, A. N. (2021) 'The digital divide: a review and future research agenda', *Technological Forecasting and Social Change*, 175, p. 121359.

Marsh, J., Hannon, P., Lewis, M., and Ritchie, L. (2017) 'Young children's initiation into family literacy practices in the digital age', *Journal of Early Childhood Research*, 15(1), pp. 47–60.

Marsh, J., Plowman, L., Yamada-Rice, D., Bishop, J., and Scott, F. (2016) 'Digital play: a new classification', *Early Years*, 36(3), pp. 242–253. doi:10.1080/09575146.2016.1167675.

Mavoa, J., Carter, M., and Gibbs, M. (2018) 'Children and Minecraft: a survey of children's digital play', *New Media & Society*, 20(9), pp. 3283–3303.

Milkaite, I., and Lievens, E. (2019) 'The internet of toys: playing games with children's data?', in G. Mascheroni and D. Holloway (eds.) *The Internet of Toys: Practices, Affordances and the Political Economy of Children's Smart Play*. Cham: Palgrave Macmillan, pp. 285–305.

Mojang Studios (2022) *Minecraft*. Available at: www.minecraft.net/en-us (Accessed 9th September 2022).

Møller, S. J. (2015) 'Imagination, playfulness, and creativity in children's play with different toys', *American Journal of Play*, 7(3), pp. 322–346.

Mundy, L. K., Canterford, L., Olds, T., Allen, N. B., and Patton, G. C. (2017) 'The association between electronic media and emotional and behavioral problems in late childhood', *Academic Paediatrician*, 6, pp. 620–624. doi:10.1016/j.acap.2016.12.014.

Odgers, C. L., and Jensen, M. R. (2020) 'Annual research review: adolescent mental health in the digital age: facts, fears, and future directions', *Journal of Child Psychology and Psychiatry*, 61(3), pp. 336–348.

Orben, A. (2020) 'Teenagers, screens and social media: a narrative review of reviews and key studies', *Social Psychiatry and Psychiatric Epidemiology*, 55(4), pp. 407–414.

Originator Kids (2013a) *Endless Numbers*. Available at: www.originatorkids.com/?p=731 (Accessed 9th September 2022).

Originator Kids (2013b) *Endless Reader*. Available at: www.originatorkids.com/?p=40 (Accessed 9th September 2022).

People Make Games (2021) *Investigation: How Roblox is Exploiting Young Game Developers*. Available at: www.youtube.com/watch?v=_gXlauRB1EQ (Accessed 14th March 2023).

Przybylski, A. K., and Weinstein, N. (2019) 'Digital screen time limits and young children's psychological well-being: evidence from a population-based study', *Child Development*, 90(1), pp. e56–e65.

Reich, S. M., Subrahmanyam, K., and Espinoza, G. (2012) 'Friending, Iming, and hanging out face-to-face: overlap in adolescents' online and offline social networks', *Developmental Psychology*, 48(2), pp. 356–368.

Roblox Corporation (2021) *Roblox*, Available at: roblox.com (Accessed 14th March 2023).

Schwartz, K. D., Exner-Cortens, D., McMorris, C. A., Makarenko, E., Arnold, P., Van Bavel, M., Williams, S., and Canfield, R. (2021) 'COVID-19 and student well-being: stress and mental health during return-to-school', *Canadian Journal of School Psychology*, 36(2), pp. 166–185.

SumofUs (2022) *Metaverse: Another Cesspool of Toxic Content*. Available at: www.sumofus.org/images/Metaverse_report_May_2022.pdf (Accessed 11th August 2022).

Taylor, M. E., and Boyer, W. (2020) 'Play-based learning: evidence-based research to improve children's learning experiences in the kindergarten classroom', *Early Childhood Education Journal*, 48, pp. 127–133.

Twenge, J. M. (2020) 'Why increases in adolescent depression may be linked to the technological environment', *Current Opinion in Psychology*, 32, pp. 89–94.

van der Hof, S., Lievens, E., Milkaite, I., Verdoodt, V., Hannema, T., and Liefaard, T. (2020) 'The child's right to protection against economic exploitation in the digital world', *The International Journal of Children's Rights*, 28(4), pp. 833–859. doi:10.1163/15718182-28040003.

Verdoodt, V., Clifford, D., and Lievens, E. (2016) 'Toying with children's emotions, the new game in town? The legality of advergames in the EU', *Computer Law & Security Review*, 32(4), pp. 599–614.

Vinci-Booher, S., James, T. W., and James, K. H. (2016) 'Visual-motor functional connectivity in preschool children emerges after handwriting experience', *Trends in Neuroscience Education*, 5, pp. 107–120. doi:10.1016/j.tine.2016.07.006.

13 Adolescents, teenagers, and youth

A time of change

Victoria Cooper, Mimi Tatlow-Golden, and Heather Montgomery

Introduction

Although the term childhood refers to anyone under the age of 18, childhood does not abruptly end when a person wakes up on their 18th birthday. Moving out of childhood is a process of change, with gains and losses, which takes place over several years and has no fixed end or starting point. The stage of life between childhood and adulthood, when people are not physically or socially mature but are no longer as dependent as younger children, has been intensively scrutinised by many disciplines. In this chapter, we show that studying this period of life holistically requires integrating perspectives to see interplays between social, biological, psychological, cultural, and historical understandings. In doing so, we discuss the invention of the teenager; historical and cultural understandings of youth; young people's views of adolescence; development in brains, bodies, selves, and peers; and young people's political activism.

Within this interplay of understandings are different terminologies and definitions that overlap with and sometimes contradict those used in everyday speech. In the contemporary UK, the word 'teenager' is perhaps the most common, but as this chapter will explore, it is a relatively recent invention. Psychologists and doctors use 'adolescence' for the years from puberty to physical maturation, noting physical changes such as menstruation, developing bodily hair and voice-breaking, and changing behaviours and identities. They typically identify adolescence as beginning at about 10 years with the onset of puberty. Social scientists usually prefer 'youth' or 'young people' to refer those from the age of 13, focusing on the social construction of this period of transition. Of particular note is how, in many countries in the 20th century, adolescence and youth became extended into the early- or mid-20s, as social change led to longer education and later work, marriage, and parenthood. As a result, both psychologists and social scientists identify the end of adolescence/youth at 24 or 25 years.

Regardless of terminology or exact starting or ending times, adolescence involves important physical, psychological, and social changes that influence one another. It is also often characterised in quite negative terms and as a time of stress and disruption. But why is this so? For many young people, navigating their developing sense of self and identity can feel daunting, but it can also be an

DOI: 10.4324/9781003358855-14

exciting time of transformation. Many young people throughout the world change schools, make new friends, gain independence, learn new skills, take on new responsibilities at work or at home, and begin to forge intimate, sexual relationships. Adolescence can be a time of firsts: first love, first job, and perhaps the first time driving a car or drinking alcohol. Not all teenagers will experience adolescence as turbulent or stressful and neither do all societies.

Adolescent studies have typically focused on experiences of young people in the global North. While these have deepened understandings of adolescent development, their focus on Europe, North America, and Australasia have led to the nuances, diversity, and different understandings of adolescent development globally being somewhat overlooked.

The invention of the teenager

The word 'teenager' is linked to social, economic, and demographic change in the USA in the 1920s although there had long been an idea of transitory, difficult stage of life between childhood and adulthood in European cultures. Ancient Greek philosophers such as Socrates and Aristotle grumbled about teenage behaviour (Blakemore, 2019a), while in Shakespeare's *The Winter Tale* (published in 1623), an old shepherd complains:

> I would there were no age between ten and three-and-twenty, or that youth would sleep out the rest; for there is nothing in the between but getting wenches with child, wronging the ancientry, stealing, fighting.
>
> (Shakespeare, *The Winter's Tale*, Act III, scene iii)

Yet the idea that young people formed a separate 'teenager' category, with their own culture, vocabulary, and importantly, spending power was unheard of before the 20th century.

In the 1920s, this began to change. Until this point, almost all children in the USA left school at about 14, started to work, and contributed their wages to their families before finding a spouse, setting up a home, and having their own children. There was little time or money for carefree transition between childhood and adulthood. The economic depression of the late 1920s and 1930s, however, meant fewer jobs were available, especially for unskilled youth, and increasing numbers of 14–18-year-olds stayed on in high school, learning a skill rather than face unemployment. In 1920, only 28% of 14–18-year-olds were in school in the US. By 1930, this had risen to 47% and 80% in 1941. Life for these young people was also becoming more age-segregated. Rather than working alongside older adults and absorbing their values, they lived and studied in a peer group who increasingly became their primary influence. A distinctive popular culture emerged, which was neither child-like nor adult-like but somewhere in between, and focused on clothes, dating, dancing, listening to music, and hanging out with friends. Many adults looked on this with concern or even alarm, but advertisers and marketers, recognising that US youth had a spending capacity of $750 million, 'began

Figure 13.1 Teenagers cluster around a jukebox in the USA, 1952.

to address high school students as teenagers on the prowl for a good time, not earnest adolescents in training for adulthood' (Paladino, 1996, p. 53).

In the UK, the school-leaving age was raised from 12 to 14 in 1918 and to 15 in 1947. This created a similar demographic: a generation of young people staying in school longer, influenced by peers rather than parents and co-workers, old enough to have independence but few responsibilities, and keen to take advantage of the social changes and greater freedoms brought about by the end of the Second World War in 1945. Social and economic changes included greater employment opportunities, greater financial independence, and the mass production of everyday items, such as food, clothes, music, and literature, providing more leisure opportunities. Teenagers were 'cool' and trendsetting, and advertisers and manufacturers chased the young who would spend money to have fun.

Although advertisers warmly welcomed the spending power of the teenager, many adults reacted with concern and alarm. Drawing on older ideas of adolescence as a period of disruption, rebellion, and disrespect, many saw the teenager as a potential challenge to social order. At the beginning of the 20th century, psychology had begun to focus on adolescence as a specific and problematic life stage. In 1904, US psychologist Stanley Hall described adolescence as a period between the ages of 14 and 24, where teenagers experienced mood fluctuations, engaged in risky behaviour, and came into conflict with parents, carers, and authority. He claimed, somewhat dramatically, that the path to maturity through adolescence was 'strewn with wreckage of body, mind, and morals. There is not only arrest, but perversion, at every stage, and hoodlumism, juvenile crime, and secret vice' (Hall, 1904, p. xiv). In other words, adolescence was risky for the individual and society.

Hall's research proved highly influential in shaping an understanding of adolescence as emotionally and psychologically turbulent. The idea of adolescence as a time of 'storm and stress' (as Hall had argued) spread widely, and by the 1950s, the 'problems' of the teenage years, young people's moods, bad behaviour, and lack of respect for their parents and adults were widely accepted, and the stereotype of the teenager as impulsive, highly self-conscious, irresponsible, self-obsessed, and – in some cases – threatening and out of control had become entrenched. These stereotypes exist to this day, and adolescents are frequently presented negatively and mockingly in the media. Often banned from shopping centres, cinemas, and recreational spaces in many (but not all) parts of the world, they have been demonised in ways which can affect both their rights to contribute and participate in society as well as their understanding of self and their developing identity. Furthermore, parenting guidance often sympathises with the perils and challenges of caring for an adolescent who won't get out of bed, is lazy, uncommunicative, and moody, offering guidance for parents on 'surviving' the teenage years.

At risk or at promise?

In English-speaking cultures across the world, the word and concept of the teenager have become ubiquitous. Even in non-English speaking countries, the words 'teenager' or 'teen' are widely known and understood so that in Japan, for example, the word 'cheenayja' has been borrowed by advertisers and in the media to describe young people's popular culture (Hinton, 2016). However, other Western ideas about teenagers have not been imported, and Japanese young people are understood differently. One of the first to look at this was US anthropologist Merry White in the 1990s. She compared experiences of being a teenager in Japan and the USA and concluded that in the US, adolescence was seen as 'a dangerous limbo period in which adolescents are at risk to themselves and others' (White, 1993, p. 10). In contrast, in Japan, adolescence was viewed more positively. Rebellion, risk-taking, and the rejection of parental authority were not considered key teenage behaviours, with antisocial behaviour, drinking alcohol, and drug-taking the exception rather than the rule. The Japanese had adopted the word 'cheenayja' but not the idea that adolescents were controlled by biological urges or that they were necessarily impulsive risk takers. White found that a young person's friends were viewed as positive reinforcements rather than as negative peer pressure. As she put it: 'Being a teen in America today, according to popular belief, means being at risk: in Japan it means, most people imagine, being at promise' (White, 1993, pp. 21–22).

More recently, there have been many more studies on Japanese teenagers, which have presented a more complex picture (see, for example, Goodman, Imoto and Toivonen, 2012). In his study of how the girl 'teen' is portrayed cross-culturally, Perry Hinton points out that cheenayja remains a widely understood marketing term but is not usually used to described young people more generally. In relation to young women, it is more common to refer to 'shoujo' (a word meaning a girl who is not yet a woman but no longer a child). Central to the traditional Japanese literature and more recently to Japanese anime (animated films) and manga (comics), the 'shoujo' is representative of a phase of life where girls experience enviable freedom before settling down to a life of domesticity and looking after others. In anime, she is often both a stereotypical Japanese adolescent, shy and naïve and pursuing typical teenage interests, such as boys, schools, friends, fashion, and music, but she is also the magical girl, or 'mahou shoujo', whose superpowers allow her to battle against evil and upset traditional gender expectations. Hinton (2016, p. 241) concludes:

> Unlike the US view of the psychologically at-risk teen requiring adult guidance to pass successfully into adulthood, in Japan the shoujo representation has positive connotations in popular culture, in both her youthful appeal and her consumer lifestyle and has been responsive to changing ideas of gender roles. The teenage girl in Japan is not necessarily a risk, or a threat, she is a promise and something to celebrate.

Key points

- While associating particular behaviours and feelings with adolescence has a long history, the teenager as a distinct social category only emerged in the 1940s.
- The idea that teenagers are always difficult drew on earlier research published by Stanley Hall in the USA in 1904 which saw adolescence as an inevitable and unchanging time of storm and stress for both the individual and society.
- While teenage rebellion is described as universal in the global North, cross-cultural evidence shows no worldwide expectation that young people should come into

conflict with their parents or that the teenage years should necessarily be a problem for young people or their society.

Understanding young people's views of adolescence

Parents and carers often report finding this a challenging stage of development where they feel less involved in their child's life (Blakemore, 2019a). For some young people, this can also feel like a difficult time. In a workshop with 28 young people aged 14 to 18 years in London, researchers Francesca Vaghi and Emily Emmot (2018) found that, as one young person aged 17 years describes, 'the bad thing about being my age is being expected to act like adults at college/work, but being treated like a child at home' (p. 4). Contradictory expectations of young people include wider society and particularly policy makers who grapple with understanding where young people fit. There are conflicting attitudes across society, and as another 17-year-old described, adolescents are 'too old in some situations but not old enough in others' (Vaghi and Emmot, 2018, p. 6).

A cursory glance at differences in how diverse cultures and societies address the ages at which young people gain permission to engage in adult activities, such as driving or voting, indicate that our understanding of adolescence is varied and still evolving. For example, most countries that permit alcohol drinking have set the minimum legal drinking age at 18 years, but others, including Cuba, Luxembourg, Belgium, Denmark, Germany, Serbia, and Zimbabwe, set it at 16 years, and minimum purchase ages vary globally from 15 to 25 years, influenced by social and cultural factors as well as by biological evidence for the impact of alcohol on the developing brain. You will learn more about the transition to adulthood in Chapter 14.

Teens' views of adolescence

The 28 adolescents taking part in Vaghi and Emmot's (2018) focus group interviews in London identified conflicting ideas and experiences about this time of rapid change in life but stressed that adolescence was not an inherently negative time of life (in contrast to the ideas suggested by Stanley Hall). These teens also felt that 'young people' was a vague term, and they preferred 'teen' or 'adolescent'. From adolescents' descriptions and insights at the workshop, Vaghi and Emmot drew the following conclusions about their experience:

- Adolescence is a time of growth and freedom but also increased responsibility.
- Adolescence can be an awkward time, somewhere between childhood and adulthood, which can lead to uncertainties and anxiety.
- Educational progress is an important marker for life transitions – from primary school (childhood), into secondary school (adolescence), into higher education (young adult).
- Financial independence was the ultimate marker of adulthood.

Vaghi and Emmot (2018, p. 3)

Brain and body: A time of rapid transformation

The field of neurobiology has significantly impacted understanding of adolescent development in recent years. By exploring changes in the brain and body, researchers have discovered that, contrary to what was previously believed, the brain changes substantially through and beyond adolescence, and indeed in adolescence the brain is particularly malleable. This goes some way to explaining aspects of adolescent thinking and behaviour.

During adolescence, the sex hormones testosterone and oestrogen stimulate puberty. Rapid growth in height and weight, maturation, and the development of secondary sexual characteristics is characteristic of adolescence globally, but its timing varies considerably between individuals as well as across cultures, depending on issues such as diet.

In addition to physical changes, adolescents also begin to think and process information in different ways. Barbara Inhelder, a developmental psychologist who worked closely with Jean Piaget, termed this period the *formal operational stage*, the fourth and final shift in thinking in Piaget's conceptualisation of cognitive development. As you learned in Chapter 7, it characterises the young person's growing capacity to think in more abstract and hypothetical terms (Inhelder and Piaget, 1958).

Contemporary research exploring adolescent cognition charts the emergence of 'executive functions', including decision making skills, self-awareness, and the understanding of others. These abilities underpin opportunities for enhanced learning and abstract thinking (Sebastian, Burnett and Blakemore, 2008). Adolescents may begin to reflect more, ask more questions, and challenge ideas which previously they might have more readily accepted. Asking questions and challenging ideas can lead many young people to question their sense of self, their future, and the future of society and the planet. These issues are discussed more later, and they may go some way to explaining why adolescents may appear argumentative as they seek to forge their own opinions and their place in the world – which is an important part of their transition into adulthood.

Since the late 1980s, new imaging techniques, such as MRI scans, create more detailed images of living brains, enabling researchers to understand more about brain structure and function. Laurence Steinberg and colleagues from Temple University in the US study neurobiological changes during puberty, affecting how young people think, feel, and behave. His research reveals that brains undergo substantial rapid development, starting from about 10 years and extending to 24 years, challenging longstanding assumptions about neurobiological development which was once thought to be mostly finished during childhood (Sawyer *et al.*, 2018). Indeed, brain changes continue throughout life but adolescence marks a particularly significant period. Plasticity is the term used by researchers to describe the brain's capacity to develop and adapt.

During adolescence, pubertal hormones oestrogen and testosterone affect the brain's plasticity. MRI scans reveal that areas of the brain's cortex develop at different stages. The

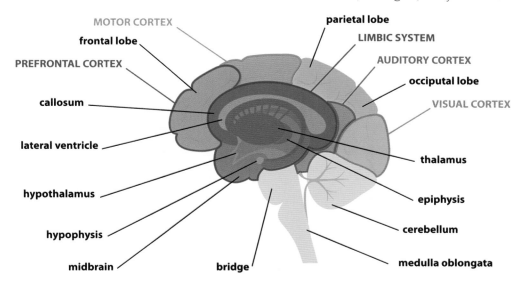

Figure 13.2 Brain development.

auditory and visual cortex (governing sight and sound) and the motor cortex (controlling movement) develop and mature during childhood and early adolescence (see Figure 13.2). Yet the prefrontal cortex is underdeveloped and still maturing during late adolescence and into early adulthood. This brain region is involved in higher-level functioning skills, such as problem solving, decision making and planning, and regulating emotions and behaviour. Furthermore, pubertal hormones stimulate dopamine production, meaning adolescents experience dopamine peaks. Dopamine is a neurotransmitter that sends messages between cells, influencing mood and our experience of reward and pleasure, and it also affects the prefrontal cortex. So adolescence is marked by two quite contrasting neurological developments: the dopamine-activated desire to seek pleasure and thrills in contrast to a still-underdeveloped 'executive function' and ability to regulate behaviour and emotions. This contrast provides a neurobiological explanation for why many, but certainly not all, adolescents may be more predisposed to engage in risky behaviours.

While neurobiological research has significantly extended understanding of adolescence, Laurence Steinberg (2014) warns against over-reliance on neurobiological explanations of adolescent behaviour and thinking. Exploring the very essence of brain plasticity reveals that *nature* (including hormones and brain activity) alone only tells part of the story and highlights the importance of the environment (*nurture*) in influencing brain development.

In the UK, psychologist Sarah Blakemore and colleagues study neuroplasticity during adolescence, its particular impact upon mental health, and the interaction of nature and nurture.

Adolescence and mental health

Some of Blakemore's early neurobiological research focused on what she perceived as a pattern in the onset of particular mental health challenges during adolescence. This prompted Blakemore and colleagues at University College London to question what it is about brain development in adolescence that marks this period as a particularly vulnerable time and increases susceptibility to some mental health conditions.

Blakemore (2019b) describes how during adolescence, the prefrontal cortex (which governs executive functions of control, insight, and decision making) is being reshaped, and at the same time, the limbic system, which is responsible for emotion, is exceptionally active. These changes can make young people particularly sensitive to adversity because the prefrontal cortex is less able to moderate the emotional responses of the limbic system. The immaturity of the prefrontal cortex and its underdeveloped capacity to regulate emotions and behaviour creates vulnerability to adverse experiences in the world around them, such as bullying, neglect, and enduring stress. In addition, young people's cognitive awareness and functioning is changing, leading them to explore new ways of thinking and feeling. With a sharp rise in abstract thinking and the capacity to plan, imagine one's future, and increasing awareness of self and how others view you, increasing pressures are placed on the developing adolescent.

Blakemore's research highlights the interaction between different parts of the brain and between nature and nurture and the importance of recognising these multiple inter-related factors when drawing conclusions about the onset of mental health difficulties.

Neurobiological research has implications for parents and carers and for practitioners who work with young people because it can reorientate and deepen an understanding of adolescence as a period of cognitive development with opportunities for learning but also a time of vulnerability where young people may require specialised support and guidance. Blakemore calls for a reframing of how adolescence is understood. Recognising the plasticity of the brain and its capacity for lifelong learning (Blakemore and Frith, 2005; Blakemore, 2019b), she draws attention to the need to understand and support young people to engage, participate, and learn through formal schooling, informal education, and work. Rather than demonising adolescents, linking behaviour with brain development can interpret certain behaviours as part of a process of development. You will learn more about how insights into brain development may affect interpretations of young people's behaviour in Chapter 14.

Key points

- Adolescence involves considerable social, cognitive, and neurobiological transformation.
- Greater risk-taking behaviour in adolescence can be understood as an adaptive development supporting transition into adulthood.
- Adolescence marks a period of vulnerability to mental health problems, reflecting considerable social and neurobiological change.
- Reframing adolescence as a time of developmental opportunities for enhanced learning and participation can challenge stereotypical perceptions of adolescents as moody, unpredictable risk takers.

Self and social relationships

An intense focus on peers

Friends are important through childhood, but one of the most striking characteristics of the transition to early adolescence is an increasing focus on peers. The amount of time spent with peers increases dramatically, leading to less time with parents, family, and other adults (Larson and Richards, 1991). Feeling accepted by a peer group becomes crucial to young adolescents, who also identify peers as important role models (Brown, 2004). Over half of contemporary adolescents also develop intense 'parasocial' relationships with media, social media, music, and sporting figures: 'symbolic, one-sided social ties' with celebrities and 'influencers' that they conceive of as a friendship or relationship (Gleason, Theran and Newberg, 2017, p. 1), a trend that has accelerated with opportunities for communication presented by social media.

Heightened prosocial behaviour and the development of reciprocal social relationships is an important aspect of adolescent development, and psychological research highlights heightened self-consciousness and the growing need for young people to feel like they fit in with a particular social group during the teenage years. Psychological research also highlights greater self-consciousness in early adolescence, and the need to receive peer acceptance has powerful effects on adolescents' behaviour. As Blakemore (2019a) and her colleagues have shown in many studies of risk-taking, adolescents are hypersensitive to social exclusion. When young adolescents are given hypothetical scenarios in psychological experiments and asked to choose antisocial or prosocial actions, they are more likely, compared to younger children, to follow what they are told their peers would do. In experiments in real-world settings, if they are with peers rather than alone, they choose more risky options and focus on their benefits rather than costs. Taken together, neurobiological and psychological research both point to reasons why adolescents may take more risks. In addition to these explanations, this is the time in life when teenagers typically face many new social and environmental situations, which require successful navigation and assessing risks and benefits. Enhanced risky and prosocial behaviours during this time are, therefore, also an adaptive development which supports the shift from childhood dependency and a young person's transition into adulthood.

Figure 13.3 Group of teenagers waiting for a bus in England.

It is important to note that family and caring relationships remain important for many young people throughout adolescence. Even in early adolescence, when peers are particularly salient, young people asked to describe their favourite people cite family members and caring relationships as most important, more so than they do friends (Tatlow-Golden and Guerin, 2017). Family members continue to be people whose approval continues to matter and whose support affects adolescent mental health. Remember as you learned in Chapter 5 that 'good adults' other than parents or outside the family can and do take on this role for adolescents. As psychologist Susan Harter notes, the challenge at this stage of life is to 'remain connected [to family] while at the same time forging an independent identity' (2012, p. 107).

After the intense peer influence of early adolescence, from mid-adolescence onwards (14 to 18 years), research shows that, in general, young people gradually decrease risk-taking and become more able to form and hold to their own values, and this applies across genders and ethnic groups (Steinberg and Monahan, 2007). In part, this comes about as their self-concept develops.

Shifting selves, identities, and self-esteem

In Chapters 2 and 4, you learned about a continuously evolving task throughout childhood and youth, the development of the self-concept (the answer to the crucial question 'Who am I?'), including self-esteem (self-evaluation of 'How good am I?'). The self-concept is compiled from diverse characteristics and preferences, and the many identities that define us, and it is shaped by culture, society, relationships, and developmental factors. Adolescence brings many shifts in the self-concept and self-esteem. For example, in seeking peer approval and potentially experiencing rejection, young people become more vulnerable to self-esteem losses, particularly so in the early adolescent years.

In early adolescence, the newly developed cognitive ability for more abstract thinking contributes to self-concept development, as young people can combine specific self-descriptions, such as 'I like to learn' and 'I get good results', to form more general ideas – for example, 'I am intelligent' (Harter, 2012). Building self-descriptive abstractions from different parts of life and then integrating them into an overall self-concept takes time and evolves rather unevenly which can create some turbulence in their sense of 'who I am'. At first, young adolescents can have contradictory ideas about themselves, such as 'I hate the world' or 'I am a happy person', but they have often not developed self-awareness about these contradictions or how to resolve them (Harter, 2012).

Part of the adolescent transition involves developing multiple identities as part of the overall self-concept because it is socially essential to be able to interact appropriately with, for example, friends, relatives, or teachers. In mid-adolescence, as abstract thinking skills increase, young people's self-awareness of different and unintegrated identities grows, sometimes leading to 'conflict, confusion and distress' (Harter, 2012, p. 108), particularly if significant others give contradictory messages about which aspects of the self-concept to value. Older adolescents (17–18 years) develop more self-awareness about how different *contexts* can elicit varying self-qualities, identities, and behaviours, thereby understanding better how different selves and values can be integrated into an overall, coherent self-narrative. For example, a younger adolescent might struggle with experiencing themselves as 'depressed', 'cheerful', and 'caring' yet later come to understand that these do not necessarily conflict but could be appropriate responses to situations they encountered or could reflect a self that is sensitive. Older adolescents' self-esteem tends to improve, probably because they become better able to identify domains that matter to them, making them less vulnerable to self-evaluations in domains they are less successful in, and less dependent on others' evaluations (Harter, 2012).

In Chapter 4, you learned about how carers scaffold the developing self-concept by telling young children stories about themselves. This continues through childhood, and in adolescence, the 'autobiographical self' becomes richer, as a collection of stories and memories about the self deepens with adolescent memory and abilities to reason. It develops in mid to later adolescence (and indeed continues to change through life), depending on what is emotionally and experientially salient (Nelson and Fivush, 2020). Importantly, building an autobiographical self, one that feels coherent even though it is made up of many different identities and self-descriptions, is further supported throughout adolescence by significant others who can contextualise experiences, offering vocabulary to describe these aspects of the self, and opportunities for discussion and reflection.

Body image and the sense of self

Another important aspect of the self that gains particular importance in adolescence is how we look. Although appearance is often dismissed as something inherently superficial, in fact, perceptions of appearance are often a powerful predictor of self-esteem (Harter, 2012). Notably, the media and peers generally influence self-evaluations of appearance more strongly than parents. This takes place even in the childhood years but even more so in adolescence, when young people's bodies are changing rapidly, and peer evaluations are so focal (Harter, 2012). Assessing factors that contributed to self-esteem in over 600 young adolescents aged 10–13 years across the Greater Dublin region in Ireland, researchers found that ratings of physical appearance were inseparable from overall self-esteem (Guerin and Tatlow-Golden, 2019). As you learned in Chapter 4, standard psychological measures assess young people's perceptions of their popularity with peers, friendship, academic and sporting ability and enjoyment, teachers' and parents' views of their behaviour, and other factors – yet self-rated appearance trumped them all.

Building self and identity in a digital era

An important issue for contemporary youth is how adolescents develop identities and an overall self-concept in their new 'hybrid reality' (see Chapter 11), where offline and online worlds connect 'dynamically and interactively . . . in a single holistic context' (Granic, Morita and Scholten, 2020, p. 196) – and whether they can be better supported than they are at present. This presents substantial challenges to those designing online worlds and to policy makers seeking to guide and regulate these. For example, Granic *et al.*'s review of research concluded that many adolescents say they have less control over their autobiographical identities in social media because content travels in ways they cannot control; that many adolescents' developing ability for self-reflection is not supported by social media which is designed and optimised to reward quick responses; and that preoccupation with appearance on social media is associated with poorer mental health. At the same time, however, Granic and colleagues found that some young people experience greater wellbeing in social media because they can express themselves honestly with peers – offering opportunities to explore their developing selves and identities in their hybrid realities. This is a field of policy, tech design, and research that is struggling to keep up with adolescents' lived experience and to offer suitable opportunities for their developing selves.

Key points

- Adolescence is a time of intense focus on peers and peer approval, yet family and other carers remain important.
- In early adolescence, risk-taking increases, particularly around peers.
- Through adolescence, the sense of self becomes more complex and insightful, building on abstract thinking, reasoning, and autobiographical storytelling skills.
- Self-perceptions of physical appearance are a powerful component of adolescent self-esteem.

- As contemporary adolescence takes place in offline/online 'hybrid reality', this offers potential but also challenges for development and wellbeing that researchers are only beginning to understand.

Transforming themselves, transforming society

Adolescence, this chapter has argued, is a time of change and transformation and this has taken place at a social and political level too. Teenagers changed society after the Second World War. They were at the forefront of civil rights movements, for example, in USA in the 1960s, where they demanded social justice and equality and played a prominent role in protests and marches. In South Africa, young people were active in the anti-apartheid movement, especially after the Soweto uprisings of 1976 in which, among others, 13-year-old Hector Pieterson and 15-year-old Hastings Ndlovu were shot dead by police while taking part in a peaceful demonstration against compulsory schooling in Afrikaans (widely perceived as the language of their White oppressors) in school. Teenagers and young people were at the vanguard of Arab Spring protests in the early 2010s. Amidst economic stagnation, corruption, and a lack of opportunities and freedoms, predominantly young protestors took to the streets in Tunisia, Libya, Egypt, Syria, Yemen, and Bahrain, leading to uprisings, social violence, and the deposing of leaders. The Jasmine or Facebook revolution of 2010–11 in Tunisia was spearheaded by the young (and several teenagers were killed in the protests), who rejected the regime's appeals to national or cultural identity and instead articulated a generational identity and clear goals for themselves and society's future. Using modern technologies, they created their own spaces for dissent and protest and new ways of engaging with the state (Honwana, 2013). In Iran, 22-year-old Mahsa Amini was arrested in September 2022 by the Iranian morality police for violating Iran's laws concerning the mandatory wearing of headscarves. She died after being, it is widely believed, beaten by the police. Civil unrest swept across Iran initiated by young people and including schoolchildren (Wintour, 2022).

Climate change has also brought extremely influential teenage activists to the fore. In India, for example, in 2018, 16-year-old Aditya Mukarji led a drive against single-use plastics in Delhi, persuading 150 different businesses in the city to go plastic free and coming to international prominence (Unigwe, 2019). Across the world, the year 2019 was characterised by mass protests in major cities, calling on governments to tackle the climate crisis, including 'Fridaysforfuture' strikes, when children and teenagers left school and joined weekly protests against government inaction. Most famously, teenage activist Greta Thunberg, then aged 16, addressed the 2019 climate summit at the United Nations and demanded that climate change be seen in inter-generational terms, denouncing those who had let her generation down:

> You have stolen my dreams and my childhood with your empty words. . . . How dare you! . . . You are failing us. But the young people are starting to understand your betrayal. The eyes of all future generations are upon you. And if you choose to fail us, I say: We will never forgive you.
>
> (Thunberg, 2019)

Figure 13.4 Young climate change protester near the British Parliament as part of a Global Day of Protest.

Figure 13.5 Civil rights protestors in Charlotte, North Carolina. In February 1960, African American young people started a series of peaceful protests at stores which had 'Whites only' lunch counters. Refusing to leave after they had been declined service, they staged sit-ins. Other young African Americans followed suit, staging sit-ins across the Southern states of the USA, when they refused to accept their status as second-class citizens.

Teenage activism, often a force for good in the world, is not always sufficiently acknowledged and celebrated. After the end of the apartheid era in South Africa, for example, the Truth and Reconciliation Commission examined its injustices, and despite its importance, it has been criticised for reducing teenagers to the role of child victims, looking at crimes against them rather than recognising their organisation, political commitment, and bravery. It is important, therefore, neither to romanticise young people's political activism nor to underplay the difficulties that teenagers have in contributing positively (Honwana and Boeck, 2005) while at the same time recognising the potential they have for political insight and engagement.

Key points

- Teenage creativity and rebellion can be highly positive, and young people have played important roles in many social justice movements throughout the world.
- The impact and potential of teenage activism is not always recognised, and their rights to contribute to public life are often not facilitated.

Conclusion

In combining psychological, cultural, historical, and biological research, this chapter has examined how adolescence involves considerable social, cognitive, and neurobiological transformation within the forces of nature and nurture, which brings a flux of gains and losses. Using their growing abstract thinking, reasoning, and autobiographical storytelling abilities, adolescents test their sense of self and their place in the wider and increasingly hybrid world. They place increasing focus on peers (particularly seeking peer approval) while still recognising the importance of family and other carers. The new social environments and neurobiological developments that characterise this transition towards adulthood prompt greater prosocial and risk-taking behaviour. Finally, reframing adolescence as a time of opportunities for enhanced learning and participation can challenge stereotypically negative perceptions of adolescents as moody, unpredictable risk takers. Teenage creativity, energy, exploration, thinking, and rebellion can be highly positive, and young people have played important roles in many social justice movements throughout the world.

References

Blakemore, S. J. (2019a) *Inventing Ourselves. The Secret Life of the Teenage Brain*. London: Black Swan.

Blakemore, S. J. (2019b) 'Adolescence and mental health', *The Lancet. The Art of Medicine*, 393(10185), pp. 2030–2031.

Blakemore, S., and Frith, U. (2005) *The Learning Brain. Lessons for Education*. Oxford: Blackwell.

Brown, B. B. (2004) 'Adolescents' relationships with peers', in R. M. Lerner and L. Steinberg (eds.) *Handbook of Adolescent Psychology*. Hoboken, NJ: Wiley, pp. 363–394.

Gleason, T. R., Theran, S. A., and Newberg, E. M. (2017) 'Parasocial interactions and relationships in early adolescence', *Frontiers in Psychology*, 8, p. 255.

Goodman, R., Imoto, Y., and Toivonen, T. (2012) *A Sociology of Japanese Youth From Returnees to NEETs*. London: Routledge.

Granic, I., Morita, H., and Scholten, H. (2020) 'Beyond screen time: identity development in the digital age', *Psychological Inquiry*, 31(3), pp. 195–223.

Guerin, S., and Tatlow-Golden, M. (2019) 'How valid are measures of children's self-concept/self-esteem? Factors and content validity in three widely used scales', *Child Indicators Research*, 12, pp. 1507–1528.

Hall, G. S. (1904) *Adolescence: Its Psychology and Its Relations to Physiology, Anthropology, Sociology, Sex, Crime, Religion, and Education* (Vols. 1 and 2). New York: AD Appleton and Co.

Harter, S. (2012) *The Construction of the Self* (2nd ed.). New York: Guildford Press.

Hinton, P. (2016) 'The cultural construction of the girl "een": a cross-cultural analysis of feminine adolescence portrayed in popular culture', *Journal of Intercultural Communication Research*, 45(3), pp. 233–247.

Honwana, A. (2013) *Youth and Revolution in Tunisia*. London: Zed Books.

Honwana, A., and de Boeck, F. (2005) *Makers and Breakers: Children and Youth in Postcolonial Africa*. Oxford: James Currey.

Inhelder, B., and Piaget, J. (1958) *The Growth of Logical Thinking From Childhood to Adolescence*. New York: Basic Books.

Larson, R., and Richards, M. H. (1991) 'Daily companionship in late childhood and early adolescence: changing developmental contexts', *Child Development*, 62(2), pp. 284–300.

Nelson, K., and Fivush, R. (2020) 'The development of autobiographical memory, autobiographical narratives, and autobiographical consciousness', *Psychological Reports*, 123(1), pp. 71–96.

Paladino, G. (1996) *Teenager: An American History*. New York: Basic Books.

Sawyer, S. M., Azzopardi, P. S., Wickremarathne, D., and Patton, G. C. (2018) 'The age of adolescence', *The Lancet Child & Adolescent Health*, 2(3), pp. 223–228.

Sebastian, C., Burnett, S., and Blakemore, S.-J. (2008) 'Development of the self-concept during adolescence', *Trends in Cognitive Science*, 12, pp. 441–446.

Steinberg, L. (2014) *Age of Opportunity. Lessons From the New Science of Adolescence*. New York: Marimer Books.

Steinberg, L., and Monahan, K. C. (2007) 'Age differences in resistance to peer influence', *Developmental Psychology*, 43(6), pp. 1531–1543.

Tatlow-Golden, M., and Guerin, S. (2017) 'Who I am: the meaning of children's most valued activities and relationships, and implications for self-concept research', *Journal of Early Adolescence*, 37(2), pp. 236–266.

Thunberg, G. (2019) 'Speech at the U.N. climate action summit', Reported in *The Guardian*, 23 March 2019. Available at: www.theguardian.com/environment/2019/sep/23/greta-thunberg-speech-un-2019-address (Accessed 18th October 2022).

Unigwe, C. (2019) 'It's not just Greta Thunberg: why are we ignoring the developing world's inspiring activists?', *The Observer*, 5 October 2019. Available at: www.theguardian.com/commentisfree/2019/oct/05/greta-thunberg-developing-world-activists (Accessed 3rd October 2022).

Vaghi, F., and Emmot, E. (2018) *Teen Views on Adolescence. A One-Day Workshop*. Thomas Coran Research Institute UCL Institute of Education. Available at: https://discovery.ucl.ac.uk/id/eprint/10054186/ (Accessed 4th October 2022).

White, M. (1993) *The Material Child: Coming of Age in Japan and America*. New York: Free Press.

Wintour, P. '"Women, life, liberty": Iranian civil rights protests spread worldwide', *Guardian*, 1 October 2022. Available at: www.theguardian.com/world/2022/oct/01/women-life-liberty-iranian-civil-rights-protests-spread-worldwide (Accessed 1st October 2022).

14 Transitions to adulthood

Anthony Gunter and Naomi Holford

Introduction

Throughout this Reader, the question has often arisen of what it means to be a child. In many ways, this also invites a further question: what does it mean to be an adult? Just as different societies and cultures have different conceptions of childhood, so they also have different conceptions of adulthood. The transition to adulthood is marked by legal boundaries, which affect people's lives in different ways, but it is also a social and economic transition. Children move from childhood structures to those of adulthood, such as work, higher education, and partner relationships, and must find their place and identity within them. These transformations and progressions are wide-ranging and may extend over a substantial time period.

One significant theme in considering the transition to adulthood is how difficult it is to pinpoint exactly when someone becomes an adult and exactly what it means to experience adulthood. Furthermore, many of the attributes or activities we think of as characterising childhood continue into adulthood: dependence on other people, play, and continuing to learn. This final chapter will utilise sociological and cultural studies perspectives concerning this life stage. It will specifically explore how young people respond, at a local level, to changes in the national and global political economic system that inform their pathways into adulthood.

Boundary crossings

As we will go on to discover in this section, and building on Chapter 13, there is no universally accepted way to determine the point at which childhood ends and adulthood begins. Youth transitions are best understood as being just one section of the longer journey across the 'life course' (a sociological and psychological concept incorporating culturally defined birth-to-death age categories, such as early years, adolescence, teenage years, and middle age, for example, that people are expected to pass through during the many stages of their lives). During their lifetime, an individual will experience and navigate many transitions: leaving the family home, starting work, and having children, for example. Consequently, youth transitions are not linear and finite but rather are dependent on a complex array of interrelated factors informed by individual, organisational, and governmental decisions and actions as well as market opportunities.

DOI: 10.4324/9781003358855-15

Young people experience movements and changes in different areas of life – in work, education, family life, housing, or relationships – through which they develop physiologically and gradually become more 'adult'. They move through these trans-itions at different rates, affected by differing individual, physiological and social factors, although their progression in one area may affect progression in another. For instance, they may go to university in another town and thus move out of their parents' house. They may sometimes appear to move 'backwards', for instance, if they have moved out to live with a partner but later break up and move back in with a parent. So the transition to adulthood is not necessarily smooth or immediate but is often made up of fragmented movements, some of which may be predictable, but others less so. It is best therefore to view becoming an adult as fluid and changeable.

There is also a significant 'in-between' stage, in which young people are neither quite children nor quite adults. Historically, there has not always been such an in-between stage, and it is not consistent across the world today. Instead, some societies have marked out defined points at which children move into adulthood. One seemingly simple way to define the boundary of childhood is through biological development. As Chapter 13 indicates, children's physical bodies grow and develop as they transition through puberty, which involves hormonal and neurological changes that influence their psychological development and behaviour and the transition to adulthood has often been divided by gender. The physical markers that a girl has reached sexual maturity are more obvious, and many societies view menarche – a girl's first menstru-ation – as marking the point at which a girl becomes a woman (see Chapters 11 and 13). In many societies, this biological event is shaped by social and cultural meanings and economic factors.

Many societies and cultures have used ceremonies or rituals to mark the entrance into adulthood. Within anthropology, the concept of the 'rite of passage' has been influ-ential in interpreting movements into adulthood. This concept was developed by Dutch-German-French ethnographer Arnold van Gennep in 1909 (van Gennep, 1960 [1909]) and suggests that social life is a process of changing states, in which people move from one role to another. These transitions, according to van Gennep, are marked symboli-cally and publicly and consist of three stages. First, an individual is separated from their familiar context within a social structure; second, there is a liminal (in-between) stage; and finally, they return and reintegrate into society, in their new role.

One of the most famous accounts we have of a rite of passage is that written by former South African president, Nelson Mandela. Mandela was a member of one of South Africa's largest tribal groups, the Xhosa, and in his book, *A Long Walk to Freedom* (Mandela, 1994), he describes Xhosa rites of passage. He describes a long process, taking several months, in which he and his peers left their homes and set-tlements and went to live in grass huts in a secluded valley (separation). Supervised by adult elders, they prepared for their circumcision by performing feats of bravery, such as killing a pig, to show that they were ready for the trials of manhood. At the end of this liminal stage, they were ritually circumcised. Once this had been done, they returned home to their villages as adult men and were allowed to take on adult duties, such as marriage (reintegration). Although the circumcision was painful, it was a necessary part of social life and a way of confirming and strengthening the tribal identity. Mandela concluded:

> In my tradition, an uncircumcised male cannot be heir to his father's wealth, cannot marry or officiate in tribal rituals. An uncircumcised Xhosa man is a contradiction in terms, for he is not considered a man at all, but a boy. For the Xhosa people, circumcision represents the formal incorporation of males into society. It is not just a surgical procedure, but a lengthy and elaborate ritual in preparation for manhood.
>
> (Mandela, 1994, p. 24)

While circumcision and initiation ritual continue to this day, and remain an important and valued part of life, there also voices from within the Xhosa community who are trying to modify the ceremonies and ensure the safety of the young people in them. It is estimated that more than 400 young men have died from shock and septicaemia after being circumcised with daggers or blunt knives, and the use of the same blade on multiple boys has been linked to the spread of HIV (Fihlani, 2019). There have been calls for better standards of hygiene and medical care for these boys and greater regulation of the ceremonies. Teachers, too, have called for shortened periods of initiation so that now, many Xhosa ceremonies last only three weeks, rather than the three months that Mandela's did.

Figure 14.1 Xhosa boys preparing for their ritual circumcision. They smear white clay on themselves to mark their liminal status.

For other societies, it is more difficult to identify rites of passage in the sense that van Gennep described. There are moments of transition and points of achievement but not such distinct public social rituals. Societies in the global North do construct defined external markers of adulthood, often based on chronological age, which impose order and standardisation on the experience of growing up. The UN Convention on the Rights of the Child (UNCRC) (United Nations, 1989), discussed in earlier chapters, defines a child as 'every human being below the age of eighteen'. This is the age of entrance into adulthood – or the age of majority – in the UK and in many other countries. There is, however, no single age at which a child is considered to become an adult under UK law. Instead, there are different ages, relating to different areas of activity, at which young people attain certain rights and responsibilities. For instance, in England, Wales, and Northern Ireland, individuals can legally drive a car or motorcycle at 17 years of age, and they can buy tobacco or alcohol at 18 years, but the age of criminal responsibility when children can be arrested or tried as an adult for a crime is 10 years. In Scotland, the age of criminal responsibility is 12 years. In England and Northern Ireland, the voting age is 18 years, yet from 16 years, young people can vote in elections to the Scottish Parliament or to the Senedd Cymru (Welsh Parliament).

These legal age restrictions are often related to particular constructions of childhood or adulthood. Many legal age limits relate to the protection of children, as they are considered vulnerable. Others restrict children's activities on grounds of competence. Some can be viewed as contradictory: for instance, those under 18 in England and

Table 14.1 Legal age restrictions and entitlements across the UK

Age	Legal Position
10	• can be held criminally responsible for actions in England, Wales, and Northern Ireland
12	• can be held criminally responsible for actions in Scotland
13	• can have a part-time job (but not entitled to any minimum wage)
16	• can consent to sexual activity
	• can have a full-time job and is entitled to the minimum wage for 16–18-year-olds
	• can apply for own passport
	• can claim some state benefits
	• can vote in elections for the Senedd Cymru/Welsh Parliament or the Scottish Parliament
	• can get married in Scotland; parental consent required in Northern Ireland. [In England and Wales, all marriage under the age of 18, regardless of parental consent, was banned in The Marriage and Civil Partnership (Minimum Age) Act 2022.]
	• can join the armed forces with parental consent
17	• can drive a car or motorcycle
18	• can serve on a jury
	• can buy alcohol and tobacco
	• can watch material that includes explicit sexual or violent content
	• can vote in elections for the Northern Ireland Assembly
	• can vote in UK General Elections
	• can marry in England and Wales
	• can stand for election as a Member of Parliament
	• is entitled to minimum wage for 18–20-year-olds
21	• can apply to adopt a child
	• is entitled to full adult minimum wage

Northern Ireland are not seen as sufficiently rational or competent in decision making to have a say in how the country is governed, yet 10–17-year-olds are viewed as sufficiently rational to be charged or tried for committing a crime.

While these age restrictions apply equally to all young people, individuals may be differently affected by them, depending on their circumstances. For instance, being able to drive may be more important to someone living in a remote rural area than it is someone living in a city with good public transport.

The case study on child and adolescent brain development (see below) and implications for criminal prosecution of young offenders provides one example of the impact of government policies on young people's lives.

Child and adolescent brain development and its impact on propensity to criminal behaviour

The treatment of young adults in the criminal justice system: Seventh Report of Session 2016–17: House of Commons Justice Committee

This report focuses predominately on 'young adults' as opposed to children. It suggests that there should be a distinct approach to the treatment of 'young adults' in the criminal justice system because their brain is still developing. It identifies that 'young adults' are still developing neurologically *up to the age of 25* and have a high prevalence of neuro-disabilities and mental disorders.

- 'In typical brain maturation, temperance – the ability to evaluate the consequences of actions and to limit impulsiveness and risk-taking – is a significant factor in moderating behaviour and the fact that its development continues into a person's 20s can influence anti-social decision-making among young adults'. [paragraph 9]
- 'Young adults offend the most but have the most potential to stop offending. They are resource intensive as they are challenging to manage. A strong case could be made for recognising that expenditure to make the system more developmentally responsive would pay dividends in reduced costs to the system in reducing incidents of violence and to society in reducing offending and the creation of further victims'. [paragraph 139]
- 'Both *age and maturity should be taken into significantly greater account* within the criminal justice system. The rationale of the system for young adults should presume that up to the age of 25 young adults are typically still maturing. A developmental approach should be taken that recognises that how they perceive, process and respond to situations is a function of their developmental stage and other factors affecting their maturity, and secondarily their culture and life experience'. [paragraph 141]

House of Commons Justice Committee (2016)

Key points

- Becoming adult can be seen as a range of different biological, legal, psychological, emotional, and social processes, which may happen at different times for different groups of people and for different individuals.
- Societies often mark entrance into adulthood at defined points, based on biological processes, social rituals, or age boundaries.
- In the UK, different age limits apply in relation to different activities, and they also vary across its four nations, reflecting particular ideas of childhood and adulthood.

Journeying into adulthood: Youth identities and subcultures

Becoming an adult involves moving out of the social structures children are positioned within and situating oneself – or being situated – within some of the social structures that adults occupy. For instance, children usually live in the household of their parents or carers, who are considered to have responsibility for the children. In the UK, moving out of the parental home is often considered a sign of adulthood, although this is by no means a universal opinion or possibility, as the chapter will explore further. But becoming adult is not just a matter of fitting into new social structures. It is also considered a time in which people find – or solidify – their individual and group identities. Moreover, the role of the peer group in young people's lives (as introduced in Chapter 13) also plays a significant role in the creation of personal identities and subcultural formations, for example, skinheads, punk rockers, rave culture, and street-based youth cultures, which can be viewed as individualised and collective responses to the expectations and responsibilities of adulthood.

The work of the Centre for Contemporary Cultural Studies (CCCS) at the University of Birmingham in the 1970s had a major impact on the development of youth studies, specifically, academic understanding of subcultures and deviance. Under the stewardship of sociologist and cultural theorist Professor Stuart Hall, the CCCS, through a number of landmark studies, sought to analyse and understand the relationship between 'culture' and 'society' by focusing in equal measure on the symbolic as well as the social – 'subcultures and style' (Hall and Jefferson, 1975). As such, CCCS researchers emphasised how the rituals and symbols associated with the subcultures of working-class youth – as distinct to those of the parent working-class 'culture' – were used as ways to resist dominant middle-class or ruling elite culture.

The UK had long been a country defined by its rigid social class structure – and this was most certainly the case during the decades following the Second World War – which has, for many generations of young people, been transmitted through and distinguished by education, language, leisure activities, culture, family life, and occupational careers. For example, young working-class males on leaving school at 15 were expected to follow their fathers in obtaining manual jobs, like coal miners and dock workers. These young men were also expected to share the same cultural pursuits as their fathers by spending their leisure time 'down the pub' and/or attending

Figure 14.2 A group of teddy boys/rockers, London, 1979.

football or rugby matches on a Saturday afternoon. CCCS researchers challenged these perspectives by demonstrating how, via the creation of their own subcultures, working-class young people were able to resist these dominant societal cultural and economic norms.

Resistance through rituals

The work of researchers at the CCCS is best illustrated by their landmark edited collection, *Resistance Through Rituals* (Hall and Jefferson, 1975). With the utilisation of ethnographic research methods, *Resistance Through Rituals* includes studies examining the subcultures of teddy boys, mods, punk rockers, skinheads, and street corner culture.

The subcultural response

> We can return, now, to the question of 'sub-cultures'. Working class sub-cultures, we suggested, take shape on the level of the social and cultural class-relations of the subordinate classes. In themselves, they are not simply 'ideological' constructs. They, too, win space for the young: cultural space in the neighbourhood and institutions, real time for leisure and recreation, actual room on the street or street-corner. They serve to mark out and appropriate 'territory' in the localities. They focus around key occasions of social interaction: the weekend, the disco, the bank holiday trip, the night out in the 'centre', the 'standing-about-doing-nothing' of the weekday evening, the Saturday match. They cluster around particular locations . . . In addressing the 'class problematic' of the particular strata from which they were drawn, the different sub-cultures provided for a section of working class youth (mainly boys) one strategy for negotiating their collective existence. But their highly ritualised and stylised form suggests that they were also attempts at a solution to that problematic experience.
>
> Hall and Jefferson (2003 [1975], pp. 45–47)

Although contemporary youth studies is greatly indebted to the pioneering work of the CCCS, in recent years, their research has been criticised for its narrow interpretation of subculture – which tended to be theorised solely in relation to youth and social class. The CCCS was also criticised for its fixation upon the 'spectacular' styles and subcultures of working-class heterosexual White males (Griffin, 2011) at the expense of researching the everyday and mundane activities of girls (McRobbie, 1978) and Black, Asian and minority ethnic youth (Gunter, 2017). Also, in the 1990s, prominent sociologists began to argue that in recent decades, societies in the global North had changed significantly, especially in terms of how the individual relates to dominant societal cultural and economic structures. Collectively, these 'late modern' theorists, such as Ulrich Beck, Anthony Giddens, and Zygmunt Bauman, have varying perspectives on social change, but they all argue to some extent that modern society is increasingly characterised by risk and uncertainty in the realm of relationships between individuals and the place of the individual within society. They see traditional social divisions, such as social class and gender, as less important in shaping paths in life and in determining identity and belonging. German sociologist Ulrich Beck (1992) argued that we are moving from 'normal biographies', where our roles and life plans are predetermined, defined by tradition and social institutions, to 'choice biographies', where we are free to choose who we are and what we become. The individual is thus considered responsible for everything that happens to them, a concept that Beck calls 'individualisation'.

Notwithstanding this 'late modern' theorising about individualisation, risk, uncertainty, and the importance of consumerism (Miles, 2000) to young people's identity creation, ethnographic research studies have challenged these perspectives. They highlight the continuing significance of 'place' (Watt and Stenson, 1998), social class (MacDonald and Shildrick, 2007), and race (Gunter, 2010) in young people's lives. In addition to ethnographic youth studies, scholars also argue that traditional divisions – such as those of social class and gender – are still very influential in shaping the experiences and possibilities of young people, even if they now do so in different ways (Bourdieu, 1986). Some researchers studying young people's experiences, education, and identities draw on the work of the theorist Pierre Bourdieu (1977, 1986) to understand how social inequalities are 'reproduced' from one generation to the next via the important concepts of social capital (your friends, networks, and social connections) and cultural capital. As discussed in Chapter 7, cultural capital refers partly to the knowledge and skills (acquired though education and formal schooling) and also to ideas and cultural ideologies. The forms of capital are linked, in the sense that those with more economic capital tend to have 'higher' levels of cultural and social capital as well. A child of wealthy parents, for instance, may be sent to an elite private school, be encouraged (by family, school, or friends) to go to 'sophisticated' cultural events (art galleries and concerts), mix with people of a similar background, or find internships – and in due course, jobs – in elite companies. This means that young people's options, chances, and choices as they move into adulthood are influenced by their background not just because of money but also because of other resources.

Key points

* Moving into adulthood involves becoming situated in new social structures, which include education and/or work.
* It is important that we don't underestimate young people's agency and their attempts to resist larger social and economic structures via the creation of individualised and group-based identities and subcultures.
* Late modern theorists argue that modern societies in the global North are characterised by uncertainty, that divisions like social class are less important influences than in the past, and that individualisation characterises this age.
* Ethnographic studies find that place, race, and social class continue to be important in young people's lives.

Post-16 transitions: Finding work and/or continuing education

The end of compulsory education is another key point in transitions to adulthood. Leaving school is a point at which young people are considered able to make their own choices about their further development. In Scotland, Wales, and Northern Ireland, young people must stay in school until the age of 16, and in England, they must stay in some form of education or training until the age of 18 (after 16, this can include apprenticeships or full-time employment combined with part-time education or training, as well as full-time education at school or college). Work is often considered the archetypal marker of adulthood, in contrast to play, which is associated strongly with childhood, and as you learned in Chapter 13, young people described working and earning money as characterising the transition. Moving into the workplace frequently plays a central part in becoming adult. In economic terms, employment allows young people to exercise their independence rather than relying on their family for support. In addition, work in contemporary UK society is often considered central to an individual's sense of self. So transitions into work are key in how young people experience and understand becoming different kinds of adult. However, as with many of the transitions discussed in this chapter, this division is sometimes blurred and much more complex than was the case for previous generations.

The decades following the Second World War were characterised by a relatively stable labour market. During the 1950s and 1960s, young people's school-to-work transitions were seen as linear. As discussed earlier, most young people would leave school at 15 and immediately enter into paid employment. However, changes in further and higher education and the collapse of the youth labour market have resulted in young people's post-16 transitions becoming more complex, prolonged, and non-linear. Given the contemporary focus on work as a central part of self-identity, this can be difficult not only in financial terms but also in terms of wider self-worth and standing in society and in achieving transition to adulthood. In periods of economic depression or recession, when rates of unemployment are particularly high, these issues can be particularly problematic for large numbers of young people, particularly for those already disadvantaged by race/ethnicity, class, disability, and demographic location. An example is youth transitions in East London (see the box).

Youth Transitions in East London

The transformation of the East London skyline at Canary Wharf and elsewhere in Docklands has not been matched by a similar sea change in the fortunes of its poorer residents. East London remains one of the poorest regions in the UK and is also increasingly multi-ethnic. An analysis of the five East London 2012 Olympic host boroughs indicates that worklessness is worse there than in the rest of London and nationally. Despite aggregate employment growth in East London from the mid-1990s, there are doubts as to how many of the new jobs, and especially professional-managerial jobs, have gone to locals: 'in London's primary financial centre, Canary Wharf, there are still relatively few people from the locality in employment within the largest concentration of financial services firms in Europe – 15 years after the first firms moved there'. Low-level and no qualifications underpin much of the labour market exclusion and disadvantage in East London, factors that are worse for young people living there than in the rest of London. Young people in East London are, for example, more likely to be 'not in employment, education or training' (NEET) than elsewhere in the city.

Worklessness, including unemployment and economic inactivity, linked to 'deproletarianization'...is undoubtedly a major problem facing deprived groups in East London and London generally, prominent among which are Black Asian Minority Ethnic youth. It is not, however, the only problem since many of the capital's new post-industrial service jobs as well as older manual jobs are characterised by insecurity, short-termism, and low pay due to increased subcontracting and informalization, detailed analysis of new jobs in the East London borough of Newham found that the majority were part-time and many East Londoners are employed in low-paid, low-skilled jobs.

Gunter and Watt (2009, pp. 517–518)

The example from East London highlights the prevalence of insecure and short-term employment. Since then, precarious and insecure work practices have become much more widespread with the growth of the 'gig economy', in which people are offered work (usually through digital platforms and apps) for services such as ride-hailing, food delivery, and other freelance activities. They are not considered employees, and the hours are unpredictable. Robert MacDonald and Andreas Giazitzoglu (2019) draw upon their own empirical work from the 1980s and currently to discuss the implications of youth precarity, insecure work, and the current 'gig economy'.

Youth precarity and the gig economy

First, we need to understand the particular conditions of 'the gig economy' as a concentrated form of a more general de-standardisation of employment that has brought multiple forms of insecure work. Second, although there is clamour and excitement about 'the gig economy' in fact it shares strong parallels with earlier forms of insecure enterprise. Third, while not uniform nor as yet fully empirically demonstrated, young adults' encounters with the 'gig economy' and other aspects of the contemporary labour market (such as the 'low-pay, no-pay' cycle, self-employment, 'zero-hours contracts') appear to be typified by a lack of choice and control, and experiences of disempowerment, low pay, degraded work conditions, alienation, anxiety and insecurity.

MacDonald and Giazitzoglu (2019, p. 724)

The landscape of work in the UK has also seen significant transformations in relation to gender in recent decades, changing the patterns of youth transition along with it. Until quite recently, there were entrenched gender divisions between the work done by men and women. Men were seen as ideally the primary earners in a family, whereas for women, getting married, becoming a housewife, and having children was seen as the norm and the ideal. In reality, women often did work because of low-earning part-ners, being widowed, separated or single, or wanting an independent income. However, the jobs they were able to secure were often low paid and part time and con-centrated in particular spheres. The primary marker of adulthood for many young women was getting married and then having children. Gender divisions have become less relevant in determining the course of a young person's life since movements for gender equality intensified in the 1960s and 1970s and brought associated legal and cultural changes. Although significant gender differences and pay differentials may still remain, most young women now expect to pursue work and a career indepen-dently just as young men do.

During the last 50 years or so, whilst the youth labour market has virtually col-lapsed, young people's participation rates in post-compulsory education have more than doubled. The proportion of 16–18-year-olds in England in full-time education and training increased from just under 35% in 1988 to nearly 63% in 2007 (DCSF, 2008). This almost doubling of the 16–18-year-old participation rates in post-compulsory full-time education and training was fueled by a combination of factors. Firstly, the introduction of the GCSE final year examination in England in the mid-1980s, which incorporated assessment through coursework, generally led to a marked increase in levels of attainment for young people completing secondary education. Secondly, the

Figure 14.3 Students celebrating and throwing their hats in the air at their graduation ceremony.

collapse of the youth labour market coupled with the withdrawal of state benefits com-
pelled many 16–18-year-olds to stay on in full-time post-compulsory education.
Thirdly, reforms in the further-education sector resulted in the broadening out of the
curriculum to include more vocational and foundation courses, lessening the perception that education was an option reserved solely for an academic elite. Lastly, the tre-
mendous expansion of higher education in the UK (as in many other higher and
middle-income countries across the world) has resulted in a broader range of higher
education options, including courses with lower entry requirements.

In 1948, just after the Second World War, only 3.7% of 18-year-olds entered higher
education in the UK. In the 1960s, a British government report recommended expan-
sion of higher education to allow all those with the qualifications and ability to enter
(Robbins, 1963). Subsequent changes in education policy have continued to see the
expansion of higher education as well as variation in government policies across the
UK since the implementation of devolved responsibility for higher education in
England, Scotland, Wales, and Northern Ireland. Published since 2004, the Higher
Education Initial Participation (HEIP) measure reports age-specific participation rates
for 17–30-year-olds in England in each academic year (16–30-year-olds in Scotland). It
can be thought of as a projection of the likelihood of a 16- or 17-year-old today participating in higher education by age 30 if that year's entry rates persisted in the future.
In 1995, 26% of 18–21-year-olds entered higher education across the UK. In 2019–20,
the HEIP measure was 53.4% (60.8% for females, 46.3% for males), and in Scotland,
in 2018–19, it was 56.6%. For over half of young people, then, the transition to adulthood involves more education. This expansion has come with government policies
aimed at 'widening access', trying to ensure that higher education is accessible to
people from across society and providing additional support for those who have not
followed a route within the school system that prepares them for university entry.

Despite these policies of widening participation, there is evidence that young people
from higher social class backgrounds are still significantly more likely to enter higher
education and complete qualifications. There are financial constraints: in addition to
living costs, new funding arrangements for higher education in the UK require most
students outside of Scotland to pay substantial fees for their tuition. Research suggests that poorer students are more likely to leave university with significant debt and
that the prospect of debt is more likely to deter students from poorer backgrounds
from studying (Callender and Mason, 2017). Decisions about whether to go into higher
education are also shaped by other factors, many of which are established significantly
earlier, such as academic success (young women outperform their male peers at
school and this corresponds to the high HEIP measure for females), the values of a
particular environment, or personal attributes. Research also indicates that when
choosing paths into college or university, children from higher social class backgrounds are advantaged by their higher levels of social and cultural capital, in
Bourdieu's terms. They have access to a greater range of information and advice from
parents, schools, and other sources. This contributes to a landscape in which students
from higher social class backgrounds tend to attend more prestigious universities,
which often have higher entrance requirements and are (rightly or wrongly) often

judged more positively by employers. Choices about whether to pursue higher education or employment greatly influence young people's transitions. These choices have a significant impact on future options and employment opportunities, as well as shaping other aspects of transitions to adulthood.

While educational transitions are often thought of as a linear process, this is not necessarily the case, with many adults now engaging in ongoing professional development or returning to education in later life as part of the continuous and 'lifelong learning' journey. Policies to expand access to further and higher education have encouraged people to return to education, often through part-time study, which may build on existing employment or explore new avenues. Although the years immediately after leaving school are often vital in shaping young people's paths, later life may also bring experiences and aspirations that lead to further educational and employment transitions.

Key points

- The landscape of work has changed significantly in recent decades, becoming more precarious.
- The emphasis on work as a key marker of identity can be problematic for those who are unemployed or underemployed, particularly in a time of economic recession.
- Higher education in the UK has expanded significantly in recent decades, making it a significant feature of youth transitions for many people.
- There are still social class inequalities in access to higher education, and social and cultural capital can affect paths into higher education.
- Choosing paths of higher education and experiences of higher education are shaped by other aspects of life, such as relationships with peers and family, and by government policies.

Conclusion

In this chapter, you have explored some of the ways in which children move into adulthood. Like childhood, adulthood is defined in multiple ways – biologically, legally, and socially – and different societies have different concepts of what it means. Some societies and communities mark boundaries between childhood and adulthood through rituals, or rites of passage, while others use age (or a range of ages) to distinguish legal boundaries. Some of these key transitions into adulthood may be seen through social changes, such as leaving formal education or entering the world of work. Other changes may come through forming and consolidating new relationships, with peers and with intimate partners. In contemporary societies in the global North, there is quite an extended 'in-between' period between childhood and adulthood. Some people have argued that this period is becoming longer and that it can be characterised as 'extended adolescence'. There is no single dividing line between childhood and adulthood. Instead, becoming adult is shaped by multiple factors. Social, emotional, and psychological transitions to adulthood are not always linear. Young people may move backwards as well as forwards in certain aspects of their lives. Throughout adulthood, indeed, people may well continue to experience feelings and states often associated with childhood: vulnerability, dependence, or lack of competence.

References

Beck, U. (1992) *Risk Society: Towards a New Modernity*. London: Sage.

Bourdieu, P. (1977) *Outline of a Theory of Practice*. Cambridge: Cambridge University Press.

Bourdieu, P. (1986) 'The forms of capital', in J. G. Richardson (ed.) *Handbook of Theory and Research for the Sociology of Education*. New York: Greenwood, pp. 241–258.

Callender, C., and Mason, G. (2017) 'Does student loan debt deter higher education participation? New evidence from England', *The ANNALS of the American Academy of Political and Social Science*, 671(1), pp. 20–48. doi:10.1177/0002716217696041.

DCSF (2008). *Participation in Education, Training and Employment by 16–18 Year Olds in England*. Available at: www.dcsf.gov.uk/rsgateway/DB/SFR/s000792/index.shtml.

Fihlani, P. (2019) 'South Africa initiation schools suspended after circumcision deaths', *BBC News*, 20 December 2019, South Africa initiation schools suspended after circumcision deaths – BBC News.

Gennep, A. van (1960 [1909]) *The Rites of Passage* (trans. M. B. Vizedom and G. L. Caffee). Chicago: University of Chicago Press.

Griffin, C. (2011) 'The trouble with class: researching youth, class and culture beyond the "Birmingham School"', *Journal of Youth Studies* 14(3), pp. 245–259.

Gunter, A. (2010) *Growing up Bad: Black Youth, Road Culture and Badness in an East London Neighbourhood*. London: The Tufnell Press.

Gunter, A. (2017) *Race, Gangs and Youth Violence: Policy, Prevention and Policing*. Bristol: Policy Press.

Gunter, A., and Watt, P. (2009) 'Goin' college, goin' work and goin' road: youth cultures and transitions in East London', *Journal of Youth Studies*, 12(5), pp. 515–529.

Hall, S., and Jefferson, T. (2003 [1975]) *Resistance Through Rituals: Youth Subcultures in Post-War Britain*. London: Routledge.

House of Commons Justice Committee (2016) *The Treatment of Young Adults in the Criminal Justice System: Seventh Report of Session 2016–17: House of Commons Justice Committee* [online]. https://web.archive.org/web/20200813104106/https://yjlc.uk/child-and-adolescent-brain-development-and-its-impact-on-propensity-to-criminal-behaviour/

MacDonald, R., and Giazitzoglu, A. (2019) 'Youth, enterprise and precarity: or, what is, and what is wrong with, the "gig economy"?', *Journal of Sociology*, Melbourne, Vic., 55(4), pp. 724–740. doi:10.1177/1440783319837604.

MacDonald, R., and Shildrick, T. (2007) 'Street corner society: leisure careers, youth (sub)culture and social exclusion', *Leisure Studies*, 26(3), pp. 339–355.

Mandela, N. (1994) *Long Walk to Freedom*. London: Little, Brown and Company.

McRobbie, A. (1978 [1991]) 'The culture of working class girls', in A. McRobbie (ed.) *Feminism and Youth Culture*. London: Macmillan.

Miles, S. (2000) *Youth Lifestyles in a Changing World*. Buckingham: Open University Press.

Robbins, Lord (1963) *Higher Education: Report of the Committee Appointed by the Prime Minister under the Chairmanship of Lord Robbins*, Cmnd 2154, London, HMSO.

United Nations (1989) *United Nations Convention on the Rights of the Child*. Convention on the Rights of the Child | OHCHR.

Watt, P., and Stenson, K. (1998) 'The street: It's a bit dodgy around there: safety, danger, ethnicity and young people's use of public space', in T. Skelton and G. Valentine (eds.) *Cool Places: Geographies of Youth Cultures*. London: Routledge, pp. 249–265.

Glossary terms

Behaviourists are a collection of theorists and researchers in the field of psychology who studied the ways behaviours are affected by a person's direct experiences of their environment in response to stimulus.

Biological determinism is the theory that an individual's characteristics and behaviour are determined exclusively by biological factors.

Bipolar disorder is a mental illness that affects moods and emotions, which can swing from one extreme (depression) to another (mania). It used to be known as manic depression.

Causal indicates that something has caused an observed effect.

Cerebral palsy is the name for a group of lifelong conditions that affect movement and coordination. It's caused by a problem with the brain that develops before, during, or soon after birth.

Conditioning is a technique used in behavioural training and associated with behaviourism. It aims to change a child's behaviour through positively or negatively rewarding their behaviours.

Cognition describes mental processing and acquiring knowledge through thought, experience, and sensory information.

Colonialism is the policy or practice of acquiring political control over another people or country, occupying it with settlers and exploiting it economically.

Culture represents the ideas, attitudes, norms, values, beliefs and practices of a society or of group(s) within a society. This includes the *objects* they create (whether toys, cars, art, fashion, tools, or other items, known as material culture) and the *symbols and meanings* attached to them. Sometimes, writers use the term 'culture' interchangeably with 'society' to mean a wider group of people, how they are organised, and their practices.

Devolved governments refers to the separate legislatures and executives, each with a different range of powers in Scotland, England, Wales, and Northern Ireland. Education across the four nations is a 'devolved responsibility', meaning that governments across the four nations have greater powers to legislate in this area of policy and to decide how to spend monies allocated to elected bodies from Westminster (England).

Ethnography is the study of individual cultures, communities, or groups of people.

Ethnographic field notes are written documents made by the researcher whilst observing in a particular setting.

Focus group interviews is a research method involving a small group of people who are interviewed together on a specific subject of interest to the research study.

Forms of capital is a term originally coined by French sociologist Pierre Bourdieu [1930–2002]. Forms of capital include both the physical and intangible social assets and resources that are accumulated by individuals as they interact with communities based on their positions in society. The concept of different forms of capital is connected to a broader theory developed by Bourdieu to explain how societies create and reproduce social class inequalities.

Gross motor skills are the abilities relating to major bodily movements usually acquired during childhood – although this depends on the child's individual development – as part of motor learning and include skills such as crawling, walking, jumping, running, and skipping.

Hippocampus is a region of the brain that is associated primarily with memory.

Hypothesis is a fundamental premise of scientific method. Researchers use the information available to them to propose a hypothesis (a theory or prediction of what will happen), then test through research whether the hypothesis can be confirmed or not.

IQ, or intelligence quotient, is used in psychology as a measure of a person's ability to reason and solve some kinds of problems. Typically associated with intelligence, the use of IQ tests has been criticised for only measuring certain abilities and as a test constructed to reflect constructs of intelligence developed in the global North.

Local authorities refer to UK elective local governments who are responsible for administering a range of public services, including social care, schools, and housing and planning. Across the four nations, local councils are the most common form of local authority, and they play a role in working with local businesses and other organisations to identify, implement, and deliver key services to local communities.

Menstruation is the regular discharge of blood and tissue from the lining of the uterus through the vagina. The menstrual cycle is also characterised by the rise and fall of hormones, also defined as menarche.

Mixed methods is a research approach where researchers collect and analyse both quantitative and qualitative data within the same study.

Muscular dystrophy is a group of diseases that cause weakness and loss of muscle mass that progressively deteriorate. Caused by abnormal genes (mutations) that interfere with the production of proteins needed to develop healthy muscle, muscular dystrophy affects movement.

Natural science is the study of the natural (physical) world and the rules that govern it using scientific methods. This encompasses parts of psychology.

Neurobiology refers to the biology of the nervous system (brain and spinal cord are the central nervous system, and nerves around the body are the peripheral nervous system).

Neurodiverse refers to the wide range of neurocognition in *all* humans. The term is often used to describe atypical, in contrast to neurotypical, patterns of thought or behaviour and particularly to refer to autistic spectrum disorder (ASD) and other conditions, including attention deficit hyperactivity disorder (ADHD).

Online grooming is where someone befriends a child or young person online and builds up their trust with the intention of exploiting them and causing them harm.

Othering is a term used to describe how people are set out as different in some ways to other people or to an imagined idea of 'normal'.

Pathologise means to think about or treat people as psychologically abnormal.

Prefrontal cortex is a region of the brain associated with a variety of complex behaviours, including planning, and contributes to personality development. The prefrontal cortex helps people plan, set, and achieve goals.

Progressive education movement is a pedagogical movement that began in the late 19th century and emphasises learning through experience. Influential thinkers for progressive education included, among others: Maria Montessori (1870–1952) and Loris Malaguzzi (1920–1994), who developed the Reggio Emilia approach.

Prosocial behaviour is a type of voluntary behaviour designed to help others. Examples include helping, sharing, comforting others, and cooperating.

Psychosis is a severe mental illness or episode of mental illness in which thought and emotions are impaired so that contact is lost with external reality.

Psychotherapy describes the use of psychological methods, particularly using talking therapies, such as one-to-one counselling with a psychotherapist, to help a person change behaviour and overcome challenging thoughts and feelings.

To refute something is to disprove it.

School ethos encompasses the local values, attitudes, and cultures that shapes teacher, parental, and children's attitudes towards learning, behaviour, and the purposes of education.

School league tables rank schools in the UK based on performance data. This includes pupil achievement in public examinations taken at key points while attending school. England and Wales publish school performance information, but the publication of this data was abolished in Northern Ireland in 2001, followed by Scotland in 2003. However, in 2017, Scotland began publishing data based on pupil performance in reading, writing, and numeracy.

Setting and streaming is a collection of practices used predominantly in UK secondary schools to hierarchically group young people based on perceived ability.

Shamanism is a religious practice, amongst some peoples of Northern Asia, Amazonia and North America, that involves a practitioner who is believed to interact with a spirit world through altered states of consciousness and who can use this practice to heal others.

Social science is the interdisciplinary study of human societies and how they are organised. It often encompasses parts of psychology.

Socialisation defines the process of internalising the norms and ideologies of a given society. Socialisation encompasses both learning and teaching.

Stakeholders is a term used within policymaking to describe individuals, communities, or organisations with a vested interest, or 'stake', in an area of interest, such as children and young people's education, where commonly cited stakeholders include governments, schools, head teachers, parents, and children and young people themselves.

The Age of Reason /The Enlightenment is a term often used to describe the emergence of modern European philosophy.

INDEX

Note: Page numbers in *italics* indicate figures and page numbers in **bold** indicate tables.

abstract thinking 61, 113, 116, 206–208, 211
achondroplasia 50
adolescence: abstract thinking and 61, 116, 206–208, 211; autobiographical self and 211; body development and 206; body image and 212; cognitive development and 61, 206–208, 211; defining 17, 46, 200, 203; executive function and 30–31, 207–208; family relationships and 210; identities and 212; limbic system and 208; menstruation and 46, 219; neurobiological change and 206–207; neuroplasticity and 207–208; parasocial relationships and 209; peer groups and 209–211, 223; as period of disruption 200–204; prosocial behaviours and 209; puberty and 17, 200, 206–207, 219; risky behaviours and 203–204, 207, 209–210; self-concept and 210–212; self-consciousness and 209; self-esteem and 211–212; sense of self and 201, 211–212; social change and 213, *214*, 215, *215*; young people's views of 205; *see also* teenagers; youth
adulthood: biological development and 219; defining 231; employment and 227–229; global North and 221; global South and 219–221; group identities and 223; higher education and 230; identity and 223; marriage and 161–162, 229; menarche and 219; motherhood and 161–162; rites of passage and 219–220; ritual circumcision and 219–220, *220*; school-leaving and 226–227; socialisation for 162–163; in-between stage and 219; transition to 161–164, 166–167, 200–201, 209, 211, 216, 218–220, 222–223, 226, 228–232; waithood and 161

African Charter on the Rights and Welfare of the Child 164–165
African Union 165
African Unity 165
agency: bodies and 46, 54–55; children and 7; mental health and 101; online platforms and 193, 195; sense of self and 60–61
Ainsworth, M. 62
Albert, D. 104
Aliens and Alienists (Littlewood and Lipsedge) 94
Allen, L. 182
Alphablocks 190
American Academy of Pediatrics (AAP) 188
American Psychiatric Association 93
American Psychological Association (APA) 35
Amini, M. 213
anti-apartheid movement 213
anti-bullying interventions 33
Anyan, S. 79
Arab Spring protests 213
Aristotle 201
artificial intelligence (AI) 186
Asian people 151, 179
Atkinson, C. 102
attachment theory 62–64
augmentative and alternative communication (AAC) 193
augmented reality (AR) 186–187
Australian University (ANU) 144
autobiographical self 211
Axon, S. 20

Backstrom, L. 50
Bauman, Z. 225
BBC Bitesize 192
Beck, U. 225–226
behaviourism 117–118

behaviour management 118, *118*
Benjamin, D. J. 38
Bhana, D. 180
Biesta, G. 110, 114
Big Bumpin' 195
biological determinism 46
biological development: adolescence and 17, 204–205, 207; bodies and 43, 46; childhood and 4, 116–117, 219; menstruation and 46, 219; puberty and 17, 170, 174–175, 200, 206, 219; sex of infants and 170, 174–175; social life and 43, 46, 166, 205
biological language 5–6
biological psychology 24, *25*
biomedical model of mental health 95–98, 134
biopsychosocial model 103–104, 134
bipolar disorder 99–100
Black children and youth: adultification of 149–150, 152; dehumanization and 149; gender identities and 179; interracial friendships and 148–149; isolation booths and 118; out-group preference and 146, *147*; protections of childhood and 149; pro-White bias and 146, *147*; punitive treatment of 149–151; racism and 144, 146, 148, 150–151; road culture and 148–149; stop and search of 150–151; worklessness and 228
Blake, J. 149
Blakemore, S. J. 208–209
bodies: agency and 45, 55–56; biological determinism and 46; characteristics of 49–50; culture and 43, 45, 47; development and 45–46, 206; disabled children and 48–51; disciplined 51–56; examined 44, *44*; gender identities and 179–180; genes and 45; menstruation and 46, 219; nature/nurture and 46–47; othered 47–51; perceptions of 43; self-esteem and 212; sense of self and 47–49; social aspects of 46–47
body work 47, 49
Bourdieu, P. 119, 226, 230
Bowlby, J. 62–63, 65
Boyce, T. 104
Bradbury, A. 113
Bragg, S. 183
brain development: adolescence and 30–31, 206–208, 222; biomedical model and 97; biopsychosocial model and 103–104; cerebral palsy and 45; child development and 30, 222; cortex development and

207–208; criminal behaviour and 222; developmental psychology and 24; dopamine and 207; environment and 104; executive function and 30–31; infants and 30; learning and 192; nature/nurture and 207–208; neurobiological change and 206–207; neuroplasticity and 104, 207–208; object permanence and 116; race science and *141*; social experience and 179; structures in *206*; *see also* cognitive development
British Psychological Society 28, 36
British Sign Language 133
Bruner, J. 117
bullying 181, 183
Butler, J. 180
Butler Act (1944) 112

Cameroon 166
caregivers 62–65, 76, 171
Carter, M. 193
Centre for Contemporary Cultural Studies (CCCS) 223–225
cerebral palsy 45, 129
cheenayja 203–204
Child and Adolescent Mental Health Services (CAMHS) 28
child and adolescent psychologists 28
childhood: African Charter on 164–165; age of majority and 163–165; biological development and 219; caregiver relationships and 62–63; conceptions of 10–12, 19, 154–157, 160–161, 167–168, 218; defining 163–164; diverse 5–6; globalisation of 157–162, 165; global South and 4; inequities in 6; interdisciplinarity and 1–2; middle 17, 46, 61; protection of youth in 154–155, 165, 168, 194; separation from adults 155–156, 162, 167–168; social construction of 4–6, 12–16, 65, 154, 221; *see also* early childhood; youth
Childhood and Youth Studies (CYS): children's participation and 21–22; children's rights and 18–19; expertise in 11–12; global childhood and 167–168; interdisciplinarity and 1–2, 17; psychology and 1–2, 167; specialist areas in 16–18, 23; study of 10–11, 16
Children Act (1989) 20
Children's Commissioner for England 79
Children's Ombudsman (Norway) 21
children's rights: as human rights 18–19; Mosaic approach and 22; right to participation 20–22; right to protection 20;

right to provision 19; Uganda and *19*; UNCRC and 7, 19–21, 159–161, 194
Chitty, C. 111
chore curriculum *161*, 163–166
Clark, A. 22
Clark, E. 99
Clark, K. 146, *147*
Clark, M. P. 146
Clearfield, M. W. 173
climate change 213, *214*
clinical psychologists 28
Coard, B. 150
cognitive behavioural therapy (CBT) 98–99
cognitive development: adolescence and 61, 206–207, 211; concrete operational stage 116; formal operational stage 116, 206; learning and 115; middle childhood and 61; preoperational stage 116; self-concept and 60–61; sensorimotor stage 116
cognitive psychology 24, *25*, 27
collective identity 60, 67, 139–140
collectivism 13, 15, 67, 86, 166
colonialism 141, 157–158, 168
comprehensive education system 113, 115
concrete operational stage 116
conditioning 118
Cooley, C. H. 47–48
coping skills 30, 77, 92, 99–100
Covid-19: digital technologies and 186–188, 196; families and 83–84; travel restrictions and 84
Cregan, K. 51
Crenshaw, K. 144
criminal justice: adolescent brain development and 222; age of responsibility and 221, **221**; forensic psychologists and 29; hate crimes and 148; punitive treatment of Black and minority people 150–152; racial discrimination and 139–140, 144, 149–150, 179; stop and search of Black people 150–151
criminological studies: brain development and 222; hate crimes and 148; protections of childhood and 149–150; racial attitudes and 145, 148–151
cultural capital 119–120, *120*, 226
culture: attitudes towards disability and 45; bodies and 43, 45, 47; caregiving and 63–64; caring networks and 63–64; childhood and 161–167; collectivism and 67; delayed gratification and 39; development and 5; environments and 33; ethnicity and 144–145; extended families and 78, 82, 86; family

storytelling and 65–67, 69, 86; indigenous people and 141, 157; indigenous psychologies and 166–167; individualism and 67; mental health and 94–95, 103; parenting and 63–65, 75–76; psychological concepts and 165–166; psychological research and 36, 41; self and 58, 60–61, 65–68; social constructions of childhood in 65; socialisation of children and 166; society and 5, 223; storytelling and 65–67; subcultures and 148–149
Cuthbert, D. 51
cystic fibrosis 44

dandelion-orchid studies 31, *32*, 33
Danielsson, U. 101
data protection 195
deaf communities 134
deaf culture 130
deep play 190
delay-of-gratification paradigm 37–39
depression: biomedical model and 97; CBT and 99; culturally-sensitive research on 94; psychological model and 98–99; quantitative research and 34; separation from parents and 86; social media use and 187–188; youth and 77, 91, 93, 99
Descartes, Rene 67
development: biological determinism and 46; biological development and 4; bodies and 45–46, 206; brain and 206, *206*; culture and 5, 33, 166; gains and losses in 4, 30–31; language and 29–30, 61, 117; marshmallow test and 37–40; physical skills and 192; process of 9, 26, *26*, 30–31; psychology and 24, 26, 40; social development and 4; *see also* biological development; brain development
developmental psychology: cognitive development and 116, 206; criticism of universal standards in 38, 165; defining 24; gender identity and 177; marshmallow test and 40; pillars of *25*; self-concept and 69; self-esteem and 69; social and cultural 2
devolved governments 107, 230
de Waal, A. 159
Dewey, J. 111, 115
Diagnostic and Statistical Manual of Mental Disorders (DSM) 93, 96
differences in sex development (DSD) 174
differential sensitivity 33, 40
digital divide 186–187
digital technologies: accessibility and 193; apps and 189–190, 193; assistive 193; augmented

reality (AR) and 187; child exploitation and 194–196; children and youth 186–191, 212; children's relationships and 191–192; children's use at home 189–190; Covid-19 and 186–188; data gathering and 195; deep digital play and 190; education and 188, 192–194; embedded advertisements and 194; identity and 212; inequitable access to 188; physical skill development and 192; play and 189–193; protection of children and youth 187; regulation of 187; schools and 187, 194; screen time and 186, 188, 196; social gaming and 187; social media and 187–188; transgressive play and 190–191; user-generated games 194; video games and 191–194; virtual reality (VR) and 187, 191, 194; youth protest and 213

disability: cultural attitudes and 45; identities and 129; medical model of 127–128, **131**, 134; models of 125–127, 132, 134–135; religious/moral model of 126; social model of 128–131, **131**, 134–135; Ubuntu philosophy and 135

disabled children: embodied experiences and 48–51; inclusive education and 123–125, *125*; interventionist beliefs and 131–132; models of disability and 125–131; pathognomic beliefs and 131–132; stigma and 132; UNCRC and 124

Disabled Children's Childhood Studies 17

disciplined bodies 51–56

discrimination 35–36, 140, 143–144

disproportionate dwarfism 50

diversity: adolescent development and 201; childhood and 5–6; gender 181, 183; genetic 142–143

dopamine 207

Dunn, J. 82

Durkheim, E. 111

dwarfism 49–50

early childhood: attachment theory and 62–64; caregiver-child relationships and 62–64; children's participation and 22; defining 16; gender in 177–179; racial attitudes and 139, 146; self-concept and 2

East London 227–228

economic capital 119, 226

education: behaviour management and 118, *118*; compulsory 107–109, *109*, 226; deficit model of 119–120; defining *126*; digital technologies and 188, 192–194; exclusion from 118, 123–125, *126*, **131**, 135; expansion of higher 230–231; fairness and 109–110, 113; formal 107–110; goals of 109; home-schooling and 108; industrial schools and *112*; integration and *126*; intelligence measurement and 112–113; key phases in UK systems *109*; kindergarten and 13, 15, 123–124, 132–134; marketisation of 114–115; mass schooling and 111–115, 156; middle/upper-class boys and 155–156, *156*; missionary values and 157; perspectives on good 107–109; post-compulsory 229–231; progressive education movement 111; segregation and *126*; suitable and efficient 108–109, 120; Sustainable Development Goals and *108*; types of UK 110, *110*; *see also* inclusive education; learning; mass schooling; schools

Education Act (1870) 156

Education Act (1996) 108

educational psychologists 29

Education Reform Act (1988) 114

Elementary Education Act (1870) 111

Ellis, B. 104

Emile, or On Education (Rousseau) 155

Emmot, E. 205

embodiment 47, 179–180, 184

employment: education for 109, 231; gendered divisions in 228–229; gig economy and 228; racial discrimination and 144; teenagers and 201, 203; transition to adulthood and 227–229; women and 63, 229; youth labour market exclusion and 227–230

Endless Numbers ™ 193

Endless Reader ™ 193

Engels, R. C. 191

Enlightenment 154, 167

environments: bodies and 44–45; brain development and 104; children's characteristics and 27, 31, 33, 38–40; culture and 33; dandelion-orchid studies and 31, *32*, 33; digital 189–190, 191–192, 194; disability and 129–132; gender norms and 172, 180; human migration and 142; learning and 115–117; nature/nurture and 33; self-control and 38; sensitivity and 104; social support and 39; stages of thinking and 116

Epstein, R. 149

Ethiopia 161

ethnicity: body judgements and 49, 51; collective identity and 139–140; culture and 144–145; defining 140; discrimination and 144;

ethnocentrism and 95; human differences and 144–145; identity and 139–140, 144; intersectionality and 144; racism and 148; sense of self and 47; stigma of mental illness and 101; teacher beliefs and 27, 118; worklessness and 227–228; *see also* race
ethnocentrism 94–95
ethnographic research: children's bodies and 49, 52; gendered behaviour and 178, 180–181; racism and 148; road culture and 148; stop and search of Black people 150–151; subcultures and 225; youth identity and 226
European Commission 194
exclusion 118, 123–125, *126*
executive function 30–31, 206–208

fa'afāfine 182–183
Facebook revolution of 2010–11 213
fakaleiti 182–183
families: adolescence and 210; childcare and 63–64, 76; child circulation in 86; children's views on 78–80, 82; culture and 78, 82, 86; defining 75; fluidity and 78, 82; forms of 75–80, *81*, 82, 87; nuclear 75–77; relationship quality and 77–80, 82; roles in 79, 86; sibling relationships in 82–83, 86; single parent 76–77, 79; stigma of mental illness and 103; storytelling and 7, 61; transnational 83–87
fathers: caregiving and 171, 173; competition and 14; racialised stereotypes and 76–77; role in childhood 63; as role models 223; transnational families and 86; *see also* parenting
Fausto-Sterling, A. 179
femininity: border crossing and 181; gender binary and 172; gender identity and 180; gender norms and 175, 179; management of violence 180; motherhood and 175; schools and 180; toys and play 178–179
finger flutings *11*
Fingerson, L. 45–46
focus groups 162, 180, 205
forensic psychologists 29
formal education 107–109
formal operational stage 116, 206
forms of capital 119–120, 226
Fridaysforfuture strikes 213
Fung, H. 65–66

Gallagher, M. 55
gender: adult expectations and 172–174; body judgements and 49; border crossing and 181;

borderwork and 181; children's peer groups and 180; children's perceptions of 179; defining 171–172; in early childhood 177–179; embodiment of 179–180; institutions and 182–183; intersectionality and 179; lived contexts and 180; overlapping normal distribution curves and 175–176, *176*, 177; performativity and 180; schools and 180–181; social construction of 101, 170, 184; stigma of mental illness and 101–102; transition to adulthood and 219; variations in 175–177
gender binary 172, 177, 183–184
gender differences 34, 36, 71, 177–178, 229
gender diversity 175, 181, 183
gender divisions 181, 228–229
gender dysphoria 21, 181–182
gender identities: bullying and 182–183; children and 4; defining 171; development of 177–179, 184; fa'afāfine and fakaleiti 182–183; fluid 177, 183; gender stability and 177; medical transition and 182; non-binary 171–172, 181, 183–184; parent influence and 178, 182; schools and 180–183; toys and play 178, *178*, 179; transgender 171–172, 177, 181–183
Gender Identity Development Service (Tavistock Clinic) 21
gender norms 172, 175, 180–183
gender stability 177
genes 45, 47, 104, 143
genetic diversity 142–143
Geneva Declaration of the Rights of the Child 19
Gennep, A. van 219, 221
Ghana: child circulation in 86; childhood and *161*; children's rights and 159; families in 76, 78, 80, 85; transnational families and 85
Gibbs, M. 193
Giddens, A. 144, 225
gig economy 228
Gillborn, D. 114
Global Day of Protest *214*
globalisation: children's welfare legislation and 159–160; colonialisation and 157–158, 168; conceptions of childhood and 157–162, 165, 167–168; defining 157–158; digital divide and 186–187; missionaries and 157, *158*, 168; psychological concepts and 165–166
global North: adolescence in 201; conceptions of childhood in 154–155, 160, 168; defining 154; digital exclusion in 187; individualism and 67, 166; mass schooling in 111; as Minority World 8; mothers as caregivers in 63; nuclear families and 76–77;

psychological research and 33, 165; social model of disability and 134–135; social structures and 225; terminology and 8; transition to adulthood and 221
Global Positioning System (GPS) 187
global South: conceptions of childhood in 4, 160–161; defining 154; digital divide and 187; extended families in 76; as Majority World 8; rites of passage and 219–221; terminology and 8
Goff, P. 149
Goffman, E. 101
Golombok, S. 77
González, T. 149
good-enough parenting 64–65
Granic, I. 186, 191, 212
gross motor skills 46
Growing Up Bad (Gunter) 148
Gruneisen, S. 39
Gunter, A. 148
Guse, T. 50

Hall, G. S. 203, 205
Hall, S. 68, 144, 223, 225
Harter, S. 60–61
Harvey, C. 50
health care 6, 19, 29, 103, 140
Hendry, J. 13, 15
Hermann, E. 39
higher education 229–231
Higher Education Initial Participation (HEIP) 230
Hinton, P. 204
HIV/AIDS crisis 165, 167, 220
Hoffman, E. 67–68
home-schooling 108
Honwana, A. 161
Horizon Worlds 187
Howell, T. 182
Hughes, B. 190–191

I am whole (YMCA) 99
identity: adolescence and 212; collective 60, 67, 139–140; defining 139; disability 129; ethnicity and 139–140, 144; group 223; online/offline worlds and 212; race and 139; self-concept and 60, 68; social change and 225–226; social class and 223–225; transition to adulthood and 223
imaginative play 190
inclusive education: defining *126*; disabled children and 123–125, *125*; Euro-American practices and 135; Indonesian kindergartens and 132–134; interventionist perspectives and 131–132; models of disability and 131, **131**, 132, 134–136; pathognomic perspectives and 131–132; social model of disability and 131, 136; storytelling and 133–134; Ubuntu philosophy and 135–136; UNCRC and 124
Indigenous Australians 143–144
indigenous people 141, 143–144, 157, 166
indigenous psychologies 166–167
individualisation 226
individualism 14–15, 67, 166
Indonesia 123–124, 132–134
Indonesian sign languages 133
inequities 4, 6, 35–36, 100, 144
infants: attachment theory and 62–63; brain development and 30; childcare and 171; defining 46; gender and 173; good-enough mother and 64–65; sensorimotor stage and 116
Ingham, N. 114
Inhelder, B. 206
institutional racism 139–140, 144
integration *126*
intelligence testing 112–114
interdisciplinarity 1–2, 17
International Convention on the Elimination of All Forms of Racial Discrimination (United Nations) 144
intersectionality 6, 144, 179
intersex conditions 174–175
interventionist beliefs 131–132
isolation booths 118, *118*

James, A. 48
James, W. 58–59, 73
Japan 13, 15, 67, 203–204
Jefferson, T. 225
Jensen, M. R. 188
Johnson, S. 86
Jones, O. 51
Jordan, A. 131
Just Dance 191

Keller, H. 63
key word signing 133
kindergarten 13, 15, 123–124, 132–134
Klein, V. 63
Kleinman, A. 94, 103
Kleinman, J. 94
Knowledge construction 116
Koomen, R. 39
Korea 67
Kruse, R. 51
Kusserow, A. 14–15

Laidlaw, L. 189
Laing, R. 134
Lalonde, R. 86
Lamm, B. 39
Lancy, D. 46, 163
language: behaviourism and 117; biological
    5–6; cultural capital and 119, 223;
    development and 29–30, 61, 117; digital
    apps and 193; family migration and 31;
    human differences and 142, 144; mother-
    infant 173; racism and 150; signing and
    133, *133*, 134; terminology and 8, 170
Lawrence, S. 148
learning: active 115; barriers to 29, 36;
    behaviourism and 117–118; brain patterns
    and 192; chore curriculum and 162–164;
    cognitive development and 115; construction
    of knowledge 116; contexts for 107, 109;
    curriculum and 115; deficit model of
    education and 119–120; digital technologies
    and 187–190, 193–192; disabled children
    and 123–127, 132–135; embodied
    experiences and 47, 51–54; environmental
    interactions and 115–117; forms of capital
    and 119–120; internal school factors and
    119; pedagogy and 115, 117; play-based
    190; scaffolding and 117; social and cultural
    capital 119–120; social-emotional abilities
    and 27; social relationships and 117; *see also*
    education; inclusive education; schools
Leavell, A. S. 173
Lee, D. 94
legal age limits 221, **221**, 222
Liang, C.-H. 65
Liegghio, M. 98, 103
Linnaeus, C. 140
Lipsedge, M. 94
Littlewood, R. 94
Lobel, A. 191
Long Walk to Freedom, A (Mandela) 219
looking glass self 48
Lost in Translation (Hoffman) 68
Lubman, D. 99
Lundtofte, T. E. 188
Lyttleton-Smith, J. 178

MacDonald, R. 228
Majority World 8
Mandela, N. 219–220
marketisation 114–115
Markus, H. R. 60, 67
Marsella, A. 100
Marsh, J. 189–193

marshmallow test 37, *37*, 38–40
Martin, D. 102
masculinity: gender binary and 172; gender
    identity and 180; gender norms and 175,
    179; help-seeking and 101; schools and 180;
    sexual prowess and 175; social/cultural
    value of 172, 178–179; stereotypes on Black
    179; toys and play 178–179
mass schooling: children's perceptions of ability
    grouping in 114; comprehensive education
    system and 113, 115; corporal punishment in
    112; global North and 111; psychometric
    testing and 112–113; reproduction of
    inequalities in 119–120; rise of 111–115;
    standardised testing regimes in 114; tripartite
    system and 112–113; *see also* education
Mavoa, J. 193
Mayeza, E. 180
McCann, T. 99
McNally, S. 50
medical model of disability 127–128, **131**,
    134–136
menstruation 46, 219
mental health: adolescence and 208, 210;
    coping skills and 99–100; culturally-sensitive
    research on 94; culture and 94–95, 103;
    defining 90–91; ethnocentrism and 94–95;
    fluctuations in 91, *91*; isolation booths and
    118; medical model of disability and 134;
    psychology and 24, 26; social media use and
    187–188, 212; social model of disability and
    129; spectrum of 91–92, *92*; transgender
    children and 183; wellbeing and 91; youth
    perspectives on 97–98
mental illness: assessment of 92–93;
    biomedical model and 95–98;
    biopsychosocial model and 103–104;
    cultural differences and 93–95; deficit model
    of 97; defining 90–91; psychiatric
    medication for 96; psychological model and
    98–100; sensitivity and 104; social model
    and 100–101; stigma and 101–103;
    strengths-based approach to 99; universality
    of 93
Me-self 59, *59*
Mesman, J. 64
Metaverse 187
middle childhood 17, 46, 61
migration: children and 84; genetic diversity
    and 142; internal 85; language and 30;
    parent-child relationships and 85–86; racism
    and 148; sense of self and 67–68;
    transnational families and 84–86

Miller, P. 65
Minecraft 191–193
Minority World 8
Mischel, W. 37–38
missionaries 157, *158*, 168
mixed methods research 35
Montgomery, H. 2
Morgan, D. 78
Moriarty, A. 99
Morita, H. 186
Morrow, V. 78, 83
Mosaic approach 22
Moss, P. 22
motherhood 161–162
mothers: adulthood and 161–162; attachment
    theory and 62–65; caregiving and 63–64, 80;
    competition and 14–15; as feminine ideal
    175; good-enough parenting and 64–65;
    infant play and 173; as one good adult 77;
    single 76–77, 85; transnational families and
    85–87; *see also* parenting
Mukarji, A. 213
Murphy, L. 99
muscular dystrophy 44
Myrdal, A. 63

National Society for the Prevention of Cruelty
    to Children (NSPCC) 148
nature-nurture: bodies and 46; brain
    development and 207–208; characteristics
    and 33; development and 45; gender and
    173; mental illness and 95
Ndlovu, H. 213
Neale, B. 79
Neary, A. 182–183
Nelson, N. M. 173
neurobiology 206–209, 216
neurodiverse children 17, 193
neuroplasticity 104, 207–208
New Ethnicities 144
Nigeria 162
Nintendo Switch™ 194
Norway 21
Nsamenang, A. B. 163, 166–167
Nso children 166–167

object permanence 116
Odgers, C. L. 188
Oliver, M. 128
Open University, The (United Kingdom) 123
operant conditioning 118
Orben, A. 187
Organisation Intersex International (OII) 175

Organisation of African Unity (OAU) 165
othered bodies 47–51
othering 47, 49, 56
Overton, W. F. 45–46

Palmer, A. 49, 51
Pan-Africanism 165
parenting: bodies and school-readiness 52–54;
    child circulation and 86; children's work and
    162–166; compulsory education and 108–109;
    conceptions of ideal 64; continuities in
    parent-child relationships *11*; culture and
    63–65, 75–76; digital media in the home and
    188–190; disabled children and 127, 132;
    family relationships and 77–79; gender
    identities and 173–175, 178, 182; good-
    enough 64–65; one good adult and 77;
    school choice and 114–115; single-parent
    families and 76–77, 79; transnational
    families and 83–86; *see also* families;
    fathers; mothers
Parreñas, R. S. 86
pathognomic beliefs 131–132
Payne, S. 192
pedagogy 115, 117
Pedley, R. 113, 115
peer groups 209–211, 223
physical health psychology 26
Piaget, J. 78–79, 116, 206
Pieterson, H. 213
play: child development and 190; children's
    rights and 195; deep digital 190; digital
    technologies and 187, 189–193, 194–195;
    gendered groups and 181; gender identity
    and 178–179; imaginative 190; mother-
    infant 173; racial bias studies and 146–147;
    recapitulative 191; rough-and-tumble 191;
    siblings and 82–83; tactile experiences and
    191; transgressive 190–191; types of digital
    190–192
play-based learning (PBL) 190
Plowden Report (1967) 113
Pokémon Go 187
post-traumatic stress disorder (PTSD) 93
Preece, V. 52
prefrontal cortex 30, 97, *206*, 207–208
prejudice 143–144
preoperational stage 116
primary sexual characteristics 171
Principles of Psychology, The (James) 59
progressive education movement 111
prosocial behaviour 209
Pryor, J. 79

psychological model of mental health 98–100
psychological research: and apology for
    oppressive and discriminatory practices 35–36;
    biological determinism and 46; culture and 36,
    41; explanatory power of 36, 40; gender
    differences and 36; global North and 33, 165;
    marshmallow test and 37–40; mixed methods
    35; qualitative 35; quantitative 33–35; racism
    and 35–36, 145–147, *147*; replication in 35,
    38; statistical analyses 34, 39
psychologists 28–29, *28*, *29*
psychology: biological 24, *25*; of children and
    youth 1–2, 24, *25*, 26–27, 40–41; cognitive
    24, *25*, 27; cross-cutting themes in *25*, 26;
    culturally-informed 41; culture and 165–166;
    developmental 24, *25*; indigenous 166–167;
    mental health and 24, 26; physical health
    26; social and personality 26; study of 24;
    teacher beliefs and 27
psychometric testing 112–113
psychosis 99
psychotherapy 29, 98
puberty: adolescence and 17, 200, 207, 219;
    biological development and 170, 174–175,
    206, 219; blockers and 21, 182; gender
    dysphoria and 21, 182; neurobiological
    changes during 207
Punch, S. 83

qualitative research 35
quantitative research 33–35

race: biological effects and 6; biological
    language and 5–6; body judgements and 49,
    51; children's attitudes and 139, 145–147;
    deficit model of education and 119–120;
    defining 139–140; discrimination and 140,
    143–144; ethnocentrism and 94; genetic
    diversity and 142–143; hate crimes and 148;
    identity and 139; 'race science' and 140–141,
    141, 142–143; social construction of 4–6, 8,
    143–144; stigma of mental illness and 101,
    103; UNESCO on 142; worklessness and
    227–228; youth and 226; *see also* ethnicity
racial attitudes: on Black children and youth
    149–151; criminological studies and 148–151;
    psychological research and 35–36, 145–147,
    147; sociological studies and 148–150;
    teachers and 27, 118, 132, 150, 152
racism: bullying and 139; children and 139,
    145–146; colonialism and 141; defining 140;
    ethnicity and 144; Indigenous Australians
    and 143–144; individual 144; institutional
    139–140, 144; mental health evaluation and
    94–95; negative stereotypes and 143–144;
    'new racism' and 144–145; pro-White, anti-
    Black bias 146, *147*; scientific 140–141,
    141, 142–143; structural 144, 150; UK
    criminal justice system and 150; UK
    education and 35–36, 150; violence and 148
Reay, D. 180–181
recapitulative play 191
relationships: adolescent peer groups and
    209–210; adolescents and family 210;
    caregiver-child 62–64; children and 70;
    individual and society 225; learning and 117;
    online/offline worlds and 191–192, 212;
    parasocial 209; parent-child *11*, 85–86;
    quality of family 77–80, 82; residence-based
    79; self-concept and 60; siblings and 82–83
Renold, E. 181
research: adolescence and 203, 205–210, 212;
    biological determinism and 46; biomedical
    model 95–98; biomedical model and 97;
    biopsychosocial model and 103–104; body
    characteristics and 48–49, 51; children's
    chores and 162–163; culturally sensitive 94;
    dandelion-orchid studies 31; digital
    technologies and 186, 188–190; disabled
    children and 17; family relationships and
    77–79; gender identity and 177–178,
    180–183; group averages and 7; inclusive
    education and 124, 132, 134; marshmallow
    test and 37–40; mental health and 98–99;
    models for 2; Mosaic approach and 22;
    neurological 104; observational 62; play-
    based learning 190; psychological 26–27,
    35–36, 40–41, 46, 58, 61–62, 67, 99;
    psychological model 98–100; psychometric
    testing and 113–114; qualitative 35;
    quantitative 33–35; racial awareness and
    145–146; racism and 148–150; self-concept
    and 69, 72–73; sensitive parenting and 64;
    separate elements in 2; social 63; social
    model 100–103; storytelling and 65–66;
    subcultures and 225–226; transnational
    families and 84–86; working with children
    21–23, 30
research psychologists 29
resilience 99–100, 104
Resistance Through Rituals (Hall and Jefferson)
    225

Rigg, A. 79

rights: adolescents and 203; African Charter on the Rights and Welfare of the Child 164–165; children and youth 7, 18–19; children's participation and 20–21; civil rights and 213, 215; impact of racism on 140; online/offline worlds and 195; participation in digital media and 187; protection of youth and 20–21; United Nations Convention on the Rights of Persons with Disabilities (UNCRPD) and 124, 128–129; *see also* United Nations Convention on the Rights of the Child (UNCRC)

ritual circumcision 219–220, *220*

Rix, J. 114

road culture 148–149

Roblox 194–196

Rose, D. 126

Rosenberg, M. 59

rough-and-tumble play 191

Rousseau, J.-J. 154–155

Rutter, M. 64

Safe Child Africa 162

Saini, A. 142

Sandel, T. 65

Sansfaçon, A. P. 182

scaffolding 117, 211

Scholten, H. 186

schools: anti-bullying interventions 33; behaviour management in 118, *118*; borderwork and 181; digital technologies and 187, 194; disciplined bodies and 51–53, 56; gender divisions in 181; gender identities and 180–183; league tables 114–115; parent choice in 114–115; racism in 36, 118, 150; readiness and 31, 52–53; resistance to surveillance 55; starting ages 17, 52; *see also* education; mass schooling

scientific method 33–34

scientific racism 140–143

screen time 186, 188, 196

secondary sexual characteristics 171

segregation *126*

self: agency and 60–61; culture and 58, 60–61, 65–68, 166; developing sense of 47, 49, 58–59, 203, 227; embodied experiences and 47–48; employment and 227; as identity 60; social construction of 60–61, 65, 73

self-concept: adolescence and 210–212; adult-devised study of 69, 73; attachment theory and 62; autobiographical self and 211; children's views on 69, *69*, 70, *70*, 71, *71*, 72, *72*, 73; cognitive development and 60–61; defining 59; formation of 2, 60–61; fun and 73; identities and 60, 68; individual characteristics and 59; meanings and 70–72; Me-self and 59, *59*; past selves and 60; possible selves and 60; progression in activities and 72; scaffolding and 211; social relationships and 60, 70–71; things and 60

self-control: environments and 38; executive function and 30; marshmallow test and 36–37, *37*, 38–39

self-esteem: adolescence and 211–212; attachment theory and 62; body image and 212; children's views on 69, 72–73; co-construction of 61; formation of 2; self-evaluation and 60; storytelling and 66–67

self-evaluation 60

sensitivity 62–64, 104

sensorimotor stage 116

Serpell, R. 163

setting and streaming 114

sex: ambiguous genitals and 174–175; assignment at birth 170–171, 174, 177; biological factors for 174–175; defining 170–171; gender identities and 184; primary sexual characteristics 171; secondary sexual characteristics 171

Shakespeare, T. 129

Shakespeare, W. 201

shamanism 94

Shildrick, T. 226

siblings 82–83

Signalong Indonesia 133, *133*, 134

Sign Supported Big Books 133

Sims, The 193

single-parent families 76–77, 79

sit-ins *215*

Skinner, B. F. 117

slavery 141

Smart, C. 79

Smith, A. 86

social and personality psychology 26

social capital 119–120

social change: end of adolescence/youth 200; gender equality and 229; identity and belonging 225–226; relationships between individual and society 225; social model of disability and 131; youth activism and 17, 213, *214*, 215, *215* social class: body judgements and 49; higher education and 230; identity and 223–226; reproduction of inequalities in 119; social/cultural capital and 119–120, *120*, 226, 230–231; subcultures and 223–225; teacher perceptions and 27, 118; United Kingdom and 223–224, 230

social constructions: childhood and 4–6, 12–16, 65, 154, 221; defining 15; gender and 101, 170, 184; intelligence measurement and 113; race and 4–6, 8, 143–144; self and 60–61, 65, 73

social-emotional abilities 27, 30, 37

social gaming 187

social inequalities 100, 226

socialisation: body work and 47; chore curriculum and 163, 165; collectivism and 13, 15; cultural traditions and 166–167; families and 75–76, 82, 86; preparation for adulthood and 162; psychological research and 24, 165–166; schools and 109, 111; siblings and 82, 86

social media 187–188, 209, 212

social model of disability 128–131, **131**, 134–135

social model of mental health 100–101

social norms 77, 178

society: adolescent transformation of 213; biological language and 5–6; culture and 4–5, 223; difference and 8, 127; disability and 128–129; individual and 160, 203, 225, 227; inequalities and 27, 36, 100; norms and 16–17; racial attitudes and 143–146

sociological studies 148–150

Socrates 201

South Africa 180, 213, 215, 219

Spock, B. 12

Stahl, R. 159

statistical analyses 34, 38

Steeves, V. 51

Steinberg, L. 206, 207

stigma 101–103, 132

storytelling: constructive shame and 66–67; cultural beliefs and 65–67, 69, 86; families and 7, 61; inclusive education and 133–134; self and 65–67; self-esteem and 66–67

Strange Situation protocol 62

Straw, J. 76

streaming 114

structural racism 144, 150

subcultures 223–224, *224*, 225

sub-Saharan Africa 76, 159, 161

SumOfUs 187

Sustainable Development Goals (SDG) *108*

Sutton, C. 80

Systema Naturae (*Systems of Nature*) (Linnaeus) 140

Taipei 65–67

Tatlow-Golden, M. 2

Tavistock Clinic (London) 21

teachers: behaviourism and 117; disabled children and 131–132; inclusive education and 132–133; interventionist beliefs and 131–132; pathognomic beliefs and 131–132; racial attitudes and 27, 118, 132, 150, 152

teenagers: activism and 213, *214*, 215, *215*; adolescence and 200; American 201–202, *202*, 203–204; anime depictions of shoujo 204; as dangerous period 203–204; invention of 201–203; Japanese cheenayja 203–204; social change and 213; spending power and 201–203; in the United Kingdom 202–203; *see also* adolescence

Temple Run 190

Thatcher, M. 114

Thomas, G. 117

Thorne, B. 181

Thunberg, G. 213

toddlers 46, 60–61, 65–66, 69

transgender people: gender identity and 171–172, 177, 181–183; medical transition and 182–183; mental health difficulties and 183; rites of passage and 219; social transition and 181–183; support for 183

transgressive play 190–191

transitions: adulthood and 161–164, 166–167, 200–201, 209, 211, 216, 218–223, 227–232; educational 230–231; employment and 227; end of compulsory education and 226–227; rites of passage and 219–221; school-to-work 227; social/cultural capital and 226, 230–231; social rituals and 221; social structures and 223–225; stages of 219

transnational families 83–87

tripartite system 112–113

Truth and Reconciliation Commission 215

Twenge, J. M. 187–188

Ubuntu philosophy 67, 135–136, 180

Uganda *19*, 62, 76

UK Centre for Mental Health 91

UNCRC *see* United Nations Convention on the Rights of the Child (UNCRC)

Ungar, M. 100
UNICEF 159
Union of the Physically Impaired Against
    Segregation (UPAS) 128
United Kingdom: 1989 Children Act 20;
    children's happiness in 80; children's rights
    and 20–21; comprehensive education system
    113; compulsory education in 107–109, *109*,
    115, 227; devolved governments in 107, 230;
    expansion of higher education in 230–231;
    families in 78–79; informal kinship care in
    76; labour market exclusion and 227–228;
    legal age limits and 221, **221**, 222; mass
    schooling in 111–112, 156; medical model
    of disability in 128; national curriculum in
    118; new racism in 144–145; post-
    compulsory education in 229–231; punitive
    treatment of Black children in 118, 150;
    single-parent families and 76–77; social class
    in 223–224; social model of disability in
    128–129, 131; teenager concept in 202–203;
    transition to adulthood and 221; tripartite
    system in 112–113
United Nations *107*
United Nations Convention on the Rights of
    Persons with Disabilities (UNCRPD) 124,
    128–129
United Nations Convention on the Rights of the
    Child (UNCRC): child development and 40;
    children's rights and 7, 19, 159–161, 194;
    definition of child in 163–164, 221;
    disability and 124; education and 107;
    ratification of 19–20; right to play and 195;
    right to privacy and 195; Western traditions
    and 165
United Nations Educational, Scientific and
    Cultural Organisation (UNESCO) 107, 142
United States: individualism and 14–15;
    socialisation of children in 14–15; storytelling
    and 65–67; teenagers and 201–202, *202*,
    203–204
Universal Declaration of Human Rights 107
Universitas Negeri Surabaya (UNESA) 123

Vaghi, F. 205
van der Hof, S. 194
video games 191–194
virtual reality (VR) 186–187, 191, 194
Vygotsky, L. S. 117

Wade, A. 79
Watson, N. 129
Watts, T. W. 38
wellbeing: attachment theory and 62–64;
    digital media and 187–188; emotional 2;
    family relationships and 64; gender identity
    support and 183; good-enough parenting
    and 64–65; hybrid reality and 213; impact of
    prejudiced beliefs on 6; medical model and
    127; mental health and 91, *92*, 118;
    resilience and 104; social media and 212
White, M. 203–204
White children and youth 146, 148–149, 179
WiiFit 191
Winnicott, D. 64–65
Winter's Tale, The (Shakespeare) 201
worklessness 227–228
World Mental Health Day *102*

Xhosa 219–220, *220*

Yosso, T. 119
Youdell, D. 114
youth: criminal prosecution of 222; defining 17;
    employment and 227–229; interdisciplinarity
    and 1–2; labour market exclusion and
    227–230; legal age limits and 221, **221**, 222;
    place and 226; post-compulsory education
    and 229–231; race and 226; social class and
    223–226; subcultures and 223–224, *224*, 225;
    transition to adulthood 161–164, 166–167,
    200–201, 209, 211, 216, 218–219, 222–223,
    228–231; views on adolescence 205; *see also*
    adolescence; teenagers
Youth Studies 17

Zambia 163